Egypt 1919

Edinburgh Studies in Modern Arabic Literature
Series Editor: Rasheed El-Enany

Writing Beirut: Mappings of the City in the Modern Arabic Novel
Samira Aghacy

Autobiographical Identities in Contemporary Arab Literature
Valerie Anishchenkova

The Iraqi Novel: Key Writers, Key Texts
Fabio Caiani and Catherine Cobham

Sufism in the Contemporary Arabic Novel
Ziad Elmarsafy

Gender, Nation, and the Arabic Novel: Egypt 1892–2008
Hoda Elsadda

The Unmaking of the Arab Intellectual: Prophecy, Exile and the Nation
Zeina G. Halabi

Egypt 1919: The Revolution in Literature and Film
Dina Heshmat

Post-War Anglophone Lebanese Fiction: Home Matters in the Diaspora
Syrine Hout

Prophetic Translation: the Making of Modern Egyptian Literature
Maya I. Kesrouany

Nasser in the Egyptian Imaginary
Omar Khalifah

Conspiracy in Modern Egyptian Literature
Benjamin Koerber

War and Occupation in Iraqi Fiction
Ikram Masmoudi

Literary Autobiography and Arab National Struggles
Tahia Abdel Nasser

The Libyan Novel: Humans, Animals and the Poetics of Vulnerability
Charis Olszok

The Arab Nahdah: *The Making of the Intellectual and Humanist Movement*
Abdulrazzak Patel

Blogging from Egypt: Digital Literature, 2005–2016
Teresa Pepe

Religion in the Egyptian Novel
Christina Phillips

Space in Modern Egyptian Fiction
Yasmine Ramadan

Occidentalism: Literary Representations of the Maghrebi Experience of the East-West Encounter
Zahia Smail Salhi

Sonallah Ibrahim: Rebel with a Pen
Paul Starkey

Minorities in the Contemporary Egyptian Novel
Mary Youssef

www.edinburghuniversitypress.com/series/smal

Egypt 1919

The Revolution in Literature and Film

Dina Heshmat

EDINBURGH
University Press

Edinburgh University Press is one of the leading university presses in the UK. We publish academic books and journals in our selected subject areas across the humanities and social sciences, combining cutting-edge scholarship with high editorial and production values to produce academic works of lasting importance. For more information visit our website: edinburghuniversitypress.com

© Dina Heshmat, 2020, 2022

First published in hardback by Edinburgh University Press 2020

Edinburgh University Press Ltd
The Tun – Holyrood Road
12(2f) Jackson's Entry
Edinburgh EH8 8PJ

Typeset in 11/15 Adobe Garamond by
Servis Filmsetting Ltd, Stockport, Cheshire

A CIP record for this book is available from the British Library

ISBN 978 1 4744 5835 1 (hardback)
ISBN 978 1 4744 5836 8 (paperback)
ISBN 978 1 4744 5838 2 (webready PDF)
ISBN 978 1 4744 5837 5 (epub)

The right of Dina Heshmat to be identified as the author of this work has been asserted in accordance with the Copyright, Designs and Patents Act 1988, and the Copyright and Related Rights Regulations 2003 (SI No. 2498).

Contents

Series Editor's Foreword	vi
Acknowledgements	ix
Note on Transliteration and Translation	xii
Introduction	1
1 The Poetics of Disillusion	38
2 The Fear of the Rabble	59
3 1919 and the Trope of the Modern Nation	79
4 The Revolution on the Screen	106
5 The Politics of Rehabilitation	133
6 Rewriting History in the 1990s	155
7 Rewriting History in the Wake of 2011	182
Conclusion	204
Bibliography	210
Index	226

Series Editor's Foreword

Edinburgh Studies in Modern Arabic Literature is a new and unique series that will, it is hoped, fill in a glaring gap in scholarship in the field of modern Arabic literature. Its dedication to Arabic literature in the modern period (that is, from the nineteenth century onwards) is what makes it unique among series undertaken by academic publishers in the English-speaking world. Individual books on modern Arabic literature in general or aspects of it have been and continue to be published sporadically. Series on Islamic studies and Arab/Islamic thought and civilisation are not in short supply either in the academic world, but these are far removed from the study of Arabic literature qua literature, that is, imaginative, creative literature as we understand the term when, for instance, we speak of English literature or French literature. Even series labelled 'Arabic/Middle Eastern Literature' make no period distinction, extending their purview from the sixth century to the present, and often including non-Arabic literatures of the region. This series aims to redress the situation by focusing on the Arabic literature and criticism of today, stretching its interest to the earliest beginnings of Arab modernity in the nineteenth century.

The need for such a dedicated series, and generally for the redoubling of scholarly endeavour in researching and introducing modern Arabic literature to the Western reader, has never been stronger. Among activities and events heightening public, let alone academic, interest in all things Arab, and not least Arabic literature, are the significant growth in the last decades of the translation of contemporary Arab authors from all genres, especially fiction, into English; the higher profile of Arabic literature internationally since the award of the Nobel Prize in Literature to Naguib Mahfouz in 1988; the growing number of Arab authors living in the Western diaspora and writing both in English and Arabic; the adoption of such authors and others by mainstream, high-circulation publishers, as opposed to the academic publishers of the past; the establishment of prestigious prizes, such as the International Prize for Arabic Fiction (IPAF; the Arabic Booker), run by the Man Booker Foundation, which brings huge publicity to the shortlist and winner every year, as well as translation contracts into English and other languages; and, very recently, the events of the Arab Spring. It is therefore part of the ambition of this series that it will increasingly address a wider reading public beyond its natural territory of students and researchers in Arabic and world literature. Nor indeed is the academic readership of the series expected to be confined to specialists in literature in the light of the growing trend for interdisciplinarity, which increasingly sees scholars crossing field boundaries in their research tools and coming up with findings that equally cross discipline borders in their appeal.

The 1919 Popular Uprising against the British occupation in Egypt, often also referred to as the 1919 Revolution, was a landmark event in the country's modern history. It played a great role in the development of Egypt's awareness of itself as a nation and in the development of the political institutions that came with such awareness. Its influence on the national imaginary has passed on from generation to generation and is still alive today a hundred years on, not only in the history books and lecture rooms but also in the wider public arena, most notably in Cairo's iconic Tahrir Square throughout January and February of 2011, which witnessed the revival of images and slogans first used during 1919. Many analysts saw the 2011 popular uprising that toppled the Mubarak regime after thirty years of autocratic rule as a natural descendant of the 1919 Revolution, bypassing Nasser's 1952 'revolution' which was in fact a military coup that kept the military in power for generations until the ouster of Mubarak.

While the 1919 revolution may have been seen to have failed at the time in that it did not gain Egypt its independence from the British, its strategic success, if not immediately comprehended, was to make Egypt feel its potential, its unity, its nationhood. Such budding consciousness naturally took form in literary and other artistic expressions, notably the then nascent genre of the novel. Indeed, the revolution is credited with helping the evolution of the genre in Egyptian literature, at the time still dominated by poetry. In turn, however, the evolving genre helped the educated class to grasp the significance of the revolution and become conscious of their nationhood. Thus, within a few years of 1919, Tawfiq al-Hakim (1898–1987), then a young writer, was to write the first major novel to celebrate the events of 1919, *The Return of the Spirit*. But it was Naguib Mahfouz (1911–2006) who eventually documented and immortalised the revolution in his magnum opus, *The Cairo Trilogy* published in 1956–7.

These are relatively early grand classics of representations of 1919 in fiction, but there are many other less-known works, not just in fiction, but also in other genres such as verse, drama, song, memoir, film, TV series, some closer to the historic event itself, but many evolving much later as 1919 became part of the national imaginary that kept reconceiving and reproducing the event in ways suitable to the present moment of later events.

The present monograph attempts to set the record straight by drawing attention to literary and other artistic representations of the revolution neglected by earlier researchers, while reassessing the canonical ones; by highlighting the role of women in the revolution; by showing the role of communities beyond the capital, Cairo, which has so far stolen the thunder of the rest of the country; and by bringing to light the contribution of the rank and file of the nation to the uprising, traditionally overshadowed by the role of the political elite and the educated classes. This revaluation could not have come at a more appropriate moment, not just because of the centenary of 1919, but also because of the ongoing renewed interest in 1919 since 2011, of which a good example, analysed here, is Ahmad Murad's recent novel, *1919*, published in 2014, just three years after the 2011 events, tacitly making the link and writing the past to make a statement about the present.

Professor Rasheed El-Enany, Series Editor,
Emeritus Professor of Modern Arabic Literature,
University of Exeter

Acknowledgements

This book has benefitted from the generous support of many individuals. I clarified my ideas about the 1919 revolution during conversations with Laila Soliman and Alia Mossallam as they were preparing for the play *Hawa al-Hurriya* (*Whims of Freedom*); these conversations have been an eye opener to me. Alia further generously shared with me insights and documents linked to her research into the peasants' contribution to the revolution; her work is an inspiration to me.

My colleagues and friends in and around the Arab and Islamic Civilizations Department at the American University in Cairo (AUC) have helped in many different ways. I want to thank in particular Amina Elbendary for her discreet and effective support and Adam Talib for his multiform advice and thorough feedback on the book proposal. Samia Mehrez' work has always been an inspiration to me. I thank her for making me believe this could become a book from the earliest stages and for her immeasurable advice and insights, not least her inspiring comments on two of the chapters. This book also owes a lot to Samah Selim's detailed feedback on several chapters and to my stimulating conversations with her; these heartening exchanges kept me going during the writing process and her inspiring insights helped me sharpen my argument.

The American University in Cairo provided one semester paid leave in Fall 2016, which gave me the time I needed to begin working on the project; the writing fellowship in the form of a course release I received in Spring 2019 from the Mellon Foundation allowed me to complete the manuscript. My research into 'Figures of Revolt and Revolution in Modern Egyptian Literature' for the course ARIC 3197 in the Fall of 2013, 2014 and 2015 helped me prepare for this book; the discussion with the students in these courses, and in my course on 'Narratives and Images of the 1919 Revolution' in Spring 2019 greatly informed my reflection. I am also thankful to Ola Seif and Katharine Halls for the presentations they gave in my class, and to Mark Muelhaeusler from the AUC Library for being an enthusiastic interlocutor about documents from 1919. For the illustrations, I thank Ruud Gielens, Eman Morgan from the Rare Books Library at AUC, and the staff at the Centre for Theatre and Music, who tried to be as accommodating as they could during my research journey at the Centre.

Throughout this research project, I have been lucky to be surrounded by people who generously sent useful documents, provided help during my research journey and gave valuable suggestions. For that, I am indebted to Roger Allen, Emad Abu Ghazi, Ferial Ghazul, Nadia al-Gindi, Peter Gran, Alain Gresh, Heba Helmi, Hala Kamal, Arab Lotfi, Sayyid Mahmud, Ahmad Mourad, Hussein Omar, Muhammad Shuayr and Amina Rachid. I also owe a word of thanks to the scholars who trained me in literary criticism, in particular to Heidi Toelle.

Earlier versions of Chapters 6 and 7 were presented at the Supreme Council of Culture in Cairo, the Annual History Seminar at the American University in Cairo, the congress of the European Association for Arabic Literature, l'Institut du Monde Arabe in Paris and the annual meeting of the Middle East Studies Association. I thank the organisers for giving me the opportunity to present my work and benefit from the criticism and questions of engaged audiences. I am thankful to the editors of *Kitab Maraya* for giving me the opportunity to publish parts of Chapter 6.

I am indebted to Rasheed El-Enany, editor of the Edinburgh Studies in Modern Arabic Literature Series, for his valuable suggestions and thorough review of the manuscript, and to the anonymous reviewers for their insightful comments. I thank as well all the EUP staff for ensuring a friendly communication and a fluid publication process. This manuscript (apart from Chapter 4), has been copy-edited by Nada Elia; I thank her for her patience with my schedule and her encouragement.

The writing process for this book has been arduous, at times painful. I am blessed with my friends, who shared my fascination for the subject, kept breathing energy into me when it was most needed and ensured that I was not losing track of my schedule. I want to thank in particular Heba Helmi,

Lamia Bolbol, Nevine Elnoseiry and Dina Kabil for all this, and for the multiform advice and stimulating conversations.

My last thankful words go to my parents and family. This book would have been a lot more fun to write if my father was still alive to share these stories of revolution and drag me playfully into stormy discussions; I remain forever indebted to him and to my late mother for the gift of education and for my interest in narratives of hope and social justice. I am grateful to Hany and Engy for their heartening presence, and to Yousra and Salma for their love, humour and for the time they awarded me. Finally, I thank Yassine Temlali for his patience, daily encouragements and, not least, for his discerning eye on earlier drafts of this book. No words can do justice to the rock solid and loving support he provided during the whole process.

Note on Transliteration and Translation

I have used a simplified version of the *IJMES* transliteration system; diacritical marks are dropped, except (') for the *hamza* and (') for the *'ayn*. Names of well-known figures, as well as authors of novels, films and plays are transliterated in accordance with their most common English spelling (Saad Zaghlul instead of Sa'd Zaghlul, Naguib Mahfouz instead of Najib Mahfuz, Laila Soliman instead of Layla Sulayman). In the transliteration of Egyptian proper names and titles, the letter *jim* is spelled (g) ('Abd al-Gawwad instead of 'Abd al-Jawwad and *Gumhuriyyat Zifta* instead of *Jumhuriyyat Zifta*). Unless otherwise stated, translation of primary and secondary sources from Arabic or French is mine.

To the memory of my parents, Yousry Heshmat and Vike Braet

Introduction

Or perhaps the abysmal tension between what is narrated and what cannot be narrated in what is collectively experienced is the unavoidable law of community. The latter, in any case, is always beyond judgement, or judged in vain. The community just is: from its celestial signs and secularized tabernacles, from the permanent negotiation that it establishes with its own inevitable myths. From its strange wisdom in survival that has generally nothing much to do with intellectual critique. (Casullo 2009: 124)

The experience of equality, as it was lived by many in the course of the movement – neither as a goal nor a future agenda but as something occurring in the present and verified as such – constitutes an enormous challenge for subsequent representation. (Ross 2002: 11)

On 12 February 2011, one day after the hundreds of thousands of people who had occupied Tahrir square for eighteen days had withdrawn, I witnessed a scene on the *midan* that left a durable impression on me. President Hosni Mubarak had just stepped down, and I expected to find in Tahrir some sense of the joy and excitement I had experienced the night before. Instead, the *midan* was pulsing with tension; heated discussions were taking place between youth who refused to fold up their tents and those who vehemently pushed them to do so. Among the many disturbing scenes I witnessed that day, I saw tens of youth frantically cleaning up the square – although it had never been dirty throughout those eighteen days. They were gathering the pavement stones demonstrators had patiently taken off one by one to be used in the battles against the *baltagiyyas* (thugs), and washing slogans off the dark green metallic fences with sponges and dish soap (Heshmat 2012: 100–1).

In the following days, not only slogans were wiped off from the walls and fences, but a more general, all-encompassing operation of erasure began, and the 25 January revolution was actively re-written in an elitist manner.[1] The complexity of the *extra-ordinary* moment we had gone through was simplified through a focus on the sit-in, detaching it from its context and from the still unfolding revolutionary momentum. The *mazar* aspect that had already existed during the eighteen days – as Tahrir became a place to *visit* and photograph – became more and more prominent in the narrative about Tahrir; rather than a site of struggle, the *midan* was now a place to be lauded and celebrated. The scene of the youth tediously cleaning the fences surfaced in my mind when I began preparing for a course titled 'Narratives of Revolt and Resistance in Egyptian Literature', which I taught in the Fall of 2013 at the American University in Cairo. As I was reading scenes of demonstrations, strikes or rioting, as they unfold in novels, short stories, plays or films, I became more and more sensitive to what had been left out of the story. Putting texts about the same event in conversation with each other, I became aware of the silences in each narrative; every narrator was offering a personal insight, packaged in his/her own ideological preconceptions and exclusions. Nowhere were these silences as familiar as in texts dealing with Egypt's anti-colonial revolution of 1919.

Like 2011, Egypt's 1919 anti-colonial revolution is framed through a central, photogenic moment. Similarly to the Tahrir sit-in, the demonstrations of Spring 1919, which erupted when the British administration exiled the nationalist leader Saad Zaghlul, have come to *signify* 1919. This occulted the diverse and complex struggles underlying that moment; it masked hundreds of stories about the strikes, sit-ins, spontaneous street demonstrations and carefully planned sabotage actions. It deadened the voices of thousands of ordinary people, muted their demands, slogans and songs, concealed their hopes, anger, pains and fears. It is this systematic politics of erasure that I am concerned with here.

This book is an encounter with stories of the 1919 revolution as they unfold in novels, short stories, memoirs, plays, films and drama series. Organised chronologically, it brings together narratives published and produced between 1923, in the immediate aftermath of 1919, and 2014, in the aftermath of yet another revolutionary moment. All the chapters place the works studied in the context of their production through a reflection about the contemporary social and political dynamics. Informed by concepts of class and gender, my analysis underlines the specific issues at stake in the memory of 1919 at different moments in Egypt's recent history. That memory, I argue, has been constantly evolving, shaped, modelled and re-modelled throughout the last century by ongoing social, cultural and political struggles.

This book is at once an illustration of the many different ways 1919 has been remembered, and a critical reading of those narratives and their reception. More fundamentally, it highlights processes of remembering and forgetting that have contributed to shaping what I call a dominant imaginary about 1919, coined by successive political and cultural elites. My main contention in this book is that literature and film, at once a mirror and a vector of the politics of erasure I referred to earlier, played a key role in shaping this dominant imaginary. As I seek to understand *how* and *why* so many voices have been relegated to the margins, I reinsert elements of the story into the dominant narrative, thereby enabling the reader to meet the revolution's marginalised voices and to reconnect with its layered emotional fabric.

Similarities 1919/2011

The striking similarities 1919 shares with 2011 are related to the fact that both can be defined not only as a combination of demonstrations and riots, or even as insurrections, but as revolutionary moments.[2] In Arabic, the term *thawra* comes from the root th-wa-ra, which signifies anger, directed either against an individual or a ruler. It is used in Egyptian historiography to designate moments of revolt and rebellion: *thawrat al-Qahira* in October 1798 during the French expedition, or *thawrat al-Sa'id* in 1824 under Muhammad 'Ali's rule. But it is also used as a translation of the modern political concept of 'revolution' in English and French, which indicates a 'challenge to the established political order and the eventual establishment of a new order radically different from the preceding one' ('Revolution' 2019). In the Marxist tradition, as developed in particular by Gramsci, a revolutionary moment is a moment in which the relations of force between classes are potentially disrupted (Martinelli 1968: 8). Accordingly, this moment, while it certainly constitutes 'a challenge to the established political order', does not necessarily lead to the 'establishment of a new order radically different from the preceding one.'

Like 2011, 1919 witnessed massive popular mobilisations, hitherto unprecedented in scale. As with the huge numbers gathering in Tahrir and elsewhere throughout the country in 2011, accounts of 1919 describe endless seas of people spontaneously bursting into the streets. Testimonies of both moments insist on the extraordinary solidarity of the people on the streets, their humorous and carnivalesque spirit and attitudes.[3] Moreover, like 2011, 1919 was a complex and multi-layered moment, that developed through a variety of struggles, including social struggles. The apex of each of those two revolutionary moments was preceded by a crescendo of social and nationalistic or democratic struggles: peasant rebellions in 1918, urban protest in the city of al-Mahalla in 2008. Finally, both moments carried hope for radical transformation – even though both failed to achieve it. Among all the slogans displayed in the *midan* in 2011, only one, *Irhal* (Leave!) was successful, with president Hosni Mubarak stepping down, whereas the demands for 'bread, freedom, social justice' were not met. Similarly, 1919 witnessed the participation of important numbers of underprivileged, both working class and peasants who carried their own social agenda – an element I discuss in greater detail below. Most of these demands were not satisfied in the aftermath of the revolution.

Following Nicolas Casullo in his article about the Argentinian revolution quoted in the epigraph to this introduction, I argue that 'the figure of the failed or revoked revolution' is helpful to the understanding of 1919's memory. According to Casullo, 'such a figure . . . disturbs and frees up the site of immobile discourses that have been installed by dominant historiographies, by reifying politics and by common sense, all of which conclude by distancing and hardening memory' (Casullo 2009: 109). The figure of the 'failed revolution' facilitates the task of questioning and deconstructing what I call, following Paul Ricoeur, an 'imposed memory', a memory 'armed with a history that is itself "authorized", the official history, the history publicly learned and celebrated' (Ricoeur 2004: 85).

1919 as Articulated in Dominant Historiography

In school curricula and the media, as well as in most historiographical material, both official and academic, the 1919 revolution has commonly been framed under a trope of national unity. According to that narrative, the 1919 revolution began on 9 March in Cairo, with student demonstrations protesting the British colonial administration's arrest and subsequent exile of Saad Zaghlul (1859–1927), the leader of the nationalist Wafd (delegation). The story presents the revolution as a mostly peaceful Cairo-centred event led by upper-middle class figures from the Wafd, and insists on the unity of the nation, especially between Muslims and Christians, and on the participation of a few hundreds of elite women.

In the history school programme of 2016, as presented in a textbook for

Figure I.1 History textbook, 2019. The title of the chapter states: '1919: Egypt's Nationalist Revolution'

graduation year at high school (*thanawiyya 'amma*),⁴ eight pages are devoted to 1919 – in contrast to eleven pages to 1952, under the title 'Egypt's nationalist revolution'. 1919 is presented as the first nationalist revolution (*thawra qawmiyya*) in modern Egyptian history (*Tarikh* 2018: 121). The chapter is summarised by its introductory picture, a drawing of people standing in front of a green flag with a cross and a crescent. The drawing brings together a man and an adolescent wearing a *tarbush* (a fez indicating an effendi background), a Christian cleric, an imam and two women whose dresses indicate an upper middle-class background. Although peasants and workers are mentioned later, their absence in the chapter's iconography eloquently illustrates the main postulate of this historical narrative. The introduction insists on the identification of 1919 as the birth of a united nation (*umma muwwahhada*) constituted of 'Egyptians only', without discrimination between Muslims and Christians (*Tarikh* 2018:121). National unity is presented in a celebratory mode, as a corollary of a comprehensive revolution (*thawra shamila*) bringing together 'all cities of Egypt, all strata of society, workers, students and peasants, men and women, and both elements of the *umma*, Muslims and Christians' (*Tarikh* 2018: 120). Although the textbook describes the historical context of the period, and mentions the oppression experienced in particular by peasants during the First World War, there is no clear link between the peasant action during the 1919 revolution and this oppression. The remark that 'revolutionary committees were constituted in order to organise the struggle against the British' gives an impression of a well-organised and coordinated movement.⁵

This mention of revolutionary committees, and the laudatory tone used to present the popular violence, is a mark of the post-1952 historiography about 1919. Anne Clément dates this apology for violence to the end of 1951, when the Wafd, in the context of a revival of the anti-colonial struggle, 'revisited' the revolution during one of its celebrations: 'it is described as a real war whose heroes are the fighters who have sacrificed their lives for their country (*al-fida'iyyin*)' (Clément 2005: 61). Moreover, starting in 1952, 1919 is inserted in a teleological narrative about the nationalist movement framed by the Free Officers, in which the July Revolution becomes 'the successful culmination not only of the failed 1919 Revolution but also of one hundred and fifty years of exhaustive revolutionary endeavor' (Di-Capua 2001: 92).

One of the consequences was that the figure of 'Saad Zaghlul passed into oblivion' (Clément 2005: 15).

Before 1952, 'the 1919 Revolution was subjected to the political interpretation of the Wafd Party and its protégés' (Di-Capua 2001: 92). More specifically, in her article eloquently titled 'Re-creating the Past: The Manipulation of the Notion of Rupture in Egyptian Revolutions', Giedre Sabaseviciute notes that in 'historiographical literature produced between 1920 and 1946, two major tendencies seem to prevail: an almost complete lack of interest in both the Urabi movement and 1919 uprising and a tendency to focus on the actions of the Wafd and its leader Saad Zaghlul' (Sabaseviciute 2011: 5). This personalisation of politics is eloquently embodied in a persistent iconisation of both Saad Zaghlul and his wife Safiyya Zaghlul.

The Metaphor of Saad Zaghlul as Egypt

Surprisingly maybe, the man who came to embody the struggle for independence was not the product of a neat and linear journey into anti-colonial activism. Although Saad Zaghlul was active during the 'Urabi revolution, and was imprisoned for a few months in 1883, accused by the British of belonging to an underground organisation called 'Gam'iyyat al-intiqam' (Abu Ghazi 2019), he later became a member of an elite that had strong ties to the British authorities. He was on good terms with Lord Cromer, Consul-general of Egypt, infamous in Egyptian memory for his repression of the Dinshway peasants in 1906, and was appointed as Minister of Education in 1909 and Minister of Justice in 1910. Born to a *sheikh al-balad* (village headman), he became a close associate of the ruling elite through his marriage, as his father-in-law, Mustafa Fahmi, was a protégé of the British who was regularly appointed prime minister. It is only in 1914 that he reconnected with the activism of his youth, becoming a voice of the anti-colonial agitation as vice-president of the new Legislative Assembly he had joined in 1913. According to Tamim al-Barghouti, it is the combination of [rural] origins and elitist upbringing that made of Zaghlul the ideal interlocutor for the British administration circles, as he could conveniently be presented as a spokesperson on behalf of the peasants.[6] Ironically, although he was born in a Delta village, Zaghlul 'had never been a peasant'[7] (al-Barghouti 2007: 68), as he belonged to a land-owning family possessing more than 200 *feddans*.

Not unlike the British administration, 'many national historians have tried to present Zaghlul as a son of a local peasant family in order to stress Zaghlul's "Egyptianness"' (Schulze 2012). This image of an authentic Egyptian peasant, in combination with his journey as a man who stood at the crossroads of a traditional education and modern upbringing, at once a sheikh, and an effendi,[8] then a bey and a pasha, was crucial in the construction of his role as leader.

His eloquence and combativeness made Zaghlul extremely popular.[9] Hundreds of thousands of people took to the streets to protest his exile in March 1919 and 300,000 partook in his funeral procession when he passed away in August 1927 (Clément 2005: 23).[10] 'In death as in life, Saad was venerated, and the cult around him [only] grew [with time]. Parents named their children Saad; shopkeepers hung his pictures and costumers bought medallions engraved with his bust and scarves imprinted with his likeness' (Baron 2005: 154).

The popular veneration of Saad is eloquently mirrored in three 1919 musical hits, two of them composed by the musician and composer Sayyid Darwish (1892–1923) and written by the poet Badi' Khayri (1893–1966).[11] Saad was invoked in a playful manner in these songs, mainly through wordplays on the double meanings of both his first and last name. The most famous one, *Qum ya Masri*, sung by Sayyid Darwish, contains a verse in which *Saad* (which means 'good omen' or 'happiness') at once refers to the leader and can be understood as 'happiness': *Yum ma saadi. Rah hadar uddam 'inayk* (*The day my happiness . . . was wasted in front of your eyes*).[12] The song was intended to be sung by every single person on the street and this verse in particular allows a strong personal identification with the leader, mostly through the possessive pronoun 'i' suffixed to the leader's name. Saad thus becomes literally *owned* by the people while his presence is framed as a condition for the happiness of every individual. The song performed by the singer Na'ima al-Masriyya (1894–1976)[13] is entirely based on a playful reference to the leader through the praise of a kind of date called *balah zaghlul*; its central verse metaphorically addresses Saad as the 'soul of your country' (*ya ruh biladak*). Finally, the song performed by the singer and actress Munira al-Mahdiyya (1885–1965) describes her love and passion for the leader through a playful reference to the meaning of *zaghlul* as 'young pigeon': 'it's a *zaghlul* and my heart aches for it' (*Zaghlul wa qalbi mal ilay*). In this song, the leader is depicted as a beloved, and as a full moon (*badr*) standing high in the sky. More generally, Saad Zaghlul was often lauded in many of the colloquial poems (*azjal*) distributed in pamphlets and publicly performed by *zajjalun* (*zajal* performers).[14]

Neo-classical poetry was another vector of this iconisation, as it efficiently contributed to articulate a more conventional metaphor of Saad as an embodiment of the nation. In addition to *qasidas* by established poets, like Ahmad Shawqi and Hafiz Ibrahim, Saad Zaghlul inspired poems by ordinary people, who wrote to celebrate his deeds, welcome him when he came back from exile, or simply greet him.[15] In many of these poems, Zaghlul's figure embodies Egypt and is metaphorically depicted as *al-umma*, or *misr*. His death further gave Zaghlul 'a kind of "sanctity" aura' (Clément 2005: 24). Two elegies by Shawqi and Ibrahim singing the praises of the deceased, describe him as Egypt's 'father', a 'sun' for whom the entire Orient is weeping (Shawqi), and a dazzling light (*shihab*) (Ibrahim). Both elegies use the leader as a metaphor for Egypt. Ibrahim underlines the exact equivalence between him and the nation: in the coffin lies a nation, he says. Shawqi describes the modern Egyptian nation as being constructed by Saad, and shaped by his qualities. Ibrahim further describes Saad's death as an earthquake (*zilzal*) and a catastrophe (*nakba*).[16] Among many other elegies, Ahmad Rami's '*In yaghib 'an Misra Saadun*' likewise frames his death as a calamity, inviting the audience to glorify Saad. As it was repeatedly sung by Um Kulthum (1904–75), a venerated diva herself, the poem efficiently contributed to fixing the leader's memory in the Egyptian imaginary.

Safiyya Zaghlul, 'Mother of the Egyptians' and the Women's Demonstrations

Although her central role in the political scene is most often ignored by historians of the nationalist movement (Baron 2005: 136), Safiyya Zaghlul (1876–1946) was no less of an icon than her husband. She became politically active during Saad Zaghlul's exile, as she de facto replaced him as leader of the national movement. She insisted his house, known as *Bayt al-Umma* (House of the Nation), should remain open during his absence; she attended meetings, organised demonstrations, welcomed delegations of protestors, and

Figure I.2 Advertisement for the 'Safiyya Zaghlul perfume' carrying the photograph and signature of the singer Umm Kulthum.

addressed the crowds from the balcony.[17] She managed to preserve her independence from her husband, taking on initiatives of her own and occasionally openly expressing her disagreements with his political views. Safiyya Zaghlul was extremely popular, and when she left to join Saad Zaghlul in his second exile on 8 October 1923, the 'dense crowd' that accompanied her, 'according to the *Egyptian Mail*, numbered "many hundreds of thousands"' (Baron 2005: 146). Similarly to Saad Zaghlul, she was glorified in poetry,[18] and had her image exploited by ephemera, as well as having it associated with that of Um Kulthum.[19]

Beth Baron argues that Safiyya Zaghlul consciously worked on her political image, presenting herself as 'Umm al-Misriyyin' (Mother of the Egyptians) and manipulating 'maternal symbolism to carve out a political role for herself' (Baron 2005: 135–6). Having no children, she frequently presented herself as the mother of young demonstrators, taking affectionate attitudes towards them (Baron 2005: 136). This family rhetoric is analysed by Baron as 'a dual-edged sword' serving the Wafd's class interests, as 'it condemned violence and stifled dissent from below, from the "devoted sons" and left decision making in the hands of the elite'. She further underlines the fact that this rhetoric 'did not seriously challenge' gender order, as it reinforced 'domesticity' (Baron 2005: 161).

Safiyya Zaghlul is associated in the imaginary of 1919 with the group of women of whom she was the dynamo, along with Huda Shaʿrawi (1879–1947),[20] a central figure of Egyptian feminism. In addition to their roles as political leaders, Zaghlul and Shaʿrawi were the cornerstones of the anti-colonial demonstration that gathered around 300 women on 16 March 1919.[21] That demonstration was immediately welcomed by Hafiz Ibrahim in a famous *qasida*, 'The fair ladies went out to protest (*Kharaja al-ghawani yahtajijna*)', which was published in nationalist leaflets.[22] Its eloquent and sarcastic depiction of the ridiculously disproportionate use of force by the British military was exploited as a propaganda tool by the Wafd to denounce the systematic repression by the colonial army of peaceful demonstrations. The narrator, who 'observes the gathering', describes the women as harmless demonstrators, carrying nothing but basil and roses, nevertheless surrounded by British soldiers, whose swords are pointed at the women's breasts. The poem salutes and glorifies the women's courageous anti-colonial stance, presenting them metaphorically as 'stars in the darkness'.[23] But, by identifying them as belonging to the elite, as it mentions 'their palaces', the poem excludes all other women from its representation, fixing and reifying female participation in that particular moment.[24]

'Visual material, and photographs in particular' further 'played a crucial role in embedding the women's demonstration in the collective memory. Photographs became a trigger for remembering the revolution and shaping the women's demonstrations as an iconic moment' (Baron 2005: 123). Baron has shown how photographs of women demonstrating in 1919 underwent a series of changes in order to turn women into a signifier of national awakening. By tracing the minor and major crops and edits and studying the accompanying captions, she proves that the photographs were taken out of their context in order to focus on the veiled woman, and to systematically associate her with figures of the new nation, like the Egyptian flag (Baron 2005: 123–7).

I argue that, in addition to this association between woman and nation, these photos were crucial for establishing elite women as standing at the forefront of the nationalist struggle. Women from under-privileged backgrounds are thus implicitly excluded from this iconic, visual representation of the revolution. More generally, these photographs were crucial in establishing 1919 as an exclusively nationalist revolution led by the upper middle class.

Six Years of Revolutionary Turmoil: 1918–23

The trope of national unity around which these iconic representations are constructed, however – in addition to most of the historiographical and literary accounts – appears to be fundamentally problematic. First of all, from a methodological perspective, this trope is based on a questionable assumption. In an article about Upper Egypt in modern Egyptian history, Peter Gran regrets that 'virtually all historians approach Egypt in terms of the idea of a center and do so according to the oriental despotism model'. He explains that, according to that model, 'the countryside and the provincial towns are areas where a simplified traditional life carries on rather statically while change and movement occur in the large cities' (Gran 2004: 80). Gran further argues: 'thus we come to assume that Upper Egyptians participated in national events, such as the 'Urabi Revolution and the 1919 Revolution, but in these exceptional moments they did so only as a result of national leadership' (Gran 2004: 82).

Moreover, this trope fails to give an accurate picture of what was going on. Instead of a movement entirely triggered by Saad Zaghlul's exile and framed by the Wafd's leadership, the 1919 revolution emerges as a moment more extended in time and space, with mobilisations of peasants and workers on their own agendas, including violent challenges to the social order. It can thus be accurately depicted as a revolutionary moment in which the balance of power is disrupted by the sudden irruption of the masses on stage, a power vacuum in some rural zones and the self-governance of some localities by popular committees.

Although there are testimonies of a coordinated preparation for a series of peaceful demonstrations if Saad Zaghlul came to be arrested,[25] the protests that erupted in Spring 1919 were much more radical than anything the Wafd leaders had expected or imagined, and their reality was very far from the image of a huge, peaceful demonstration organised and led by the Wafd, in which all other segments of society would form a procession carrying nationalist slogans. People did not keep to the instructions of the Wafd: to organise peaceful demonstrations 'that were to be an image of civilization' (Mossallam, forthcoming).[26] Peasants attacked and destroyed railroad stations, cut roads, railroads and telegraph lines; they looted granaries and attacked and killed

British soldiers and officers.²⁷ 'Over 100 villages were destroyed, 63 railroad stations were burnt, and the railway itself was damaged at over 200 points' (Schulze 1991: 188). According to al-Rafi'i, 3000 peasants lost their lives during the revolution (Diyab 2011: 158). Bedouin tribes 'advanced on the provinces of Buhaira and Fayyum and occupied them the following day. On March 17 they engaged in battles with the British forces in Damanhur/Buhaira and Madinat al-Fayyum' (Schulze 1991: 193).

Not only were the demonstrations and riots of Spring 1919 accompanied by a peasant uprising on a major scale; in fact, that uprising had already been going on for a while. Schulze notes that 'in spring 1918 collective resistance to the presence of grain confiscation agents and draft officers could be seen in the villages of the Faqus and Sharqiyya districts' (Schulze 1991: 186). Alia Mossallam writes that

> in 1918 reports in the British Foreign Office Archives indicate that some people had been arrested for inciting others against resistance – songs that sing of the war and its temptations also start to be sung to warn others against taking part in the war. The resistance becomes more confrontational until it becomes violent, with broken railways, murders and fires raging through the villages. (Mossallam, forthcoming)

Kyle Anderson confirms that

> mass uprisings took place encompassing [large] groups of actors – up to and including entire villages. At least seven examples of mass resistance connected to recruitment for the ELC [Egyptian Labour Corps] and CTC [Camel Transport Corps] are preserved in the Foreign Office records. The largest example of mass resistance reported in the archives comes from the Delta province of Daqhiliyya. (Anderson 2017: 16)²⁸

If the peasants rebelled, and did so violently, it was not necessarily thus upon the initiative of the Cairene elite,²⁹ nor chiefly to protest against Saad Zaghlul's exile, but for reasons linked to the British requisition of livestock and grains, and forced conscription during the First World War. Schulze argues that the peasants' uprisings in 1919 were in fact a large scale rebellion against the economic restructuring of cotton plantations in which the Egyptian state played a central role. Most rural riots were thus rooted in the daily oppression the peasants confronted, and carried radical aspirations in terms of social organisation. The contradictions and tensions between landowners and peasants were in some provinces so violent that 'the peasants revolted against the landowners and looted the large estates' (Barakat 2009: 63). Although he disagrees on the importance of those attacks on landowners' property, Nathan Brown documents a 'series of estate seizures' that 'occurred throughout Egypt during the Revolution' (Brown 1990: 207–8). In addition, 'peasants also began to expropriate moveable and untraceable property-the cattle, sheep, fodder, and foodstuffs that had been amassed by the wealthy during the war' (Goldberg 1992: 272). Moreover, vital institutions in some cities were occupied,[30] and popular revolutionary committees took over their organisation, as happened most notably in the Delta town of Zifta,[31] but also in Minya and Asyut (Brown 1990: 207).

As with the rural riots, urban protests also preceded the explosion of March 1919. At the end of the war severe food shortages and high inflation were felt in the big cities, and triggered growing unrest that materialised in a wave of strikes for wage increases in Cairo and Alexandria in February 1918 (Beinin and Lockman 1998: 84–5). The two leading sectors of the Spring 1919 strikes, the tramway and railway workers, had already mobilised during the winter of 1918–19 for improved work conditions and wage increases (Beinin and Lockman 1998: 91, 95).

Unlike the situation in the countryside, where poor peasants were under the yoke of Egyptian landowners, working class people had as their bosses governmental institutions or foreign company owners, and there were a lot of grievances against foreign foremen. The link between nationalism and class struggle was thus natural, and 'the events of 1919 had fused national and class consciousness into one composite world-outlook for most Egyptian workers' (Beinin and Lockman 1998: 105). The Wafd understood the importance of the strikes for the destabilisation of the colonial power, especially in the strategic sector of transportation, and supported them in a number of ways. In addition, organisational ties linked nationalist and working class circles, through the leadership of some strikes by nationalist lawyers connected to the Nationalist Party or to the Wafd (see Beinin and Lockman 1998: 100).

However, it is incorrect to read the mobilisation of the working class in

Figure I.3 Demonstrations in Cairo on 8 and 9 April, 1919. Rare Books and Special Collections Library, the American University in Cairo.

1919 as if the workers were merely one procession in a demonstration led by the Wafd. Indeed, the large scale mobilisation of working class segments that was crucial to building the power struggle against the colonial administration was largely based on a social agenda. In addition to the tram and railway workers,

> workers at the ESR printing press, the Government Press, the Arsenal and the government workshops, the Alexandria tramways, the Hilwan electric railways, the Cairo electric company, postal, port, lighthouse and customs employees, taxi and carriage drivers' were among the many others to go on strike in the Spring of 1919, as well as 'peasants working in industry'. (Beinin and Lockman 1998: 98)

The demands included higher pay and shorter working hours, and by the end of the Spring, the most combative of the sectors had succeeded in winning some of their demands: in the case of the railway workers for instance 'a substantial increase in wages' (Beinin and Lockman 1998: 98). Working class unrest did not stop, however, when Zaghlul was released in April 1919; August of the same year, for instance, witnessed an important strike wave (Beinin and Lockman 1998: 105).[32] Some sectors experienced deception towards the Wafdist leadership; the 1919 movement was a privileged moment in the development of the class consciousness and union movement of the Egyptian working class, as shown by Beinin and Lockman, since the workers were seeking to organise themselves independently from the nationalist movement.

Dynamics of National Unity in Context

As these elements do not fit into a simplistic national unity discourse, they are dropped in most of the historiographical material. Hence, the struggle against the colonial power is idealised and disconnected from both its local and international contexts, including from other contemporary anti-colonial struggles.[33] However, literary narratives show that not only were Egyptian nationalists aware of these struggles, they were also popular in the street. The way the Irish independence struggle is mentioned in several narratives I analyse (see Chapters 3 and 6) confirms that it stood 'as a frame of reference in relation to which emergent nationalist and/or anti-colonial movements elsewhere might encode their own attitudes to British rule.' (Boehmer 2005: 10). A *qasida* by Ahmad Shawqi, recited on the occasion of a commemoration of the revolution, mentions Sinn Féin by way of analogy to the Egyptian revolutionaries,[34] sarcastically noting that the British were afraid the Egyptians would become a similar threat.

Likewise, all elements that could tarnish the image of an idealised religious and ethnic unity are dropped. The fact that unity intervened in a context of confessional strife is ignored.[35] The violent acts against members of the Armenian community, after an Armenian shot at a demonstration from a window are rarely evoked.[36] Moreover, anything beyond the limits of what is commonly accepted in terms of confessional diversity is not mentioned. Thus, the presence in and support of members of the Jewish community for the nationalist struggle (Fahmy 2011: 141) is systematically omitted, and references to their presence in that struggle are censored.³⁷ The massive dimension of inter-confessional fraternisation, maybe deemed threatening because of the popular mobilisation it entails, is also not publicised. For example, the visit by 10,000 Muslims to *al-dar al-batrirarkiyya* on the occasion of Easter on 22 April 1919 (Mikha'il 1980: 30) is not a widely known fact. Although it is mentioned that priests orated in mosques and imams in churches (*Tarikh* 2018: 120), the radical implications of this permeability of houses of worship is not fully explored, neither is it said that both Christian and Muslim women gave speeches in at least one mosque, in Sayyida Zeinab.³⁸

Instead of an orderly demonstration, as it is metaphorically embodied in the canonical narratives I analyse in Chapters 3 and 4, the 1919 revolution would be more accurately described as a carnival, a concept Mikhail Bakhtin defines as a 'temporary suspension of all hierarchic distinctions and barriers' (qtd in Fahmy 2011: 165). Ziad Fahmy gives a vivid depiction of the 'public dancing', 'collective singing' and cheering common on the streets. Although the Wafd presided over a powerful propaganda network, efficiently disseminating slogans through pamphlets collectively read at cafes and popular gatherings, the happy chaos was an indicator that the movement was too radical to be entirely under the control of the nationalist elite. 'Alternative centers of power were created. The streets, and by extension the public squares, cafes, bars, mosques, and churches, became the necessary carnivalesque spaces outside the reach of the centralized authorities' (Fahmy 2011: 165).

Al-Azhar became 'the nerve center of the revolution' (Fahmy 2011: 147). Although the mosque was besieged by colonial troops, it welcomed daily meetings gathering more than 10,000 people. In his memoirs, Husayn Fawzi (1900–88), at the time a student of medicine, gives a humorous account of the strategies Azhar students developed to enter the mosque through dark passages and secret entrances unknown to the British (Fawzi 1968: 101). Open discussions were led during these huge daily meetings, and tensions and power struggles among political groups were exposed to the masses. A report in the *Washington Post* quoted by Fahmy eloquently describes these meetings:

> So, day after day, morning, noon and night, the strikers and the nationalists assembled by the thousands in El Azhar to discuss their grievances and

demands, as well as methods of procedure. It is a grand and glorious carnival of speechmaking. Moslem ulemas and sheikhs, Coptic and Armenian priests and bishops, lawyers, doctors, professors, students, merchants and whoever has something to say, gets up to address the crowd. When the audience does not like a man or have had enough of him they say so. Up to date the most popular speaker is a Christian priest, a Copt, named Sergius. The only woman ever to speak at Azhar was a Jewess, a nationalist. (Fahmy 2011: 147)

Women in the Streets

Unlike iconic depictions discussed above, many testimonies document a large mobilisation of underprivileged women. As Nawal al-Saadawi has noted,

> little has been said about the masses of poor women who rushed into the nationalist struggle without counting the cost, and who lost their lives, whereas the lesser contributions of aristocratic women leaders have been noisily acclaimed and brought to the forefront. (Qtd in Baron 2005: 122)

Women from different class backgrounds were omnipresent in the street demonstrations throughout the struggle. In his depiction of the 7 April spontaneous demonstrations celebrating Zaghlul's release, 'Abd al-Rahman Fahmi

> took notice of the role played by the female urban masses. After recounting how . . . the elite women "paraded in their cars, waving flags and throwing flowers", Fahmi described how the "lower class women ['ammat al-nisa'] were not to be outdone as they rode on the back of trucks and [donkey-drawn carriages] and proceeded to dance and chant to the rhythm of drums and trumpets" (qtd in Fahmy 2011: 140).

In his memoirs of the revolution, Sheikh 'Abd al-Wahab al-Naggar describes a procession for

> the burial of one of the freedom martyrs marching in a very organised way, preceded by Musiqa Hasab Allah . . ., then the students from all kinds in two lines on the side, and an important number of women and girls walking in the midst of the two lines, preceded by flags. (Al-Naggar 2010: 186)

In the 'dense crowd' that accompanied Safiyya Zaghlul on 8 October 1923, when she left to join Saad Zaghlul on his second exile, 'there were ladies everywhere. There were black-robed ladies, lightly veiled, riding in luxurious motorcars . . ., but there were a great many more than that; there were middle class mothers and daughters on roofs and balconies and leaning from every window; there were women of the people, veiled in coarse black crepe-stuff, standing among the crowd in the streets' (Baron 2005: 146). In addition to their presence in the demonstrations, women partook, side by side with men, in blocking the roads, and attacking property in the countryside.[39] Besides the well-documented role of Safiyya Zaghlul and Huda Sha'rawi, women from different class backgrounds held key positions in the nationalist groups and contributed to organising the anti-colonial struggle.[40]

Moreover, contrary to what is suggested by the dominant narrative, violence was not exerted exclusively by peasants. Rather, violence – including assassinations of and attacks on British officials and high-ranking Egyptian personalities collaborating with the British authorities – was part of the nationalist movement's strategy. It is by now well established that, although this was ignored by most of its leaders, the Wafd had an underground organisation (see Chapter 5)[41] led by 'Abd al-Rahman Fahmi, an efficient organiser with a military background. Besides assassinations, it coordinated the demonstrations and financed a large network of informers. In addition, other underground armed organisations, not necessarily linked to the Wafd, were active.[42] Revolutionary violence was sometimes encouraged or even exerted by members of the Egyptian police, as some of them reportedly refused to obey orders to repress the movement. There are three documented cases of *ma'murs* (police chiefs) who either resigned from their posts, attacked a superior, or delivered weapons to the insurgents and joined them.[43]

Finally, long after the Spring of 1919, the revolutionary momentum expanded, in the form of several waves of street demonstrations, strikes and rioting. One of these waves took place when the Milner mission arrived in Egypt on 7 December 1919. Alfred Milner was the United Kingdom's colonial secretary and had come to Egypt intending to negotiate a solution to the crisis[44]; but the Wafd had circulated a boycott watchword:

> The mission was preceded and accompanied by disturbances. . . . At the Great Mosque of Alexandria, at the mosque of Abu'l-'Abbas al-Mursi, there were mass meetings of 15,000 nationalists. . . . Lawyers struck; the judicial machine broke down. Tradesmen, reaching their shops on 9 December, found notices saying 'Closed' on their doors. (Berque 1972: 315)

When Saad Zaghlul came back on 5 April 1921, he was welcomed by huge street demonstrations, hundreds of thousands of people gathering on his passage, from the port of Alexandria, throughout his entire journey to Cairo, where delirious crowds welcomed him at the railway station.[45] In the aftermath of his return, violent discussions took place 'over the composition and leadership of the official delegation which was to negotiate with Lord Curzon' (Berque 1972: 321). In that context, violent rioting took place in Tanta, Cairo and most prominently Alexandria, where 'unemployed workers from Sa'id, who (it was whispered) had founded an illegal trade union, mobilised the crowd. There were strikes among the employees of the Discount Bank, cab drivers, tram drivers, printers' (Berque 1972: 322). Moreover, when Zaghlul came back from his second exile, in October 1923, hundreds of thousands of people again welcomed him in the streets.

History as Narrative

Many of these fascinating, often surprising or disturbing facts, are ignored in most historiographical material, which describes an all-encompassing national movement led by a charismatic leader. Although I hope this book will contribute to reviving an understanding of some of these events, it is not my purpose to rewrite the history of 1919. Rather, through a close reading of a selection of narratives about 1919, I hope to contribute to a reflection about the way 1919 has been narrativised at different pivotal historical moments and in diverse media, both fiction and nonfiction.

This book is based on the assumption that the vision of the past embedded in any narrative, including literary and cinematic narratives, is a reconstruction, not a restitution of a sequence of events as they 'really' happened. On the contrary, 'the events of the past are . . . "conceptualized" as a story of a particular kind', as Hayden White has argued (Spiropoulou 2015: 118).

The events are made into a story by the suppression or subordination of certain of them and the highlighting of others, by characterization, motific repetition, variation of tone and point of view, alternative descriptive strategies, and the like – in short, all of the techniques that we would normally expect to find in the emplotment of a novel or a play. (White 1978: 84)

White further notes that 'most historical sequences can be emplotted in a number of different ways, so as to provide different interpretations of those events and to endow them with different meanings' (White 1978: 85).

These different interpretations are in turn a product of the period in which they are produced, alongside the class and gender dynamics, the reflection of the author's position in the literary field and the multiple power struggles taking place between the state and the cultural actors, as Pierre Bourdieu has argued (Bourdieu 1998). The contextualised reading I offer is based on Walter Benjamin's notion that 'every present invents its own past' (Spiropoulou 2015: 119). In his *Theses on the Philosophy of History*, Benjamin argued that 'every image of the past that is not recognized by the present as one of its own concerns threatens to disappear irretrievably' (Benjamin 1969: 255); and hence those images that survive are only those that the present recognises as one 'of its own concerns'. What remains, and what is lost, of those 'flashes' of memory, is ultimately a function of the present, of the power struggles of each historical period, between the 'victor' and the 'oppressed'.

For Benjamin, if 'victim and defeat were always voiceless, lacking their own narrative, their own past', it is because 'nothing makes them historically intelligible for the present' (Casullo 2009: 109). Hayden White echoed this idea that something needs to be 'historically intelligible for the present' in order to be remembered when he wrote about the historians of the French Revolution who 'shared with their audiences certain preconceptions about how the Revolution might be emplotted, in response to imperatives that were generally extra historical, ideological, aesthetic, or mythical' (White 1978: 85). In the way they presented the past, those historians were deeply influenced by considerations of the present, including their own ideological precepts. White's observations on historians' relations to the past are entirely valid also for reflecting on the way creative writers narrate the past.

In addition, White introduces the idea of the 'familiar', which is useful to my argument. He argues that events 'take on a familiar aspect . . . in their functions as elements of a familiar kind of configuration' (White 1978: 86), further explaining that:

> in looking at the ways in which such structures took shape or evolved, historians familiarize them, not only by providing more information about them, but also by showing how their developments conformed to one or another of the story types that we conventionally invoke to make sense of our own life-histories. (White 1978: 87)

So, in a sense, historians make sense of events, and familiarise them for their audiences by making them fit into a certain kind of story type. Hence, only a narrative that matches the contemporary audiences' 'ideological, aesthetic, or mythical' acceptations, has a chance to survive oblivion.

In *Memory, History, Forgetting*, Paul Ricoeur links both remembering and forgetting to narrative: it is through narrative that what he calls a 'manipulated', or an 'ideologized' memory is framed:

> the ideologizing of memory is made possible by the resources of variation offered by the work of narrative configuration. The strategies of forgetting are directly grafted upon this work of configuration: one can always recount differently, by eliminating, by shifting the emphasis, by recasting the protagonists of the action in a different light along with the outlines of the action. (Ricoeur 2004: 448)

More specifically, he argues that 'it is on the level where ideology operates as a discourse justifying power, domination, that the resources of manipulation provided by narrative are mobilised' (Ricoeur 2004: 85). Kirstin Ross similarly argues that 'dominant narrative configurations' are 'mostly reductions or circumscriptions of the event adopted by the official story' (Ross 2002: 8). She identifies these configurations as 'a temporal reduction', which is 'geographic' and involves a reduced 'cast of characters' (Ross 2002: 8–10). Her book, quoted in the epigraph to this introduction, focuses on what she calls the 'afterlives' of May 1968 in France and is relevant when studying the memory of other revolutionary moments.

Remembering and Forgetting 1919

My close reading of some key literary and cinematic narratives dealing with the 1919 revolution enables me to analyse those 'dominant narrative configurations' in an Egyptian context. The questions I raise throughout my analysis allow me to deconstruct what Ross calls 'defiguring strategies' (Ross 2002: 4) and to identify recurring patterns of distortion: what are the spatial and temporal delimitations of the event? What are the class and gender identities of the main characters or participants in the revolutionary action? How are they presented and what are the terms used to glorify or to denigrate them? And, most importantly, what has been left out of the narrative?

Scholars have underlined the exclusion and marginalisation of the subaltern's voice in both national histories and literatures.[46] They have pointed to the limits of Anderson's *Imagined Communities*, in which he argues that the novel and the newspaper 'provided the technical means for "re-presenting" the *kind* of imagined community that is the nation' (Anderson 2006: 25). Partha Chatterjee contends that 'the specifics of the colonial situation do not allow a simple transposition of European patterns of development' (Chatterjee 1991: 522). In an Egyptian context, Zachary Lockman further argues that

> Anderson's formulation elides diversity and ignores the problem of cultural translation: because he privileges the written over the spoken word, he cannot adequately account for the ways in which nonliterate subaltern groups may appropriate and construct nationalism through orally transmitted indigenous discourses of individual and collective identity and agency. (Lockman 1994: 178)

Hence, although the underprivileged massively participated in the revolution, their participation was not properly recorded in an historiography written by the nationalist elite, state institutions (in the case of school curricula), or produced by writers and filmmakers. In the context of the Egyptian society of the end of the nineteenth and beginning of the twentieth century, Hoda A. Yousef shows that although

> both women and lower-class urban and rural Egyptians were active participants in the anti-colonial street protests . . ., 'the largely non-literate

elements of Egyptian society were almost completely absent as authors of the circulars, petitions, notices, advertisements, and secret newspapers that emerged in the post-1919 period'. (Yousef 2016)

She convincingly argues that the shift from a 'handwritten scribal' tradition to the 'new visual culture of printed materials' contributed to the further marginalisation of these voices, as:

> women of the lower classes, both rural and urban, were active petitioners on behalf of themselves and their families in the handwritten scribal petitions of the previous century. So, even as protesters were 'writing to be seen', the very 'public' and privileged nature of the new visual culture of printed materials imposed its own rebalancing of *who* could be seen in public life. (Yousef 2016: 128)

The Politics of Erasure in Egyptian Literature and Film

Among these printed materials, the modern Arabic novel was instrumental in articulating a dominant narrative about the nationalist movement.[47] Its rise has been widely analysed as closely linked to the development of 'a specifically nationalist mode of thought' and the genre has been considered as 'instrumental not only in the dissemination of that thought, but in its very formation as well' (Shalan 2002: 213). In his study of *'Awdat al-Ruh* (*The Return of the Spirit*, 1933) by Tawfiq al-Hakim, Shalan underlines 'the rhetorical power of such a fiction-of the work of art which . . . can in a quite literal and self-conscious way write the nation into being' (Shalan 2002: 245). Similarly, the novel has played a key role in reifying the 1919 revolution in the frame of the national unity story type. More specifically, I argue that the Egyptian novel has been central in imposing a class-biased narrative about 1919, one that sublimates the role of the organised middle class.

It is often highlighted that 1919 created a 'national literature' to express the 'national character through new media, and to recover the authentic face of Egypt, which had been obfuscated by dependency and occupation' (Hafez 1993: 158). This 'national' literature was in reality an expression of the 'Egyptian bourgeoisie's sense of its own identity and its role as a cultural and political vanguard' (Selim 2004: 73), stimulated by the 1919 revolution. And thus, it is only natural that contributions to the anti-colonial struggle made by people who were not Cairene upper middle-class males have been consistently erased from that 'national' literature, or included in the form of a contribution to a movement initiated and led by the Cairene elite. Both al-Hakim's *'Awdat al-Ruh* and Mahfouz' *Bayn al-Qasrayn* (*Palace Walk*, 1956) have contributed to identifying the revolution's main actors as the effendiyya (see Chapter 3). Film further played a key role in shaping the dominant imaginary of 1919 as a series of Cairene demonstrations for the liberation of Saad Zaghlul. Melodrama from the Nasser period has contributed to stripping the memory of the revolution of any of its social or democratic subversive power; Hasan al-Imam's popular film adaptation of the first volume of Mahfouz' trilogy fixed the national unity slogans in the viewers' minds in a pompous incantatory fashion.

I put those canonical narratives in dialogue with both historical sources and marginalised literary texts. To borrow Ross' terms, 'I have made a special effort to locate memories that do not conform to the pre-dispositions of the present, that do not serve to legitimate contemporary configurations of power' (Ross 2002: 18). Among these narratives are novels from the sixties whose authors were seeking to produce an alternative history, which I analyse in Chapter 6. In her book about 're-writing history', Samia Mehrez notes that these writers were 'effectively participating in a process of rewriting the dominant historical record from (an) other point of view' (Mehrez 1994: 7). She furthermore underlines that this enterprise is not that of writers considered as individuals. Rather, it is part of 'that group of texts that continue to be produced and which all seem, despite their differences, to be engaged in one common project, the construction of a narrative on history' (Mehrez 1994: 80). In the context of oppressive regimes, writers chose to engage in that project so as to 'question the referential authority of the historical archive', as argued by Noha Radwan in her analysis of two short novels dealing with the negative consequences of Sadat's policy in the seventies (Radwan 2008: 94). Authors motivated by an ambition to 'rewrite history' produced novels attentive to the social dynamics of 1919, featuring peasants (and urban underprivileged) as key actors of the revolution and narrating their resistance in a laudatory mode.

In addition to these non-canonised works (which include an unpublished manuscript), I refer to a large number of primary literary sources, some of them unknown or forgotten to both Arabic and English-speaking audiences. This enables me to show *what* exactly was left out of the story and *how* both dominant historiographical and literary narratives obliterated nuanced and very dense accounts of the turmoil. It also enables me to unearth layers of meaning and feeling that have been forgotten in the process, literally erased from our collective memory.

Building on recent scholarship about affect and emotion in Arabic literature,[48] and on the assumption that emotion is central to our understanding of revolutionary moments, this book reopens a connection to the feelings of hope and bitterness, pride and fear, joy and despair as expressed in the tone, style and structure of those narratives. Emotions are central to human experience and thus essential to understanding 'the landscape of our mental and social lives' (Nussbaum 2001: I). Being attentive to the articulation of emotions can help understand, I contend, the stakes underlying narratives about 1919. Following Martha Nussbaum's argument that 'emotions include in their content judgements that can be true or false, and good or bad guides to ethical choice' (Nussbaum 2001: 1), I contend that fear, especially fear of the so-called 'rabble' in a revolutionary context, is an emotion that is particularly relevant to understand the class dynamics at stake. Not only is that kind of fear a good illustration of 'the role of "social construction" in the emotional life' (Nussbaum 2001: 6), but more fundamentally it includes in its content, to again use Nussbaum's terms, judgements that are useful to highlight patterns of exclusion and inclusion in the nationalist discourse. I am attentive to emotions as expressed and narrated in the literary and cinematic works I analyse, but also in my study of the critical and popular reception of these works. More specifically, I question the emotional response to those narratives, especially in the case of the film *Bayn al-Qasrayn* (*Palace Walk*) I analyse in Chapter 4, and the drama series and the play I examine in Chapter 6.

Overview of the Chapters

The following chapters are based on a close reading of a corpus of nearly fifteen novels, short stories, memoirs, plays, films and drama series, in addition to a number of works that I treat more briefly. Although I do refer to poetry, both *'amiyya* and *fusha*, my main corpus is made up of prose texts, both fiction and nonfiction. Among the many texts I ended up with after a sometimes arduous research process, I selected those which express an articulated vision of 1919 and that are well rooted, in one way or another, in their context. Canonical literary and cinematic narratives about the revolution are included; others were selected precisely because of their enduring marginality in the literary field. Although I have endeavoured to locate works by women, those I have remain limited in comparison to the corpus I am dealing with. This dearth is an expression of both the political marginalisation of women and the writing of a history and literature that marginalises the many contributions of women to this struggle.

The first chapter deals with the vaudeville of the mid-twenties, through an analysis of two plays by Amin Sidqi (1890–1944), *al-Intikhabat* (*The Elections*, 1923) and *Imbratur Zifta* (*The Emperor of Zifta*, 1924), an unpublished manuscript. These plays preserve to some extent the irreverent spirit of the revolution's songs and slogans, offering an example of subversive humour and bitter sarcasm as performed in the immediate aftermath of the revolution. The first play exposes the limits of the liberal parliamentary system usually presented as one of the gains of the 1919 revolution and frames the effendiyya's electoral ambitions as dictated by self-serving concerns. The second play underlines the ambition for social change, more specifically the declaration of independence of a Delta city during the 1919 turmoil, as a bitter failure. I examine the way these narratives narrate subversive and dramatic episodes of the anti-colonial struggle, and address the apparent paradox between the comic tone and the feelings of bitterness expressed in both plays.

In the second chapter, I examine an effendi representation of the revolution in Asyut, namely Fikri Abaza's (1896–1979) *al-Dahik al-Baki* (*The Weeping Laugher*, 1933), the only novel by an otherwise prolific journalist and well-known liberal intellectual. A narrative of disunity and chaos, *al-Dahik al-Baki* does not fit in with any dominant tropes of nationalist unity; rather, it offers a class-biased narrative about the revolution, written by an effendi and addressing an effendi readership. The autobiographical mode is key, I argue, in conveying a representation of self that is cemented by a sense of collective belonging to the middle class and a need for differentiation from the so-called 'rabble'. I contend that analysing the feelings of fear and compassion displayed by *al-Dahik al-Baki*'s narrator further helps with understanding the dynamics of inclusion and exclusion at stake in this particular narrative, and, more broadly, in the nationalist discourse coined by the effendiyya. The chapter also contains a brief examination of a short text about the revolution in Asyut by Mahmud al-Badawi (1908–86), a writer best known for his contribution to the genre of the short story.

The third chapter is an analysis of two famous literary representations of 1919, Tawfiq al-Hakim's *'Awdat al-Ruh* (*Return of the Spirit*, 1933), and Naguib Mahfouz' *Bayn al-Qasrayn* (*Palace Walk*, 1956), the first volume in his trilogy. These two canonical works have been central, I argue, to polishing a class-biased narrative about 1919 that sublimates the organised middle class' role and imposes a myth-like image of Saad Zaghlul. In addition to its articulation of the concept of a modern Egyptian Nation, *'Awdat al-Ruh* posits 1919 as a key moment in the birth of that nation and identifies Saad Zaghlul as the embodiment of historical continuity with the country's Pharaonic past. Likewise, *Bayn al-Qasrayn* insists on the trope of national unity through a depiction of the emergence of Egypt as a 'new nation', and presents the effendiyya as the main actors of the revolution. In addition, the chapter contains a brief analysis of an earlier short story about 1919: *Mudhakkirat Hikmat Hanim* (*The Memoirs of Hikmat Hanim*, 1921) by 'Isa 'Ubayd (189?–1922), a pioneering short story writer.

The fourth chapter analyses Hasan al-Imam's famous film adaptation of *Bayn al-Qasrayn* (1964). Here I read cinema as a genre that further 'defigurated', to use Ross' expression, the 1919 events by fitting it into the Free Officers' ideological reframing of the nationalist movement. The novel's central trope of unity is taken to another level, both in terms of form and content, through a number of compelling additions to the original plot presented in a melodramatic fashion. Unlike historian Joel Gordon, who claims that al-Imam accurately 'recreated the spirit of national unity in a way that does capture the political sub-text of Mahfouz's novel' (Gordon 2002: 82), I argue that al-Imam transformed Mahfouz's liberal representation of the revolution into a Nasserist rhetoric. Fahmi turns from a nationalist student into an armed resistant fighter, the discourse about religious unity between Muslims and Copts is significantly radicalised, and women are granted a much more active role than in the novel – as they are placed at the centre of the film's rhetoric about progress. Moreover, I show, through a detailed analysis of *mise-en-scène* elements – montage, style of acting, music (including songs by Sayyid Darwish), – how al-Imam efficiently exploited the genre of melodrama, playing with emotions of grief and joy in order to build a cathartic expression of unity. The chapter contains references to two other films of the period, *Mustafa Kamil* (1955) and *Sayyid Darwish* (1966) both directed by Ahmad Badrakhan, as well as elements of comparison with *'Awdat al-Ruh*, a television drama aired in 1977.

The fifth chapter focuses on memoirs of 1919. While most autobiographical recollections of the revolution are written by well-known actors in the events, this chapter looks at a different type of memoir, published in the seventies by a privileged witness. In *Min Wahid li-'Ashara*, (*From One to Ten*, 1977), the well-known journalist Mustafa Amin (1914–97) recollects his childhood in his grandfather[49] Saad Zaghlul's home, narrating the chaotic 1919 days from inside *Bayt al-Umma*. Amin's documenting of the revolution is one, I argue, that unsettles dominant representations of 1919. Instead of orderly demonstrations glorifying national unity, it is chaos, conflict and carnival that prevail in Amin's narrative. *Min Wahid li-'Ashara* rehabilitates revolutionary violence, both spontaneous and organised, and opens a space for the *parole* of the revolution's marginalised actors. Moreover, I contend that Amin's memoirs are marked by the historical and personal moment in which he writes, and function as a conscious attempt at restoring Zaghlul's legacy in the post-Nasser era. The chapter also contains a brief analysis of autobiographical narratives by Saad Zaghlul himself, Mustafa al-Nahhas, Fakhri 'Abd al-Nur, 'Abd al-Rahman Fahmi, Huda Sha'rawi, 'Iryan Yusuf Sa'd and Shaykh 'Abd al-Wahab al-Naggar.

The sixth chapter analyses narratives published, performed or screened between 1968 and 1999 that have attempted a 'rewriting of history' in a context of defeat, in the aftermath of the 1967 *naksa* (setback, as the state apparatus referred to the military defeat). Belonging to different genres (a play, two novels, a television series) all these works feature peasants (and urban underprivileged) as key actors in the 1919 revolution and narrate their resistance in a laudatory mode. The chapter starts with an analysis of *al-Masamir* (*The Nails*, 1968) by Sa'd al-Din Wahba, an agit-prop play that revisits the 1919 revolution in order to urge people to resist in the wake of the 1967 defeat. It goes on with readings of *Qantara al-Ladhi Kafara* (*Qantara Who Became an Infidel*, 1966) by Mustafa Musharrafa and *al-Faylaq* (*The*

Legion, 1999) by Amin 'Izz al-Din. Both novels end with scenes of revolutionary violence led by working class and peasant characters, framing it as a necessary consequence of oppression. Finally, it examines *Gumhuriyyat Zifta* (*The Republic of Zifta*, 1999), a television drama written by Yusri al-Gindi and directed by Isma'il 'Abd al-Hafiz, in which the peasant community of the Delta village is given a much more important role than is generally admitted in the historiography of the village's declaration of independence during the 1919 revolution. Special attention will be given to language, as all the authors of these works are keen on using peasant and working class dialects, from *Qantara al-Ladhi Kafara*, entirely written in colloquial Arabic, to the Zifta series, in which the songs are based on colloquial poems written by the poet 'Abd al-Rahman al-Abnudi.

More recently, in the aftermath of the 2011 revolution, younger novelists and playwrights have similarly undertaken the role of 'underground historians'. The last chapter focuses on a novel by Ahmad Mourad, *1919* (2014) and *Hawa al-Hurriyya* (*Whims of Freedom*, 2014), a play by Laila Soliman. While Mourad's text focuses on the events of 1919 through a large range of both historical and fictional characters, Soliman's play goes back and forth between documents and voices from the past and painful moments from the present. I argue that both authors contest dominant narratives about 1919, shaped in part by their predecessors, and attempt to 'rewrite history' in a context of socio-political turmoil, albeit in very different ways. Murad's text mainly rehabilitates the memory of middle class activists from the underground 'Black Hand' organisation, including women. Soliman's narrative focuses on processes of remembering and forgetting, seeking to highlight resemblances between 1919 and 2011. By *excavating* the past to understand the present, *Hawa al-Hurriyya* draws intimate bonds with that past, integrating the 'historical Other' (Rousselot 2016: 8) into its reflections about the 2011 revolution.

Notes

1. For an analysis of the discourse about Tahrir, see: Rabab El-Mahdi (2011), 'Orientalising the Egyptian Uprising', *Jadaliyya*, 11 April, available at <http://www.jadaliyya.com/Details/23882> (last accessed 24 March 2019). For the

2011 revolution, see: Bahgat Korany and Rabab El-Mahdi (2012), *Arab Spring in Egypt: Revolution and Beyond*, Cairo: AUC Press.
2. Most writers and historians define 1919 as a revolution (Al-Surbuni 1919, al-Rafi'i 1946, Anis 1963, Lashin 1975, Barakat 2009, Berque 1972, Baron 2005, Fahmy 2011).
3. This attitude and spirit on the streets in 1919 is depicted in detail by Ziad Fahmy in Chapter 6 of his book *Ordinary Egyptians*, titled 'The Egyptian Street Carnival, Popular Culture, and the 1919 Revolution' (2011: 134–66). In his memoirs, Mustafa Amin also gives vivid depictions of the popular joy and expressions of happiness during street demonstrations in both Cairo and Dumyat (see Chapter 5). There are countless accounts of the carnival aspect of the 18 Days in Tahrir and the Egyptian revolution more generally. See for instance Ahmad Zaghlul al-Shiti (2011), *Ma'at Khatwa min al-Thawra, Yawmiyyat min Maydan al-Tahrir* (*A Hundred Steps from the Revolution, Diary from Tahrir Square*) and Muna Brins (2012), *Ismi Thawra* (*Revolution is My Name*), English translation by Samia Mehrez (Cairo, AUC Press, 2014).
4. In addition to other supports. See for instance 'Tarikh Thawrat Misr al-Qawmiyya 1919 lil-Saff al-Thalith al-Thanawi 2016', a YouTube video featuring a professor giving a synthetic overview of the material. Available at <https://www.youtube.com/watch?reload=9&v=szCDG41CQ9k> (last accessed 24 March 2019).
5. Unlike most of the historiographical material about 1919, the textbook insists that the revolution is not only aimed against British colonialism. Rather, it seeks 'total independence from any foreign country (Turkey or England)' (Tarikh 2018: 121). The use of 'Turkey' instead of the 'Ottoman Empire' is anachronistic, as is the reference to independence from 'Turkey' (Egypt had been, since 1914, a British Protectorate). These anachronisms are typical of the textbook; for instance, elsewhere, the term *muthaqqaffun* (intellectuals) is used instead of *effendiyya*, which is indicated only between brackets (120).
6. Al-Barghouti further insists on Zaghlul's ties with the colonial institution by quoting a number of his statements belonging to the period between 1908 and 1909, in which Zaghlul declares that 'colonial presence is necessary to enhance the Egyptian political culture' (69), attacks the National Party and its leader Mustafa Kamil, including after his death (68) and agrees, while he was in charge of the Education Ministry, with Sir Gorst-the British administrator, on a merciless repression should students revolt in the aftermath of Mustafa Kamil's death (70). All quotes are taken from Zaghlul's diaries, quoted in Lashin and/or in Ramadan (64–70).

7. All translations from Arabic or French are mine, unless otherwise stated.
8. Hussein Omar notes that Zaghlul identified himself in his youth as both effendi and sheikh, arguing that 'to his mind these categories were not as mutually exclusive as they are to historians' (Omar 2014: 302–3).
9. For Saad Zaghlul see: 'Abbas Mahmud al-'Aqqad [1936] (2017), *Saad Zaghlul: Sira wa-Tahiyya*. Cairo: al-Hay'a al-Misriyya al-'Amma lil-Kitab; 'Abd al-Khaliq Lashin (1975), *Saad Zaghlul wa-Dawruhu fil-Siyasa al-Misriyya*, Cairo-Beirut: Dar al-'Awda; Rif'at al-Sa'id (1976), *Saad Zaghlul Bayna al-Yamin wal-Yasar*. Beirut: Dar al-Qadaya; Tamim Al-Barghouti, (2007), *Al-Wataniyya al-Alifa. Al-Wafd wa Bina' al-Dawla al-Wataniyya fi Zill al-Isti'mar*. Cairo: Dar al-Kutub wal Watha'iq, (64–70); Reinhard C. Schulze (2012), 'Sa'd b. Ibrāhīm Zaghlul', in P. Bearman, Th. Bianquis, C.E. Bosworth, E. van Donzel, W.P. Heinrichs (eds), *Encyclopaedia of Islam, Second Edition*, available at <http://dx.doi.org.libproxy.aucegypt.edu:2048/10.1163/1573-3912_islam_SIM_6397> (last accessed 16 January 2019); *Saad Zaghlul*, directed by Tamir Muhsin, *al-Jazeera al-Watha'iqiyya*, 2009, a documentary available at <https://www.youtube.com/watch?v=IbGbiEcBwMM> (last accessed 24 March 2019). There is no English biography to date of Saad Zaghlul. In French, a biography titled *Saad Zaghloul, le père du peuple Egyptien* was published in 1927, the year of Zaghlul's death, by Fouad Yéghen, nephew of 'Adli Yakan (a leader of the Wafd who was in strong disagreement with Zaghlul and one of the founding members of its rival party, the Liberal Constitutionalists) (Paris: Cahiers de France, 1927).
10. For images of the masses of people mobilised to welcome Saad Zaghlul back from his second exile, see *'Awdat Saad Zaghlul min al-Manfa* (*Saad Zaghlul's Return from Exile*,1923), a short documentary directed by Muhammad Bayyumi.
11. All three songs are mentioned in Ziad Fahmy (2011).
12. Apart from this song, all other songs in this paragraph are quoted in Ziad Fahmy's translation.
13. About Na'ima al-Masriyya see: Negar Azimi (2004), 'A Life Reconstructed: A Lost Musical Legacy Finds its Voice in Cairo', *Bidoun*, Fall, available at <https://bidoun.org/articles/a-life-reconstructed> (last accessed 17 July 2019).
14. Ziad Fahmy translates a *zajal* mentioning the leader held in captivity: 'Ye who seek independence/long live our nation, o, Egyptians/We are on strike from all work/and we locked the doors of all institutions/O prime minister- he's held hostage Zaghlul/you know his rights, of this I am certain/We as freemen demand a constitution/and will resist the schemes of the occupiers' (Fahmy 2011: 158).

Fahmy gives an overview of the *zajal*'s development; a more systematic thematic analysis of *azjal* performed during the revolution is still to be done.

15. See for instance two poems 'Misr tuhayi Saadaha', and 'Nida' al-Wida'' mentioned in Rif'at al-Sa'id (2014: 145–6).
16. See Ahmad Shawqi [1927] (1950), *al-Shawqiyyat, vol.3,* Cairo: Matba'at al-Istiqama, p. 174; Hafiz Ibrahim [1927] (1937), *Diwan Hafiz Ibrahim, Dabatahu wa-Sahhahahu wa-Sharahahu Ahmad Amin wa Ahmad al-Zayn wa Ibrahim al-Ibyari vol.2*, Cairo: Wizarat al-Ma'arif al-'Umumiyya, pp. 218–19.
17. See *Fina Vidal* (publication date not available), Beth Baron (2005), Mustafa Amin (1977).
18. See for instance a poem by Khalil Mutran (1872–1949) written on the occasion of Saad's death, whose last part is addressed to Safiyya under the title 'ila umm al-misriyyin'.
19. For instance, an advertisement with a picture of the diva advertises a soap carrying the name of Safiyya Zaghlul. The slogan announces: 'to be charming, use the odour/scent (*ra'iha*) of Safiyya Zaghlul'. The advertisement carries a handwritten sentence by Um Kulthum stating she 'liked the odour/scent of Safiyya Zaghlul'. The term *ra'iha* has multiple semantic associations in colloquial Arabic: *al-ra'iha* designates both the perfume (and by extension the soap), and the smell of a person, in literal and figurative meaning, her odour and her soul. The advertisement mirrors the cult status of Safiyya Zaghlul, in which every aspect of her persona becomes an object of veneration.
20. See Huda Sha'rawi (2013), *Mudhakkirat Huda Sha'rawi*, with an introduction by Huda Elsadda. Cairo: Dar al-Tanwir; and Sania Shaarawi Lanfranchi (2012), *Casting off the Veil: the Life of Huda Sha'rawi, Egypt's First Feminist.* London: I. B. Tauris. Sha'rawi's memoirs are translated by Margot Badran under the title *Harem Years: The Memoirs of an Egyptian Feminist 1879–1924* (London, Virago, 1986). About this translation and its reception see: Mohja Kahf (2000), 'Packaging Huda: Sha'rawi's Memoirs in the United States Reception Environment' in Amal Amireh and Lisa Suhair Majaj (eds.) *Going Global: The Transnational Reception of Third World Women Writers*, New York: Garland.
21. About this demonstration, see Huda Sha'rawi's memoirs (see note 20, this chapter); Beth Baron (2005) 'The Ladies Demonstration' in *Egypt as a Woman: Nationalism, Gender, and Politics*, Berkeley: University of California Press, pp. 107–34. Nabila Ramdani (2013), 'Women in the 1919 Egyptian Revolution: From Feminist Awakening to Nationalist Political Activism.' *Journal of International Women's Studies*, 14(2), pp. 39–52.

22. According to the editor of Ibrahim's diwan, who states that the poem was not published in the press until 12 March 1929. Hafiz Ibrahim [1919] (1937), ibid. p. 87. Huda Sha'rawi also mentions that the poem 'was printed and circulated anonymously' (Baron 2005: 115).
23. The translation quoted by Beth Baron (by L. O. Schuman in *Salama Musa, The Education of Salama Musa* (Leiden, 1961, pp. 106–7) mistakenly translates 'yat-akhidhna min sud al-thiyabi shi'arahunna' (literally, 'taking their black clothes as emblems') as 'from underneath the black of their clothes, their hair is shown free', confusing shi'ar (slogan, emblem) with sha'r (hair).
24. The poem remained very well-circulated, across times and genres; Baron traces it in al-Rafi'i's chronicles and in Salama Musa' memoirs (Baron 2005: 116); it also figures in Naguib Mahfouz' *Bayn al-Qasrayn* (see Chapter 3) and in Laila Soliman's *Hawa al-Hurriyya* (see Chapter 7).
25. In his memoirs, Mustafa Amin explains that Saad Zaghlul was consciously provoking the British into taking a measure that would trigger a large protest movement. According to Amin, the underground organisation of the Wafd, under the leadership of 'Abd al-Rahman Fahmi, coordinated the demonstrations that are most often depicted as a spontaneous outburst of anger (Amin 1977: 159)
26. See Alia Mossallam (forthcoming): 'there was a coordinated call for a general strike – pamphlets were distributed in Cairo and various governorates depicting how protesting processions should emerge . . ., including the order of protesters, the slogans to be called, and the banners to be carried'.
27. See 'Ali Barakat (2009: 57–62) for an overview of the most significant attacks by peasants, and British repression thereof.
28. About conscription during the First World War and resistance to forced conscription see: Amin 'Izz al-Din (1969), 'al-Shughl fil Sulta, Qissat Faylaq al-'Amal al-Misri wa Faylaq al-Jimal', *al-Musawwar* 7 March; Latifa Muhammad Salim [1984] (2009), *Misr fil-Harb al-'Alamiyya al-Ula*, Cairo: al-Shuruq; Alia Mossallam (forthcoming), 'Strikes, Riots and Laughter. A Close Reading of al-Himamiyya Village's experience of Egypt's 1918 Peasant Insurrection', *Social Movements and Popular Mobilisation in the Middle East and North Africa Series*, London: London School of Economics and Popular Sciences; Mario M. Ruiz (2013–14), 'Photography and the Egyptian Labor Corps in Wartime Palestine, 1917–1918', *Jerusalem Quarterly* 56 & 57, pp. 52–66. Kyle J. Anderson 'The Egyptian Labor Corps: Workers, Peasants, and the State in World War I', *International Journal of Middle East Studies* 49 (2017), pp. 5–24.

29. Although students from rural families constituted a link with the capital (Fahmy 2011: 157)
30. About the revolution in Asyut and Bani-Sueif, see 'Asim al-Dusuqi (1981), *Thawrat 1919 fil-Aqalim, Min al-Watha'iq al-Britaniyya* (Cairo: Dar al-Kitab al-Jami'i).
31. See Ahmad Baha' al-Din (1990), 'Imbraturiyyat Zifta' in *Ayyam laha Tarikh*, Cairo: al-Hilal. *Gumhuriyyat Zifta*, directed by Muhammad Farid, Documentary including an interview with Nadia al-Gindi, Yusuf al-Gindi's granddaughter. Available at <https://www.youtube.com/watch?v=WTx17i5aa1Y> (last accessed 12 June 2019).
32. 'The great strike wave of August 1919 included the tramways of Cairo, Heliopolis, and Alexandria, omnibus drivers, the 'Anabir and Jabal al-Zaytun railway workers, numerous cigarette factories, the Abu Qirqas sugar mill, the Hawamdiyya refinery, waiters and kitchen workers in the major cafes, restaurants, and patisseries of Cairo and Alexandria, shop and bank employees, bakery workers, the Ma'sara quarrymen, the Candida engineering works in Alexandria, Bonded stores warehouses and the Spathis soda factory. There were also strikes in Suez, Tanta, and Mansura' (Beinin and Lockman 1998: 111).
33. In reality, '1919 was a year of travelling revolutions across the Middle East and North Africa', not only in Egypt, but also in Libya, Palestine and Tunisia. Iraq and Morocco witnessed similar protest movements in 1920, Sudan in 1924 and Syria in 1925 (Omar 2019).
34. The qasida '*Atafa al-'Asru 'ala Nahdatikum* is published under the title 'Dhikra Thawrat Sanat 1919' in Ahmad Shawqi's diwan, and is only eleven verses long. It is taken from Husayn Shawqi's book *Abi Shawqi* (1947: 93). There is no mention of the year this celebration took place.
35. Although testimonies by activists show that they were extremely conscious of this aspect. In his memoirs, 'Iryan Yusuf Sa'd states that, as he was a Copt, it was best he took upon himself the task of throwing the bomb at minister Yusuf Wahba. He explains that he was worried it would otherwise be interpreted as an act of confessional strife from a Muslim against a Copt (Sa'd 2007: 40).
36. Al-Naggar mentions in his entry for 9 April 1919 three incidents involving Armenians. In all three cases an Armenian shot at demonstrators or passers-by and was subsequently pursued or killed by the people (al-Naggar 2010: 168). In his entry for April 10, al-Naggar mentions a 'delegation of the Jewish and Armenian going to the Wafd to complain about abusive acts the Armenians and Jewish confronted from the rabble (*al-awbash wal ghawgha*)'. According

to al-Naggar, the Armenian patriarch, the rabbi and 'wise' members of both communities attended the evening assembly in al-Azhar and argued that the innocent among them should not be punished for the crime of one man. They were welcomed by other orators and the people attending the assembly (al-Naggar 2010: 172).

37. Ziad Fahmy notes that the line of the song *Qum ya Masri* by Sayyid Darwish that mentions Jews 'has been changed (censored) in the recently printed addition'. In the newly printed edition *yahud* (Jews) becomes *gunud* (soldiers) (Fahmy 2011: 216).
38. See Jacques Berque (1972: 310) and Ziad Fahmy (2011: 147).
39. Kyle Anderson shows that women were 'involved in resistance against conscription', including through 'outright physical resistance' (Anderson 2017: 16).
40. See 'Thawrat 19 Rafa'at al-Hijab wal-Yashmak 'an Wajh al-Mar'a al-Misriyya', *al-Musawwar* 2317, 7 March 1969, pp. 42–7. This article brings together testimonies by women who were active during the revolution.
41. See Muhammad Anis [1963] (2019), *Dirasat fi Watha'iq Thawrat Sanat 1919* (Cairo: Anglo-Egyptian Bookshop); Mustafa Amin [1974] (1991) *Asrar Thawrat 1919*, Cairo: Kitab Akhbar al-Yaum.
42. About the development of underground armed organisations see Malak Badrawi (2000), *Political Violence in Egypt, 1910–1924: Secret Societies, Plots and Assassinations*. Richmond, U.K.: Curzon. For memoirs by members of these clandestine organisations, see: 'Iryan Yusuf Sa'd (2007), *Mudhakkirat 'Iryan Yusuf Sa'd*, Cairo: al-Shuruq; Muhammad al-Gawadi, (2009), *Al-'Amal al-Sirri fi Thawrat 1919, Mudhakkirat al-Shubban al-Wafdiyyin, Ibrahim 'Abd al-Hadi, Sayyid Basha, Iryan Yusuf Sa'd, Muhammad Mazhar Sa'id*, Cairo: al-Shuruq al-Dawliyya; Yahya Haqqi (1984), "Abd al-Hayy Kira' in *Nas fi Zill wa Shakhsiyyat Ukhra*, Cairo: al-Hay'a al-Misriyya al-'Amma lil-Kitab.
43. Ma'mur Asyut, ma'mur Farskur and ma'mur Damanhur (see 'Ali Barakat 2009: 46). Two of them were sentenced to death by a military court.
44. For a detailed account of the visit, see *Yawmiyyat Lord Milner fi Misr wa Watha'iq Ukhra* (2019) ed. Mona Anis, trans. Salah Abu Nar, Cairo: Dar al-Shuruq.
45. There are detailed accounts of these demonstrations available in Mustafa Amin, *Min Wahid li-'Ashara* (see Chapter 5). See also Tamir Muhsin, *Saad Zaghlul al-Jazeera al-Watha'iqiyya*, 2009, a documentary available at <https://www.youtube.com/watch?v=IbGbiEcBwMM> (last accessed 24 March 2019).
46. See, for instance Gayatri Chakravorty Spivak (1987), 'A Literary Representation

of the Subaltern: A Woman's Text from the Third World' in *In Other Worlds: Essays in Cultural Politics*, Methuen: New York and London.

47. See Jeff Shalan (2002) 'Writing the Nation: The Emergence of Egypt in the Modern Arabic Novel' *Journal of Arabic Literature* 33, no. 3, pp. 211–47; Hoda Elsadda (2012), *Gender, Nation and the Arabic Novel, Egypt, 1892–2008*, New York: Syracuse University Press and Edinburgh: Edinburgh University Press, and Samah Selim (2004), 'Novels and Nations' in *The Novel and the Rural Imaginary in Egypt, 1880–1985*, London: Routledge.

48. See Tarek El-Ariss (2013) *Trials of Arab Modernity*, New-York: Fordham University Press, and Christian Junge, (2015), 'On Affect and Emotion as Dissent: The Kifāya Rhetoric in Pre-Revolutionary Egyptian Literature', in Friederike Pannewick and Georges Khalil, eds. *Commitment and Beyond: Reflections on the Political in Arabic Literature since the 1940s*. Wiesbaden: Reichert, pp. 253–71. El-Ariss argues that 'reading affects as a counterpart to the question of representation, which has governed literary studies for so long, is key for identifying new crossings between the literary and the political, experience and writing' (5). He further contends that it is specifically useful in the study of Arabic literature, and the critique of the way modernity has been framed, as it enables one to displace both the Enlightenment's oculocentricity and the primacy of the 'Western gaze' when examining Arab modernity (6). Christian Junge analyses 'affect and emotion as expressions of political dissent in pre-revolutionary Egyptian literature' (253).

49. Mustafa Amin uses both the terms 'grandfather' and 'grandmother' to designate Saad and Safiyya Zaghlul in his memoirs. See for instance Amin 1977: 165.

I

The Poetics of Disillusion

> The elections must ensure total freedom for everyone. This freedom, I consider, is threatened by the Wafd's influence and its bluffs (*tahwish*). The Wafd keeps the people, the newspapers and the whole country busy with its committees: its general committees, its central committees, its village committees, its principal and secondary committees.

This expression of irritation towards the Wafd was part of an article published on 11 August 1923 in *al-Ahram*, Egypt's leading newspaper, by Muhammad Salih al-Dahri, a lawyer in a small Delta town named Farskur. It was a warning sign of larger protests that would follow the establishment of the first 'People's Government' in January 1924. Although Saad Zaghlul was immensely popular, as attested by the hundreds of thousands of people who came to greet him after his return from his second exile on 17 and 18 September 1923, the Wafd's politics disappointed the rural and urban underprivileged who had been at the forefront of the revolutionary struggle. Once in power, the party that had led the nationalist movement for five years turned out to be a faithful representative of the interests of the Egyptian landowning class and the urban upper middle classes.[1] The government led by Zaghlul – who became prime minister in January 1924 – increasingly assumed the aggressive class nature of its politics. When it became clear that the social demands at the core of the struggles that had taken place throughout the revolution would not be met, discontent became vocal. Both Saad and Safiyya Zaghlul exploited their popularity in many instances to neutralise explosive situations and convince workers or peasants to delay expressions of anger;[2] when this proved inefficient, the 'People's Government' resorted to systematic repression against rising popular mobilisations. In February–March 1924, tramway workers who 'attempted to foment a strike' were arrested, and communist-led unions in Alexandria were repressed (Beinin 1998b: 317–18). Moreover, Zaghlul exerted a 'tight-fisted control of the chamber' (Botman 1998: 291) as well as an accentuated control on the press. Some of the newspapers and magazines that publicly expressed their disagreement were closed down.[3]

Echoes of that irritation and anger can be found in popular cultural genres. Ziad Fahmy has argued that 'recorded colloquial music, vaudeville, *azjal*, and the popular press' were 'the most effective tools for the dissemination of nationalist ideas to the majority of Egyptians' (Fahmy 2011: xii). In this chapter, I contend that the vaudeville was a site for both conveying and challenging the nationalist discourse. Focusing on the vaudeville in the aftermath of the 1919 revolution, I show that, as early as 1923, playwrights produced texts that were critical of the new political system, echoing the shared concerns of the underprivileged and of radicalised and/or impoverished segments of the effendiyya. These expressions of concern and disillusion mirror a wide awareness of the pitfalls of the new system. Moreover, they give a glimpse into the expectations triggered by the revolution. They indirectly allow us to imagine the sheer radicalism of mobilisations involving hundreds of thousands of people over the span of four years. They confirm that 1919 was not only about the return of Zaghlul, or even about the end of the British occupation. Rather, it was a revolutionary moment that unfolded at the crossroads of a multiplicity of social movements (see Introduction).

Both plays I analyse in this chapter are a product of a collaboration[4] between the playwright Amin Sidqi (1890–1944)[5] and the actor 'Ali al-Kassar (1887–1957).[6] The first play, *al-Intikhabat* (*The Elections*, 1923) sarcastically exposes the limits of the liberal parliamentary system usually presented as one of the gains of the 1919 revolution[7] and frames the *bey*'s electoral ambitions as dictated by self-serving concerns. The second play, *Imbratur Zifta* (*The Emperor of Zifta*, 1924) frames the declaration of independence of a Delta town during the 1919 turmoil as a failure.[8] Both are comic plays – one of them featuring al-Kassar himself – in which laughter functions as a relief mechanism, a way of dealing with the pitfalls and failures of the revolution. In a bleak post-revolutionary context, this kind of sarcastic humour eloquently mirrors popular feelings of disillusion and bitterness.

Unfortunately, as is the case for most of the plays of that period, there is no recording available of the performances. This chapter is thus based on a textual analysis of both plays. Many scripts written at the beginning of the twentieth century are missing or difficult to access; however, I was fortunate to be able to read the script of these two plays. *Al-Intikhabat* is included in a volume of plays by Amin Sidqi edited by Nagwa 'Anus, and I was able to look up the unpublished manuscript of *Imbratur Zifta* at the Centre for Theatre and Music's library.[9] Regrettably, my search for reviews about both performances – which would have provided welcome details about the reception of the plays, the interaction with the audience, and the performance of the actors themselves – was unsuccessful. The collections of journals that could contain these reviews are incomplete at the Library of the American University in Cairo and are reported missing at Dar al-Kutub.

The Genre of the Vaudeville

The explosion of theatre in Egypt as 'mass-entertainment' is dated to the first decade of the twentieth century, when 'playwrights, actors and singers began performing in, and later opening, their own Arabic theaters in the district west of the Ezbekiyyah Gardens, in the region of 'Imad al-Din Street' (Gitre 2011: 90–2). Among the plays performed there, most were vaudevilles. Defined in the Western tradition as a 'light, theatrical entertainment of a knockabout kind, with musical interludes' (Cuddon 2013: 962), the genre was extremely popular in Egypt at the beginning of the century.

Vaudeville theatre has been read as a site of expression for anti-colonial politics before, during and after the 1919 revolution. In *al-Tarikh al-Sirri lil Masrah* (*The Secret History of Theatre*), Ramsis 'Awad identifies an important number of plays dealing with nationalist topics between 1900 and 1919. In *Creating the Modern Nation through Popular Culture*, Ziad Fahmy asserts that 'for several years before the 1919 revolution, the Egyptian recording industry and the vaudeville music theatre openly supported the Egyptian nationalist agenda. This trend dramatically accelerated during and after the revolution' (Fahmy 2011: 159). In 1919, theatre thus literally accompanied the revolutionary turmoil. As the theatres had been closed by the colonial authorities for around one month starting from 10 March (Fahmy 2011: 160), the troupes performed in the streets, actively participating in the demonstrations.[10] In particular, the troupe of Naguib al-Rihani, in which Sayyid Darwish played an important role, performed *Ululuh* (*Tell him*), 'by far the most significant' of 'all the plays that dealt with the events of the revolution' (Fahmy 2011: 161). The play contained several nationalistic songs 'representing the manner and language of all the varied socioeconomic groups that demonstrated in the streets', including 'Um Ya Masri' (Rise up, O Egyptian) (Fahmy 2011: 161).

A vector of anti-colonial sentiment, vaudeville also had a marked sensibility for the social struggles of Egypt's underprivileged. The theatre of al-Kassar, explains 'Ali al-Ra'i, 'abounds in different social categories (*tawa'if*), washerwomen, street sweepers, vendors, muleteers and other lower social classes. Al-Kassar allowed them firstly to present themselves, and secondly to present their complaints and opinions of ongoing events' (al-Ra'i 2003: 294). Laughter triggered by humour and sarcasm, key to the genre, is often used as an instrument of social critique. That criticism englobed characters from diverse class and cultural backgrounds. According to al-Ra'i, in Sidqi and al-Kassar's theatre, 'most of the characters are stereotyped' (al-Ra'i 2003: 284), presented with caricatured attributes in order to trigger laughter. The best known of those characters is 'Uthman 'Abd al-Basit,[11] the black *bawwab* of Nubian origin,[12] a role 'Ali al-Kassar started playing in 1916 (Powell 2001: 27). However, I argue in this chapter that Sidqi both conveys and challenges social clichés expressed in popular cultures. In the case of *al-Intikhabat*, he challenges the dominant construction of several characters, in particular the effendi, the *fallah* and the *bey*.

Theatre goers who could afford a ticket to attend the performances were mostly from a middle-class background.[13] This should not mask the fact that the vaudeville enjoyed a privileged relationship with broad popular audiences. The writers often borrowed melodies, lyrics and anecdotes from the street, which means that vaudeville was in tune with the working class and underprivileged moods.[14] Moreover, there existed a tradition of *muqalliddun* (mimics) who imitated the songs and effects performed on stage in the streets. 'In this way, mimics expanded the audience for Arabic stage performance' (Gitre 2011: 131–2). The vaudeville was thus shaped by a dialectical relationship with popular audiences, at once borrowing from popular culture and inspiring it.

Vaudeville's special performativity was key to achieving this popular symbiosis. According to al-Ra'i, what dissociates the genre from what he calls 'the written theatre', among other elements, is 'its particular way of celebrating the spectator' (al-Ra'i 2003: 23).[15] In that relationship, improvisation is central, hence the expression of *al-Masrah al-Murtajal* (improvised theatre) which al-Ra'i uses to describe the genre as performed in Egypt in the first decades of the twentieth century. It gives the comedian 'the opportunity to become a creative artist' (al-Ra'i 2003: 23). A successful artist could exert his or her freedom of improvisation to trigger frenetic laughter among the audience by establishing unexpected references to the contemporary context, drawing on rumours or anecdotes. For the vaudeville to be successful, the actors had thus to be in tune with the audience, its expectations, feelings and moods. If the actor was creative, he or she could provide his or her audience with a cathartic experience, connected with the contemporary context, in which laughter functioned as a relief mechanism.

Al-Intikhabat

Al-Intikhabat (*The Elections*) was performed for the first time on 27 September 1923.[16] The performance had initially been planned for a week earlier, but was postponed because of 'the arrival of his excellency Saad Pasha', as reported in *al-Ahram* on 20 September 1923. Saad Zaghlul came back from his second exile while the electoral campaign was in full swing. The pages of *al-Ahram* were filled with advertisements for electoral meetings, those very same advertisements that had irritated the lawyer from Farskur. Ironically, despite its acerbic sarcasm towards the elections and the Wafd, the play was extremely popular. It was performed nearly every day in the Majestic from 27 September till 24 October, literally accompanying the first stage of the elections.[17]

The play tells the story of two Beys running in the elections, Ragab Bey, head of the majority party and Shawwal Bey, head of the minority party. Act 1 opens with an electoral meeting to support Ragab Bey, who is absent, replaced by his secretary, Muharram effendi. When Ragab Bey finally appears on stage, after his supporters have left, his primary concern has nothing to do with the elections: he is courting a married woman whom he is arranging to meet in Tanta. In Act 2, the woman appears to be none other than Zubayda, the wife of Shawwal Bey. This coincidence is aggravated by a set of circumstances, whereby Ragab Bey is forced to present himself as Zubayda's husband and is mistaken for Shawwal Bey by the latter's supporters. The comic situation that unfolds as Ragab Bey tours the city of Tanta met by the frenetic applause of his opponent's supporters culminates when he insults himself and his party (Sidqi 1989: 130). Ragab Bey is then mistakenly arrested by the police, on the basis of a complaint lodged against Shawwal Bey. The play ends after Ragab Bey, who is protesting in vain that he is not Shawwal Bey, is finally set free when his mother-in-law arrives, announcing he won the elections in Tanta.

Despite what one could expect from such circumstantial text, the performance is far from indulgent towards the actors involved in the electoral process. On the contrary, and unlike most posterior narratives, which present the parliamentary elections as one of the most important gains of the 1919 revolution (see fn 7, this chapter), this contemporary narrative depicts the whole electoral process as nothing other than a huge fraud. Indeed, all elements of the play – plot, characterisation, songs and, most prominently, its comic effects – function as a systematic critique of the political system. In addition to its cutting-edge political sarcasm, the play contains a social critique of the post-revolutionary society. It ultimately offers a cathartic experience in which laughter functions as a relief mechanism in a context of deep disillusion towards the outcome of the revolution.

The play's engaged bias against the elections is made clear from the very beginning. Its inaugural song (*lahn iftitahi*) describes the 'session' (*al-jalsa*), the electoral meeting gathering at the beginning of Act 1, as an inefficient one in which there is no space for divergent opinions. The first verses of the song instruct people not to breathe, not to philosophise, comically describing the session as *bismarkawi* and its plans as *nabuliyuni* (85)-referring to the despotic ruling methods of German chancellor Bismarck and French emperor Napoleon Bonaparte. It further describes the session's work as *kushari fi kushari* (86), a reference to the mixing-up technique at the basis of the Egyptian meal by the same name. The song also explicitly states that 'there are many people who sell their votes' (86) and ironically criticises the authoritarianism of the Wafd leaders in the following verse: 'Where is the bey the president so we can gather around him, and tell him "yes"' (86). Most comic elements – hilarious word play,[18] irony, comedy of situation – further function as a systematic critique of the electoral process represented as mostly built on powerful influence networks.

The characterisation showcases both candidates as somehow disreputable men. Ragab Bey is an untrustworthy womaniser and Shawwal Bey an arrogant *baltagi* or thug – I will say more hereunder about their names. Instead of a devoted nationalist militant, as would be expected from a Wafd candidate, Ragab Bey is caricatured as a Bey with all the characteristics of a feudal notable: he is an absentee, a futile, carefree and unprincipled man.[19] Shawwal Bey, head of the minority party which likely represents the Liberal Constitutionalists, has similar personality traits.

Despite all the pitfalls, the candidate of the majority easily wins the elections; the play hereby underlines the utterly predictable nature of the outcome. In so doing, the plot frames the elections as a non-event, in which things are determined in advance. The plot's strongest element, which is the central comic scene of the play, namely the imbroglio that emerges when Ragab Bey is forced to pretend he is Shawwal Bey, confirms that message. This scene implicitly asserts that Ragab Bey and Shawwal Bey are interchangeable – not only as partners of Zubayda, but most fundamentally as candidates. Indeed, nothing much differentiates them: neither of them is connected in any way to the demands, nationalist or social, of the people and both of them are more concerned with their personal interests than with those of the nation. Ultimately, the play insinuates that unlike what is loudly asserted in the ongoing political competition, there is not so much difference between a Wafd or a Liberal Constitutionalist candidate. The play hereby echoes anti-government and anti-Wafd sentiments in chants and slogans during the 1919 revolution (Mossallam, forthcoming).

The choice of names, an essential element of the play's comic effects, further strengthens the idea that the elections are led by laughable people all belonging to the same coterie. Most of the characters involved in the elections borrow their names from the Islamic calendar, which further guarantees this feeling of coterie. The fact that the two main candidates carry an Islamic month as their name reinforces the idea of the interchangeability suggested above. Although 'Ragab' is commonly used as a proper name, 'Shawwal' is not, and this funny, unexpected choice of name contributes to ridding the character of any serious presence on stage. The secretaries of Ragab and Shawwal carry similar names, Muharram and Safar, also two Islamic months.

The parties both men lead are named *mi'aysin* – the majority party led by Ragab – and *mitlayyissin* – the minority party led by Shawwal. *Mi'ayis* comes from the Arabic root a-ya-sa, which expresses despair, like the root ya-'i-sa. Although the term *mi'aysin* is spelled by 'Anus with a *qaf* (as *miqaysin*) this meaning is attested by a wordplay elsewhere in the text: when Ragab Bey is arrested by the police at the end of the play, the policeman who guards him reports his words as follows: 'every word or two, he says 'I am desperate', come what may' (kul kilma wal tanya yi'ul ana mi'ayis zayy ma tigi tigi' (Sidqi 1989: 152)). Ragab Bey is at once reiterating that he belongs to the *mi'aysin* party, as he has been arrested because the policemen mistook him for the head of the opposing party, and expressing his despair that anyone would believe him, as indicated by the end of the sentence: 'come what may'. In their *Dictionary of Egyptian Arabic*, Hinds and Badawi define 'ayis' as 'to act with desperate courage' (Hinds and Badawi 1986: 46); it thus translates the ambivalent position of the majority party, which, although it is about to win the elections, has been unable to successfully lead the people to achieve independence. In the context of the play, the term *mi'aysin* acquires an ironic connotation, as the leader of the party provides no particular effort to lead his party to an electoral victory. In the same dictionary, Hinds and Badawi define 'layyis' as the slang for shut-up, and notes that 'mitlayyis' can also be translated as 'stupefied with hashish' (Hinds and Badawi 1986: 807). *Al-mitlayyissin* can thus be understood as people who are being forced to shut up, in other words a party whose members do not enjoy much space for expression and are under the influence of drugs. This suggests that the minority party, which probably stands for the Liberal Constitutionalists, is not as 'liberal' as it pretends to be, and that its members are no more serious politicians than those of the majority party.

However, the most eloquent naming is that of the *mitlayyissin*'s journal, *al-Khazuq*. The name literally means 'the pike', and it is often used in a figurative way to crudely depict something that will rob the people of their rights, be it a ruler or a specific policy. In this case, it implies the discourse of the Liberal Constitutionalist is nothing but a huge fraud meant to swindle the people. Although the name applies to the minority party's paper, the fact that both candidates appear to be interchangeable suggests that the name designates the whole process. Ultimately, this implies that there is nothing to be won for the people in those elections.

Through this circumstantial critique of the elections, the play questions the Wafd and the Liberal Constitutionalists' ambition to speak on behalf of the people. Moreover, it challenges the dominant nationalist narrative by subverting its class categorisation, which associates leadership with upper middle classes. This is achieved by casting the politically active *bey* as the main target of the play's comic rhetoric and ridding the effendi of any political charisma, instead attributing this to the *fallah*. The play further completes this depiction of post-revolutionary society with a number of characters representing social categories actively involved in the revolutionary struggle: a cart conductor, a marginalised city dweller, an *azhari* sheikh and a woman from the elite.

Apart from the woman, all three characters are not involved in the electoral process. They have stopped fighting for their rights, instead complaining bitterly about their situation. They systematically mention the fact that their demands still remained unaddressed after the revolution. Ga'las (the cart driver), Duqduq (the city dweller) and Abu Qura'a (the sheikh) either bitterly note that their struggles have been in vain, or comically focus on the narrow interests of their social category. Ga'las explains that the '*arbagiyya*'s situation is becoming increasingly difficult because of the rising prices and the new traffic regulations (92). Duqduq, who represents 'all those with bad luck' (*kull wilad al-hazz al-'itir*, 93) attacks the pharmacists for delivering cocaine and speaks in favour of a legalisation of *hashish baladi*, a 'local hashish/marijuana product' (94).[20] Abu Qura'a has abandoned any nationalist concerns and adopts a reactionary agenda, calling for a more 'suitable' dress for women and a tighter control on comic plays (*riwayat hazliyya*) as well as a name change for the 'Imad al-Din street – where, ironically, the play is performed (95).[21]

Only women escape this acerbic humour. The play was first performed a few months after the constitution of the Egyptian Feminist Union (EFU) by Huda Sha'rawi. The only 'real' electoral meeting in the play is a scene in which Ragab Bey receives a delegation of women who have come to present their demands. Moreover, the only character genuinely concerned about the electoral process is Ragab Bey's mother-in-law, who is connected to this delegation of women. When Ragab Bey is absent, she replaces him, giving speeches and meeting his supporters. Although she is systematically referred to as *al-hama*, 'the mother-in-law' does not function as a stereotypical characterisation. Rather, she emerges as a politically active woman more concerned with public debates than with the domestic imbroglio in which her daughter finds herself. Although her efforts are ridiculed by Ragab Bey (101–2), she remains actively involved in the political process. This characterisation might be read as an effort by the playwright to raise awareness among popular and middle-class audience about the feminist agenda.

Like the *hama*, both the effendi and the *fallah* remain unnamed, designated only by their social quality; and like her, they do not correspond to stereotypical representations. Rather, the play's characterisation is an invitation to overcome dominant representations of the effendi as literate, hence competent in the field of public affairs and capable of leading the nation, and the *fallah* as illiterate, hence ignorant and incapable of playing any significant role in the nationalist struggle. The effendi is sarcastically depicted as a politically impotent character – despite all the modernising ambitions this class was associated with during the first decades of the twentieth century.[22] During the electoral meeting at the beginning of the play where the main candidate is absent, he is unable to deliver a proper discourse (88). His attempts at opening his speech with 'Ladies and Gentlemen' (*ayyuha al-sada*) are repeatedly mocked by the *fallah*. As the text hereby points to the difference of language code between the effendi and the audience, it underlines that the effendiyya are unable to efficiently communicate with the majority of the people.

When the audience aggressively urges him to leave the stage, the effendi is replaced by the *fallah*, who, unlike the effendi, is immediately able to address the audience in its own language as he introduces his discourse by a ritualistic religious expression: 'Come on, you guys, say with us "All Prayers and Blessings of Allah be upon the Prophet"' (*baqu sallu bina 'ala al-nabi ya gada' inta wa huwwa*, 89). The *fallah* represents rural inhabitants from a modest background, who, although they have been actively involved in the revolutionary struggle, are not taken into account in the political system about to be established. He questions the electoral operation as a whole, cynically advising everyone in the audience not to give away their vote unless they are invited for lunch and dinner, in a reference to the systematic bribing in which the candidates engaged. He then further elaborates on his critique of parliament, which he describes as a hotchpotch (*sakalans*). In his words, parliament is a space for *shuyukh*, effendiyya and *khawagat*, hence a space excluding people like himself. He concludes his discourse with a word play on the expression *Hisbina Allah wa niʿma al-wakil*, used to express despair in a situation so dark no positive outcome can be imagined. By replacing *Hisbina* Allah (Allah is sufficient for us) with *Hizbina* Allah (Allah is our party) he implicitly expresses his deception towards 'our party' (the Wafd) and its politics, by stating that the party he belongs to is that of Allah. Although the *fallah* as a character is not important in the plot, his discourse echoes the text's critical depiction of the post-revolutionary society.

The popularity of the play, built like other vaudevilles on the dialectic interaction with the audience, allows for a reading of *al-Intikhabat* as an expression of popular disenchantment with everything political. The play is at once shaped by, and contributes to raising, broad popular awareness about the fact that some-pre-revolutionary class structures and reflexes are being reproduced into the very realm of so-called revolutionary politics. It both mirrors and magnifies the disappointment with social classes casting themselves as the leaders of the nationalist struggle. Its daring sarcasm and bitter disillusion give a deep insight into the radicalness of revolutionary demands and the hope that prevailed during the preceding years. This message is very similar to that of the second narrative I analyse in this chapter.

Imbratur Zifta

This play was first performed on 24 January 1924, in the aftermath of the 1923 elections. It was popular and played nearly every day for approximatively one month.[23] It tells the story of two fishermen, ʿAbdu and Zaqzuq. ʿAbdu wants to marry off his sister Ghandura to Zaqzuq, but first needs to save some money. He is also obsessed with the memory of a princess whom he saved from drowning. The princess has announced she will marry nobody but her saviour, who only has to remind her of the words she said while drowning. The prince's advisor, Qaddur, forces ʿAbdu to disclose these words to him, thus becoming the princess' fiancé. The prince, his sister and

Qaddur then decide to abduct the fisherman and to crown him emperor. In the second act, Zaqzuq wakes up in the role of the emperor; he orders the distribution of money to his fellow fishermen and a special gift for Ghandura. In the third act, when he comes to, he realises this was nothing but a dream. When the prince suggests he becomes one of his courtiers, he refuses, stating the only thing he aspires to is to be married to his fiancée. The play concludes: Ghandura and Zaqzuq get married, as well as 'Abdu and the princess. I argue that this play sarcastically frames the Zifta experience of self-governance of 1919 as disproportionate. Its poetics is entirely built on a sense of disproportion, from the title to its comic effects, including the sequence of events. By framing it this way, it creates a sense of distance, which is further strengthened by the use of the tale to allegorically refer to Zifta events. The play thus constitutes at once a mirror of the post-revolutionary bitterness, and a vector of a disillusioned understanding of these events.

I first came across the play in a book by Nagwa 'Anus about Amin Sidqi's theatre in which she provides a short synopsis titled *Imbraturiyyat Zifta* (*The Zifta Empire*). However, in the advertisements for the play in the contemporary press, it is titled 'Imbratur Zifta'.[24] When I was finally able to put my hand on the unpublished manuscript, at the Centre for Theatre and Music, I discovered the frail hand-written document was titled 'al-Imbratur'. I first doubted this was the manuscript of the play I was searching for, but the date appended in red by the censor (1924) and the fact that the synopsis corresponded to the one provided by Nagwa 'Anus, settled my doubts. One can guess that the title was either not part of the original manuscript as written by Amin Sidqi, and was added after the rehearsals or not included in order not to draw the attention of the censor.

This shifting title is one of the most intriguing aspects of the play. Indeed, nothing in the text directly refers to the declaration of independence of the Delta city of Zifta during the 1919 revolution. The apparent discrepancy between title and text, I argue, produces meaning in itself. The choice of this particular title for a text devoid of any element clearly related to the Zifta events guides the reader towards an allegorical interpretation of the play. It invites the audience to understand the story as an allegory of this particular episode in the anti-colonial struggle. In an article titled 'Title, Text, Meaning', Josep Besa brings together reflections by theorists, philosophers and literary critics about the title and its relationship to the text. Among these is a contribution by Harald Weinrich, who 'wrote accurately that one of the hermeneutic conditions of receiving a text is that the reader should have a prior idea of it, however vague, from the very beginning of his act of decoding'. According to Weinrich, 'the reader normally receives specific orientative signs from the author that shape a certain structure of expectation, which guides the reception of the elements of the text (Besa 1997: 326). As Besa himself summarises it, 'the title anticipates, guides and situates' (Besa 1997: 327).

Widely advertised in the press, the title 'Imbratur Zifta' presupposes a certain significance of Zifta in the collective imaginary of the time. Although the Zifta events were nearly five years old in January 1924, it is clear the name of the Delta city was still remembered for its achievements during the revolution. Zifta had come to *signify* the possibility of self-governance, a dream much more ambitious than the political changes about to be undertaken at the beginning of 1924. Furthermore, the oxymoron of the title, underlining the discrepancy between its two terms, eloquently conveys a sense of disproportion. In this case, the disproportion lies in the lack of proper relationship between the nature of the position of emperor – who is by definition at the head of a large empire – and the small scale of the city he is ruling. An emperor is a powerful man of state whereas Zifta is a small city. This disproportion in itself triggers a comic effect.[25] In addition, the choice of the term 'emperor' instead of 'president' contains in itself an exaggeration and contributes to the comic dynamics of the play. The term 'president' belongs to the realm of contemporary politics and involves an electoral process. The term 'emperor,' on the other hand, belongs to the realm of the past, of the tale; moreover, an emperor is often associated with the image of a despot.

According to Michel Butor, 'the title and the text that follows it are two poles between which there circulates an electricity of meaning' (Besa 1997: 327). In this case, the dialogue between text and title contributes to linking the events of the play with Zifta as an experience of self-governance. Although the text does not mention any specific place, the structure of the plot recalls the sequence of events in Zifta. The main event, the transformation of a poor fisherman into a man of power for a short lapse of time before he returns to his initial situation, resembles the journey of Yusuf al-Gindi (1893–1941), a lawyer from the village who was named president of Zifta during the 1919 revolution before returning to his initial vocation. Moreover, this sequence of events echoes the sense of disproportion conveyed by the title, thereby strengthening the comic effect.

Furthermore, most of the comic effects of the play likewise focus on this sense of disproportion. Laughter is triggered by the comedy of situation that arises when a man from an underprivileged background finds himself in the situation of a powerful ruler. A theatrical tool to trigger laughter, disproportion is more fundamentally used as a way to understand and frame one of the most daring self-governance experiences of the revolution. This insistence on disproportion in a post-revolutionary context ultimately conveys a sense of disillusion and bitterness. As I showed above, the play's plot structure relates it to the Zifta experience, echoing the disproportion contained in the title and triggering a comic effect. It also conveys bitterness. The second act of the text opens a range of possibilities: the poor fisherman becomes a man of power and is able to implement a social measure and a decision regarding foreign affairs. But in the third act, things are back as they used to be. Regardless of the happy ending, which focuses on the personal lives of the characters, nothing changes in the social organisation of society.

Moreover, the use of a tale as an allegory for these events strengthens this sense of disillusion. The play is reminiscent of a tale from the *Thousand and One Nights* titled *The Sleeper Awakened* (*al-Na'im wal Yaqzan*, also translated as *The Sleeper and the Waker*), in which the main character, Abul Hasan al-Mughaffal, a trader impoverished after he squandered his father's inheritance, becomes caliph for one day instead of Harun al-Rashid.[26] However, it seems that Sidqi did not draw the inspiration for *The Emperor of Zifta* from this tale. In her work about the influence of the *Thousand and One Nights* on Egyptian theatre, Hiam Aboul-Hussein shows that the plotline Sidqi uses in *The Emperor of Zifta* is directly adapted from the French Opera *Si j'étais roi* (*If I Were King*) by Adolphe Adam, first performed in Paris in 1852.[27] Its libretto's plot presents many similarities to that of Sidqi's play: the main character is a poor fisherman who saved a princess from drowning and longs to marry her. The evil advisor to the prince, likewise named Kadoor, tries to impose himself instead of the fisherman and to marry the princess. In the Second Act, the poor fisherman is then made to sit on the throne and to rule for one day, before he returns to his initial condition in the third act.[28] The plotline Aboul-Hussein describes, however, is that of another play by Sidqi, entitled *Law Kuntu Malikan* (*If I Were a King*)[29] which, she mentions, was replayed under the title *The Emperor of Zifta* and *The Dreams of Kings*.[30] The fact Sidqi uses a nearly identical plotline for at least two plays,[31] with minor adaptations in the name of characters, strengthens my argument regarding the choice of the title for *The Emperor of Zifta*. It gives additional substance to this circulation of meaning between text and title; as the title seemingly presents no relation to the plotline, it is thus clearly meant to comment on the political context.

Sidqi, who held Marxist ideas ('Anus 1989: 14), invests this circulation of meaning between text and title to deliver a political message in the post-revolutionary context. Consistent with the anti-wafdist stances he articulates in the previous play I analysed in this chapter, he also uses it to comment on the election of Yusuf al-Gindi as a deputy for Zifta, eleven days before the first performance of the play.[32] The plotline of the play indeed highlights the extreme brevity of the experience of ruling for a poor fisherman, hence reminding al-Gindi that his experience as a ruler of the Delta town, at the head of the Zifta republic, has been short-lived and is definitively over.

The tale-like universe, which the play shares with Adam's opera, set in an Indian scenery, further triggers a sense of the distance between reality and dream, present and past. It thereby frames the Zifta events as belonging to an inaccessible world. This distance ultimately conveys a sense of disillusion, more specifically a disillusion with the post-revolutionary present. The hopes that, in the preceding years, had fuelled the people's mobilisation, are made to seem as legendary as a *Thousand and One Nights* tale. This artistic expression of bitterness would soon leave space for more class-conscious narratives, in which the demands and actions of the underprivileged are assimilated to an aggressive behaviour.

Notes

1. As noted by Joel Beinin, 'the Wafd had strong rural electoral support, but never felt obliged to take the side of the peasants against their *'umdas*, landlords, or local notables, the backbone of its rural base' (Beinin 1998b: 317)
2. In her book titled *Safia Zaghloul*, Zaghloul's head housekeeper, Fina Gued

Vidal, relates one of the instances in which Safiyya Zaghlul was able to calm an angry crowd. After Saad's second exile in December 1921, as protests were in full swing in the whole country, 'trams burnt, phone and telegraph lines cut, train stations destroyed, ... one day, at ten o'clock in the morning, a delegation from Ghalioub arrived in Cairo, "carrying ship masts, butcher knives, tree branches" and "stationed in front of the House of the People". While the women inside were frightened, Safia went out to talk to the crowd, "a veil on her head, face unveiled for the first time". Addressing a crowd made, according to Fina, of "workers, peasants, boatmen and butchers", Safiyya managed to make them leave after addressing them in the following way: "Saad told you so many times he didn't want a revolution. He told you so many times that it is not by using violence that you will be able to win your freedom". The crowd replied by shouting 'long live Saad' 'long live the mother of Egyptians' (Vidal na: 41–2).

3. In his memoirs, Mustafa Amin relates that Zaghlul presented a court case against the newspaper *al-Siyasa* that represented the Liberal Constitutionalists (Amin 1977: 370).
4. Sidqi and al-Kassar's troupe performed in the Majestic, a theatre in 'Imad al-Din street al-Kassar had founded in January 1919 (al-Kassar 1993: 32). It competed for some years with actor Naguib al-Rihani's troupe which brought together writer Badi' Khayri (1893–1966) and composer Sayyid Darwish. However, as appears from Khayri and al-Rihani's memoirs, Sidqi was also a close friend of al-Rihani, and was a member of his troupe before collaborating with al-Kassar (al-Rihani na: 42).
5. Sidqi was a prolific playwright and translator from French into Arabic (al-Rihani na: 43; advertisements for the play Cyrano de Bergerac in *Tawthiq al-Masrah wal Musiqa* 1924). For an analysis of his plays, see al-Ra'i (2003). Some of his plays have been published and analysed by Nagwa 'Anus and Sayyid Isma'il. See Nagwa 'Anus (1989), *Masrahiyyat Amin Sidqi*, Cairo: al-Hay'a al-Misriyya al-'Amma lil-Kitab and Sayyid 'Ali Isma'il (2006), *Masrah 'Ali al-Kassar*, Cairo: Wizarat al-Thaqafa, al-Markaz al-Qawmi lil-Masrah wal-Musiqa wal-Funun al-Sha'biyya. However, not much is available about his life. In his memoirs, Naguib al-Rihani recalls some anecdotes that brought them together. In English scholarship, an extensive study of his work has still to be done.
6. Born in the popular neighbourhood of Sayyida Zaynab, al-Kassar worked as a cook for some time after the death of his father, a saddle maker (al-Kassar 1993: 12–13). His mother played an important role in his career, consistently encouraging him. It is from her that al-Kassar inherited his name. He started

playing roles with non-Egyptian troupes at Le Théâtre de Paris before founding his own theatre, the Majestic, on 6 January 1919.

7. See the history school programme of 2016, as presented in a textbook for graduation year at high school (*thanawiyya 'amma*), which I analyse more in detail in the introduction.

8. For this experience, see 'Imbraturiyyat Zifta' in Ahmad Baha' al-Din (1990), *Ayyam laha Tarikh*, Cairo: al-Hilal. A novel by Mahfuz 'Abd al-Rahman, *al-Yaum al-Thamin* (*The Eighth Day*) deals with the events and was adapted for the small screen. Unfortunately, neither the book nor the television series are easily available. Dar al-Thaqafa al-Jadida, a small publishing house owned by Muhammad al-Gindi, son of Yusuf al-Gindi, published a novella for adolescents entitled *Kushk al-Musiqa* (*The Music Kiosk, 1980*) by novelist Majid Tubya (b. 1938). It tells the story of the Zifta republic as narrated by a young adolescent who finds out that both his mother and his father were actively involved in the events. The story begins when the parents of the boy discover that the music kiosk, set at the centre of Zifta and one of the main venues of the 1919 events, will be destroyed to allow the construction of a new road. This brings the old comrades together, as they spontaneously organise a sit-in to prevent the destruction.

9. Markaz al-Masrah wal Musiqa. The centre owns hundreds of manuscripts of plays performed at the beginning of the century, most of them unpublished manuscripts. They are only accessible for researchers who can provide a letter from their institution. Photocopy, scan or photography is not allowed.

10. For an account of theatre troupes' participation in the demonstrations see *Mudhakkirat Badi' Khayri, 45 sana taht adwa' al-masrah*, i'dad Muhammad Rif'at, Beirut: Dar al-Thaqafa, 43 (publication date not available), Fatima al-Yusuf (2010), *Dhikrayat*, Cairo: Ruz al-Yusuf, pp. 61–2 and Mustafa Amin, *Min Wahid li-'Ashara* (1977), Cairo: al-Maktab al-Misri al-Hadith, 190.

11. For the political significance of this character, see Eve M. Troutt Powell (2001), 'Burnt-Cork Nationalism: Race and Identity in the Theater of 'Ali al-Kassar', in Cherifa Zuhur, *Colors of Enchantment: Theatre, Dance, Music and the Visual Arts of the Middle East*, Cairo: The American University in Cairo Press.

12. There are also 'the Greek *khawaga*, the *lahluba* maid, the lying Moroccan, the European tourist, the arrogant Turk, the hard of hearing Armenian and the *fiqi* who talks in *fusha* to hide his opportunism' (al-Ra'i 2003: 288–91).

13. Upper-class people most often frequented the opera or private shows, as the vaudeville was considered improper in conservative upper middle-class families.

In a telling scene of *Bayn al-Qasrayn*, Amina is offended when she hears that Yassin takes his wife Zaynab to watch Kishkish Bey (Mahfuz 2014: 356).
14. Not only did the vaudeville play a role in familiarising middle-class audiences with the situation and demands of the underprivileged, it also efficiently conveyed the shared concerns of the underprivileged and of radicalised and/or impoverished segments of the effendiyya.
15. Al-Ra'i's book *al-Kumidya al-Murtajala fil Masrah al-Misri* (*Improvised Comedy in Egyptian Theatre*) is published together with two other volumes under the title *Masrah al-Sha'b* (*The Theatre of the People*, 2003). It deals with theatrical genres that, al-Ra'i argues, have not received the scholarly interest they deserve. In his introduction, al-Ra'i explains that he campaigned against the fact the improvised comedy has for a long time been disregarded by scholars and describes the contemptuous reception of his work about popular theatre (8).
16. With Bishara al-Wakim (1890–1949) in the main role (*Tawthiq al-Turath al-Masrahi, al-Mawsim al-Masrahi 1923*, vol 2, Cairo: al-Markaz al-Qawmi lil-Masrah wal Musiqa wal Funun al-Sha'biyya, 2005, 182).
17. This first stage, held on 27 September 1923, consisted of the elections of the electoral representatives. The second stage, held on 12 January 1924, consisted of the election, by the representatives, of the members of parliament.
18. An example from the sheikh's discourse, which goes as following: 'we should not allow our daughters to wear a transparent burqu', ... otherwise our life will become *accentagiyya*, accent grave' (95). This allusion to the complications of French phonetics in the form of its many accents mainly triggers laughter because it comes as totally unexpected. These references, common to what has been labelled 'franco-arabe' theatre, were of course only accessible to the middle-classes in the audiences.
19. In addition, there is a hint in the play that Ragab Bey is corrupt. One of the policemen who arrest him discovers in his drawer documents about the amount of money spent on the elections and mocks 'those who want to defend the rights of the nation' (152).
20. This was an ongoing debate at the time. When the play was first performed, on 27 September 1923, the papers were full of obituaries for Sayyid Darwish, the well-known composer and singer who had just died at the age of thirty, allegedly from a cocaine overdose.
21. 'Imad al-Din is a common name which literally translates as 'the pillar of religion', hence the sheikh's irritation over the fact the street is famous for its night life. Abu Qura'a's intervention seems to refer to contemporary debates

during which some sheikhs and writers were calling to impose restrictions and censorship on theatre. Among other examples, see Mustafa Lutfi al-Manfaluti, 'al-malaʿib al-hazliyya' in *al-Nazarat wal ʿabarat*, p. 536 and following.

22. See Lucie Ryzova (2007), 'My notepad is my Friend: Effendis and the Act of Writing in Modern Egypt', *The Maghreb Review* 32, no. 4, pp. 323–48 and Lucie Ryzova (2014), *The Age of the Effendiyya. Passages to Modernity in National-Colonial Egypt*. Oxford: Oxford University Press.

23. It was rescheduled several times in and outside Cairo until 1927. In addition to the first performances in January 1924, it was performed on 23/4/1924 (*Tawthiq al-Turath al-Masrahi, al-Mawsim 1924* vol. 1. p. 453; al-Ahram 23.4.1924 for a performance starting 24 April), on 3/6/1924 at Teatro Majestic (*Tawthiq al-Turath al-Masrahi, al-Mawsim 1924* vol. 1 p. 588). In Tanta on 11/8/1924 and at the Casino Monte Carlo in Rud al-Farag on 16 and 17/8/1924 (*Tawthiq al-Turath al-Masrahi, al-Mawsim 1924* vol. 2, 99, 101, 103). During the summer season, the play was performed in the theatres of Suez, Port Said, Mit Ghamr, Tanta, Mansura, Alexandria (Ismaʿil vol. 2 2006: 20). It was also performed during the summer season of 1929 for five months in the Casino of Rud al-Farag.

24. See *Tawthiq al-Turath al-Masrahi, al-Mawsim al-Masrahi 1924*. Cairo: al-Markaz al-Qawmi lil-Masrah wal Musiqa wal Funun al-Shaʿbiyya 2006, pp. 80, 82, 100 and 232. The advertisements mention the dates, the author and the troupe (Guq Amin Sidqi and ʿAli al-Kassar), the space (Majestic theatre) and the main actor, ʿAli al-Kassar, probably in the role of Zaqzuq the fisherman/emperor.

25. It is difficult to ascertain how this title was understood at the time. It might be interpreted as sarcastic towards the young lawyer and member of the wafd's underground organisation who had been nominated 'president' of a small city, Yusuf al-Gindi. Al-Gindi had been on the run since the crackdown on Zifta in April 1919. When the advertisement for the play appeared for the first time in al-Ahram, on 15 January 1924, the results of the elections had just been published two days earlier; al-Gindi had been elected member of parliament for the city of Zifta. He was the only candidate (Al-Ahram, 13 January 1924).

26. This plotline was invested in very diverse ways by a number of playwrights. Marun al-Naqqash used it in his play *Abul Hasan al-Mughaffal* (*Abul Hasan the Fool*, 1849–50). More than a century later, Saʿdalla Wannus uses it in *al-Malik huwa al-Malik* (*The King is the King*, 1977) to criticise the fundamentally corruptive nature of power: whoever sits in the chair of the ruler becomes a

despot. For an analysis of the intertextuality between the tale and the plays by al-Naqqash and Wannus, see Rosella Dorigo 'Intertextual and Intratextual processes in *al-Malik huwa al-Malik* by Saʻdallah Wannus' in Luc Deheuvels, Barbara Michalak-Pikulska and Paul Starkey, eds (2009), *Intertextuality in Modern Arabic Literature Since 1967*, Manchester; New York: Manchester University Press, pp. 117–32.

27. Sidqi adapted, according to Aboul-Hussein, more than 250 plays from the French. For an analysis of translation practices in Egypt during the nineteenth and beginning of the twentieth century, see Samah Selim (2019), *Popular Fiction, Translation and the Nahda in Egypt*, New York: Palgrave Macmillan, and Maya Kesrouany (2019), *Prophetic Translation: The Making of Modern Egyptian Literature*, Edinburgh: Edinburgh University Press. See also Latifa al-Zayyat (2017), *Harakat al-Tarjama al-Adabiyya min al-Injiliziyya ila al-ʻArabiyya fi Misr 1882–1925*, Tahrir wa Taqdim Khayri Duma, Cairo: al-Markaz al-Qawmi lil-Tarjama.

28. However, it is plausible that Adam's opera is itself inspired by the tale 'The Sleeper and the Waker', which was first published in the ninth volume of Galland's translation of the *Thousand and One Nights* in 1712. For a study of the origins of the tale and an analysis of its manuscripts, see Ulrich Marzolph (2015), 'The Story of Abu al-Hasan the Wag in the Tübingen Manuscript of the Romance of ʻUmar ibn al-Nuʻman and Related Texts', *Journal of Arabic Literature 46*, pp. 34–67.

29. She states that her description is based on a manuscript she obtained from the prompter of Fawzi Munib's company, dated 1936 (Aboul-Hussein 1968: 43). The manuscript of *Law Kunt Malik* by Amin Sidqi, kept in the Library of *Markaz al-Masrah wal Musiqa*, reveals a different date and a different plotline. It carries the red stamp of the British Political Censorship, with the mention 'Passed Cairo 29/2/1927' (in English). In Arabic, it is mentioned that the authorisation for this play (*riwaya*) was re-issued on 28/2/1927, and that there was a previous authorisation on 7/7/1924. The characters of the play (Badawi, 'Uf, the princess Qamar al-Zaman, and Bahlul) as well as the plotline are different from that described by Aboul-Hussein, although it contains a series of comic effects around the fact that one of the characters is mistaken for a king. It is possible that the same title was given to different plotlines, played by different theatre companies.

30. Aboul-Hussein does not give the original Arabic titles, only their French translation: *L'Empereur de Zifta* and *Les rêves des rois*. However, in an article titled 'Les

Mille et Une Nuits et le théâtre arabe au XXème siècle', published in 1977, Rachid Bencheneb gives another title for the third play with the same plotline: *Mamlakat al-'Aja'ib* (*The Kingdom of Wonders*). The first part of Bencheneb's article is entirely based on Aboul-Hussein's findings and reiterates her argument about Sidqi's plotline being borrowed from Adolphe Adam's opera. He mentions in a footnote, quoting Aboul-Hussein, that the play he describes (*Mamlakat al-'Aja'ib*) was replayed under the titles *The Emperor of Zifta* and *If I were King*. It is in Bencheneb's article that I first came across Aboul-Hussein's thesis.
31. It seems that this was current practice at the time (Isma'il 2006: 93, note 217).
32. See note 25 (this chapter).

2

The Fear of the Rabble

In 'Maksur ya Iqa'', ('Broken Rhythm'),[1] a song performed in the wake of the 2011 revolution, the author plays with the connotations of the term *ghawgha'*. He claims the insult: 'ihna al-ghawgha', 'we are the rabble', he says, we, the people, are the riff raff, the mob, the dangerous crowds. By using 'we', he subverts the term, ridiculing those who seek to separate the 'good' from the 'bad' people. In his 1946 history of the 1919 revolution, 'Abd al-Rahman al-Rafi'i expresses his dismay at the use of the terms *ghawgha'* (rabble) and *ri'a'* (riff-raff) in British military reports about the demonstrators.[2] However, it was not the term itself, nor its use in an Egyptian context, that upset al-Rafi'i. Rather, it was the fact that the British mistook for *ghawgha'* the intellectuals (*muthaqaffun*) or youth (*shabab*) who constituted, according to him, the majority of the protesting crowds (al-Rafi'i 1946: 190). In doing so, he was seeking to differentiate between 'good' and 'bad' demonstrators, implicitly stripping the so-called 'rabble' of any positive role in the anti-colonial struggle. He was no exception: *ghawgha'*[3] – and its many synonyms – is a term that has a long history in Egyptian discourses about the nationalist movement, and is recurrent in narratives about the 1919 revolution.

One of those narratives, *al-Dahik al-Baki* (*The Weeping Laugher*, 1933),[4] an autobiographical novel by Fikri Abaza (1897–1979), focuses on the revolution in Upper Egypt. Set between 1917 and 1926, the novel narrates the sentimental tribulations of a young Cairene lawyer, Shukri, who is unable to find a suitable wife. After one of his failed romantic relationships, Shukri finds himself in Asyut in 1919 and actively participates in the organisation of the nationalist movement, along with Mariam, a sixteen-year-old girl from a middle-class Christian family. Unlike al-Rafi'i, it is not the confusion between *ghawgha'* and *muthaqaffun* or *shabab* that upsets Abaza. Rather, it is their very presence in the streets of Asyut, and their role during the revolutionary struggle, which he identifies as a dangerous threat to the nationalist movement.

The revolution's representation in the novel initially caught my attention because of its setting in Asyut,[5] which places the Upper Egyptian city at the centre of the narrative about 1919, and de-facto marginalises the capital. This choice distinguishes the text from discourses that systematically present the capital as leading the revolution. Abaza's reading of the 1919 events in the south hereby departs from the broader narrative about 'Upper Egypt in Modern History'. In his article bearing that title (see Introduction), Peter Gran explains that Upper Egypt has been marginalised in dominant historiography since the nineteenth century, and that, according to prevailing assumptions 'Upper Egyptians participated in national events, such as the 'Urabi Revolution and the 1919 Revolution . . . only as a result of national leadership' (Gran 2004: 82).

Al-Dahik al-Baki further questions dominant historiography by stripping the landowning elite of its leading role during the revolution in Asyut, highlighting its absence – including that of the Wafdist leaders – at crucial moments. Unlike canonical narratives about the 1919 revolution, which depict a national movement united behind its Wafdist elite (see Introduction), the novel describes the movement as divided by ruthless class tensions and presents youth belonging to the middle class as the real driving force of the revolution. Moreover, its condemnation of the 'rabble' – in the text called *al-ashrar al-fuqara* (the evil poor) – is unusually violent. I argue that the bold class articulation of the narrative is mainly due to the text's didactic nature. An autobiographical and educational narrative, *Al-Dahik al-Baki* is primarily written in order to provide a young effendi readership with an edifying lesson about changing mores. Yet the complicity the narrator establishes with a clearly identified middle-class male reader goes beyond its romantic reformist aims, by seeking to establish a discourse about 1919 common to that particular statum of society, a discourse in which the concept of class is central.

Class, Gender and Effendiyya

Class was a central concept in the process of the formation of the effendiyya's worldview. A 'cultural category of educated men who saw themselves as standing between the illiterate peasants and the landowning aristocracy in their bid to make Egyptian state and society modern' (Omar 2014: 287), the effendiyya were at the heart of many debates about modernity and its meaning in the Egyptian context. In her recently published *The Age of the Efendiyya*, which delves into many aspects of 'effendihood', Lucie Ryzova defines effendis as 'the first self-consciously modern generation in Egyptian history'; 'the efendis [sic] are well known to have been the major actors of modern Egyptian nationalism in its many forms: they were the makers, as well as the primary consumers, of modern Egyptian political life, social institutions and cultural production' (Ryzova 2014: 4). In his article about representations of the working class in literature and newspapers from the early twentieth century, Zackary Lockman notes that 'the lower classes in Egypt' are 'being imagined by segments of the effendiyya in new and different ways' (Lockman: 1994: 179). To him, it is at the beginning of the century that members of the 'effendiyya -especially but not exclusively the nationalists among them-adopted, adapted, and deployed (elements of) a 'model,' or discourse, positing class as a significant feature of the social order' (Lockman 1994: 161).

Likewise, gender was an important element in the effendiyya's worldview. Among the many pillars of modernity as imagined by effendis, the 'New Man,' but also, especially, the 'New Woman', are important.[6] The 'New Woman' was expected to be at once educated and prepared to assume her traditional gender roles (Elsadda 2012: 4). Her education would contribute to a better upbringing of the new generations, as advocated by Qasim Amin (1863–1908),[7] Malak Hifni Nasif (1886–1918) and Nabawiyya Musa (1886–1951) among others. During that transitional phase, however, the 'New Man' had a hard time finding a suitable wife. The contemporary press talked of a 'marriage crisis', an expression used 'to refer to a supposed rise in the number of middle-class men who were choosing bachelorhood over marriage in early twentieth-century urban Egypt.' (Kholoussy 2010: 1). A representative of the category of the effendiyya,[8] Fikri Abaza himself was a living example of that 'marriage crisis'. In December 1932, he gave a lecture on that topic at the American University in Cairo, confessing that he was unable to find a suitable wife and lamenting the fact that marriage had come to resemble a commercial pact (*al-Hilal*, January 1933, 320–9), a theme also central to *al-Dahik al-Baki*.

Effendi Autobiography

Although its author did not formally acknowledge it as an autobiography,[9] *Al-Dahik al-Baki* was widely perceived as such by Abaza's peers. One reviewer at al-*Muqtataf* states that the 'book is a page of its author's life' (*al-Muqtataf*, June 1933, 121) and defines it as an effort by the author to 'translate himself'.[10] Another reviewer, at *al-Hilal*, shares this point of view, noting that the change of the 'fa'' in the author's first name into a 'shin' – from Fikri to Shukri- alludes to the 'shin' of 'shabab', youth (*al-Hilal*, June 1933, 1130). Similarly, historical sources consider *al-Dahik al-Baki* as an 'autobiographical novel' (Brown 1990: 208).

Scholars of Egyptian and Arab autobiographies from the opening decades of the twentieth century underline that these texts were narratives of success and social mobility. Ryzova 'argues that the *afandī* autobiography chronicles a success story of *takwīn* or character formation and social legibility' (Booth 2016: 345). Valerie Anishchenkova states that 'the twentieth-century Arab autobiographer was expected to present himself to his audience as a distinguished individual' (Anishchenkova 2014: 20). Shukri's story, however, does not fit neatly into that description. Although the main character is successful in his professional life, the narrative is marked by bitter failures (hence its title), the most prominent one being the young man's inability to find a suitable wife. Moreover, it expresses persistent doubts towards the dominant values displayed by the Cairene upper middle class – specifically the cynicism of potential brides' families. Finally, *Al-Dahik al-Baki*'s allusions to the young man's multiple encounters with prostitutes -which may explain why the author did not wish to clearly assume its autobiographical nature – render the narrative difficult to present as a conformist life-lesson for young effendis.

Nevertheless, *al-Dahik al-Baki* is clearly a narrative of character formation, with a strong didactic aspect aiming at shaping young effendis' behaviour, especially in the domain of gender relationships. It is through a didactic approach that the text deals with tensions of gender and masculinity the effendiyya were at the centre of, including the thematic of sexual and marital relationships. A main theme of the book is its inclusion of female characters forced by their life circumstances to resort to prostitution. Towards the end of the narrative, edifying remarks about prostitutes dominate the text, as the main plot fades to make room for the stories of the women Shukri welcomes in his *garçonnière*, all cheated or abandoned by men. These women, all of whom belong to middle-class or wealthy families, are depicted as having either fallen prey to fate or to immoral lovers and husbands, and should therefore not be deemed responsible for their situation. The narrator thus urges the reader to abandon his misconceptions and his cruel behaviour towards prostitutes and women in general. This didactic tone is strengthened by the explicit address to a male reader[11] and an identification of the narrator with the targeted group, the effendiyya, by the use of the first-person plural in several instances. Those 'efforts to bond with the audience by comparing his or her personal life with their readers', are, according to Anishchenkova, an 'indication of a collective aspect of Arab conventional autobiography' (Anishchenkova 2014: 24). *Al-Dahik al-Baki* shares with that genre its collective ambitions. The narrative does not reflect exclusively an individual journey; rather, it carries a clarifying meaning for the community, the effendiyya, in a moment of national tensions.

The Anti-Colonial Movement of the 1930s: Challenges and Debates

The early 1930s were still marked by the general climate of disillusion that had prevailed since 1924, after the intense social and political struggles of the years 1919–23 had come to an end. As I explained in Chapter 1, although the Wafd won the elections of 1923 with an overwhelming majority, its politics soon triggered broad discontent. Most importantly, the experience of institutionalised democracy came to an abrupt end in November 1924 after the assassination of the British commander-in-chief and commander of the Sudan. Zaghlul was forced to resign, and both the British and the palace used the conjunction of events to reinstitute heavy interventionism in the country's political life. After several years of political instability, with successive parliaments and governments led either by the Wafd or by politicians subordinate to the British and the palace, the investiture of Isma'il Sidqi as prime minister in 1930 confirmed the anti-democratic turn. Sidqi, a one-time member of the Wafd who had founded his own party, had acquired a reputation as a dictator after he served as Minister of Interior in 1925 (Botman 1998: 292). In 1930, true to this reputation, he abrogated the post-revolutionary 1923 Constitution, imposed a more conservative text, and dissolved parliament. This triggered a broad protest movement, with recrudescent street demonstrations, during which, after years of internecine tension in the Wafd, Zaghlul was posthumously 'presented as a model of the struggle against tyranny, and the defence of the Constitution and the parliamentary system' (Clement 2005: 29).

Abaza however was not a supporter of the Wafd.[12] He was an active member of the National Party (NP)[13] founded in 1907 by Mustafa Kamil and marginalised in the wake of the 1919 revolution. The NP's positions were considered more radical than those of the Wafd, as it advocated uncompromising stances in the negotiations with the colonial power. In his *Hawadit* (*Stories*), a volume that brings together anecdotes spanning from 1906 to 1966, Fikri Abaza summarises the NP's principles as he presented them to a potential elector: 'no negotiations before complete liberation, Egypt and the Sudan are ours, total independence without conditions or restrictions' (Abaza 1969: 91). The NP repeatedly critiqued the Wafd's and Zaghoul's handling of the 1919 revolution and of the negotiations with the British (Abaza na: 83). This rivalry between the Wafd and the NP extended to the memory of 1919, around which there was an intense debate between 1920 and 1937. The NP's marginalisation was reflected in the way its figures were remembered and celebrated: their memory was 'in eclipse' during that period (Gershoni 2004: 174).

In addition to his political activities, Abaza was an established intellectual, well known as a virulent polemicist and editor-in-chief of the journal *al-Musawwar* from 1925 on. He used this position to place a full-page advertisement for *al-Dahik al-Baki* in his weekly editorial, in May 1933. Two advertisements in *al-Ahram* announced the publication, and, in June, at least two reviews appeared in the main literary and cultural journals of the time, *al-Muqtataf* and *al-Hilal*, praising the book's interesting contribution to social debates. According to Abaza himself, the book was widely distributed, reprinted four times, and all copies systematically sold out (Abaza 2000: 170).[14] In addition to the author's renown, the book's plausible success can be explained by its bold treatment of issues related to gender relationships. The most relevant aspect of the narrative for our purposes, however, is its original articulation of the 1919 revolution.

The Revolution's Time and Space Frame

Al-Dahik al-Baki's narrative of 1919 is characterised by its unusual geographical and chronological organisation of the events and its imagery of disunity and chaos. The book does not mention the Cairo demonstrations and student strikes on 9 March 1919, following Saad Zaghlul's exile, usually presented as the beginning of the 1919 revolution. Instead, without specifying an exact date, the text states that 'the first bomb of the Egyptian revolution exploded in al-Munufiyya' before 'the spark extended to other provinces' (Abaza 1933: 59).

In Asyut, according to *al-Dahik al-Baki*, everything begins with a massive gathering in a church, where Shukri sings a nationalist anthem he himself had written and composed, of which 20000 copies were distributed in the city and the neighbouring countryside. When the crowds leave the church in a huge demonstration, they are confronted by threatening British forces; violence bursts onto the scene and the city immediately plunges into an all-encompassing chaos (67). The revolutionary scenes are described in dysphoric terms and are dominated by obscurity, distressing sounds and fire. Electric power is cut off and the city is plunged in darkness. The soundscape is made up of bullets whistling, 'monsters' shouting and screaming, and people wailing and crying. The fire engulfing the 'authority's hay (61)[15] and the modern buildings (64) turns the scene into an embodiment of hell, with its billowing flames and smell of smoke (64). References to the Day of Judgement further strengthen the analogy with hell, and a metaphor of the hay as a 'volcano' (64) reinforces that frightening end-of-the-world imagery, evoking the destructive power of nature and threatening an imminent catastrophe that might destroy an entire human community. The city is totally isolated because of the disruption of transportation, in particular the railway system, which leads to the spread of wild rumours. For instance, a 'respectable man swears that al-Basil's Arabs [a tribal leader and member of the Wafd exiled with Zaghlul] occupy the citadel . . . and the tracts of the Egyptian Black Hand [organisation], backed by the Italian and Spanish anarchists, proclaim that the occupation has been eradicated' (60).

According to the testimony of a British official living in the city at the time,[16] as well as other historical sources,[17] the violent uprising Abaza summarises in a few pages unfolded over a time span of nearly two weeks. Asyut was the theatre of a rebellion led by inhabitants of environing villages who attacked main administrative buildings, including the police station,[18] cut the railroads at several places and set fire to the authorities' granaries. This rebellion is the subject of at least two other literary narratives, both published approximatively three decades later: a novella by the Greek novelist Stratis Tsirkas, *Nur al-Din Bumba*[19] and a short story by Mahmud al-Badawi, 'Dhata Layla' ('One Night', 1965). Both stories give a laudatory account of the armed struggle that took place in Asyut. Set in Dayrut, a small city north of Aysut, Tsirkas's narrative revolves around the character of Nur al-Din Bumba, a figure of resistance against feudal notables who becomes a leader of the popular uprising in 1919. 'Dhata Layla' is narrated by one of the 500 men, mostly belonging to the Arab tribes living in the Eastern mountains, who led the armed rebellion.

Ghawgha' and Effendiyya: 'Evildoers' Versus Civilised People

In contrast, *Al-Dahik al-Baki*'s narrator explicitly condemns Asyut's armed rebellion, which he identifies as a revolution against wealth (*al-thawra didd al-tharwa*, 62), as distinct from the nationalist struggle. There are 'two revolutions' taking place according to this narrator: one against the colonial power led by 'some enlightened people' (62) and one against 'wealth' led by 'an ignorant and infidel poverty' (64).[20] Irritated by the 'strange mix between the nationalist battle and a naive socialism',[21] the narrator does not see the possibility of a concurrence between those two types of demands (63). This Manichaean vision structures the narrative according to a dichotomy between 'good' and 'bad', 'civilised' and 'uncivilised' ways of struggling. On one hand, the effendiyya, on the other, the disenfranchised poor of the city, depicted as the main actors in the chaotic violence.

The neatly dressed and well-behaved students play no role in the 'revolution's army': it is an army of *jalalib* and *za'abit* (61), (*jalalib* is the plural of *jalabiyya*, a loose garb worn by men and *za'abit* the plural of *za'but*, a headgear similar to a cap). The image could refer to peasants, the disenfranchised or unemployed workers, or most probably Bedouins, as their leader, according to the rumour, is Faysal, Shaykh al-'Arab (61). With its powerful generalising image, the synecdoche symbolically differentiates the underprivileged from the effendiyya, embodying the tradition/modernity dichotomy at the centre of the worldview of many effendiyya at the time. The dress image effectively contributes to the process of 'othering' upon which the effendi identity hinges. To describe this process, Marilyn Booth talks about 'the *afandī* and his others', 'those who give boundary and illuminate, dialectically, his middle-strata existence and his sense of social mission' (Booth 2016: 343). In *al-Dahik al-Baki*, the 'revolting monsters' are the effendi's ultimate other, embodying the exact opposite of the values central to effendi identity.

Depicted as belonging to the realm of tradition and backwardness, the underprivileged masses are unable to grasp the meaning of the ongoing nationalist struggle. Even though they are 'rebelling', the disenfranchised of Asyut are depicted in *al-Dahik as-Baki* as insensitive to the nationalist demands. When the narrator tries to stop those 'revolting monsters' from setting fire to the building in which non Egyptian families had taken refuge, he tells them it is the property of the father of Muhammad Mahmud [one of the Wafd leaders exiled with Saad Zaghlul] and that there are no English men in the building, only foreign families. In the dialogue that follows, the young men shout: 'Shut up! Did Mahmud Pasha distribute bread for the hungry? We want bread!' (63).

Moreover, the terms used to depict the 'unarmed wretched' (61) mostly belong to the semantic field of evil. The poor are first depicted as 'ferocious lions' when they attack the British 'munitions storeroom' (61). Although the metaphor of the lion evokes power and bravery as much as ferocity, they are not praised in the text as heroes, martyrs or even actors in the revolutionary struggle. Instead, they are prey to a specific kind of malefic force, namely 'the bloodthirsty sacred nationalist evil' (60). Their spontaneous patriotic energy seems to be necessarily bloody, harmful and immoral. The powerful associations of the term 'evil' flesh out the dichotomy between 'good' and 'bad' ways of struggling already established in the text *before* that 'malefic' energy turns against another target: Christian jewellery shops and foreign civilians.[22] The looting is led by people successively described by the narrator as 'the evildoers' (*al-ashrar*, 62),[23] the deprived evildoers (*al-ashrar al-fuqara'*, 62), 'the rebels' (*al-tha'irin*) and 'the gangs of thieves' (*'isabat al-lusus*, 64). Evil power seizes them and turns them into 'monsters', into threatening creatures that refuse to abide by the laws governing a human community, and who are thus outside its defining boundaries. More importantly, their violent, irrational contribution disrupts and threatens the nationalist movement; Abaza calls upon his readership to take this threat seriously. This alarming depiction of the underprivileged constitutes the cornerstone of *al-Dahik al-Baki's* class discourse.

Fear, Compassion and Exclusion

In those scenes, the focalisation through Shukri's perspective, as he actively tries to protect potential victims of looting, highlights feelings of fear on the part of the characters Shukri attempts to help, and of compassion on his side. Building on Martha Nussbaum's work about the importance of emotions for understanding 'the landscape of our mental and social lives' (Nussbaum 2001: I), I contend that analysing these feelings can help us to better understand the dynamics of exclusion at stake in *al-Dahik al-Baki*, and in discourses about the underprivileged in the context of the 1919 revolution more broadly (see Introduction).

Nussbaum devotes the entire second part of *Upheavals of Thought* to compassion, beginning her discussion with Aristotle:

> Compassion, Aristotle argues, is a painful emotion directed at another person's misfortune or suffering (Rhet.1385b13 ff.). It has three cognitive elements ... The first cognitive requirement of compassion is a belief or appraisal that the suffering is serious rather than trivial. The second is the belief that the person does not deserve the suffering. The third is the belief that the possibilities of the person who experiences the emotion are similar to those of the sufferer. (Nussbaum 2001: 306)

The first cognitive element perfectly applies to those scenes, as the terrified foreign women and children are described in a moment of extreme vulnerability, weeping and begging for help. Moreover, the narrator describes Shukri's reaction to those people's suffering in hyperbolic terms, insisting on the 'horror' (62) of the scene. The second cognitive requirement is achieved through the narrator's mapping out of the lives of these non-Egyptian people *before* the trauma they were subjected to as once normal family or professional lives interrupted by the violence. That is not only the case of the foreign families he tries to save from lynching, but also of the Christian merchants whose shops are looted.

The third cognitive requirement is more problematic, as Nussbaum states that it is largely based on 'social and familial teaching', and that 'errors may easily occur' (316). She refers to both Aristotle and Rousseau as insisting 'that compassion requires acknowledgment that one has possibilities and vulnerabilities similar to those of the sufferer. One makes sense of the suffering by recognising that one might oneself encounter such a reversal' (316). And, further: 'All kinds of social barriers – of class, religion, ethnicity, gender, sexual orientation – prove recalcitrant to the imagination, and this recalcitrance impedes emotion' (317).

In the case of Shukri, neither the barrier of gender, nor those of religion and ethnicity, seems 'recalcitrant'. Not only does he clearly express feelings of compassion, he also acts upon them by actively intervening to protect women, Christians and non-Egyptians from violence or looting. Moreover, in his depiction of the foreign families to the insurgents, Shukri underlines their identities as 'mothers' and 'children', thus insisting on what they share with Egyptians.

The barrier of class, in contrast, proves particularly 'recalcitrant to the imagination' (317). In this particular scene, the poor's need for bread, expressed by one of the rioters, does not trigger Shukri's compassion but is instead depicted as a subject of discord since it disrupts the nationalist movement. None of the three requirements applies to them. First of all, Shukri does not identify the poor's hunger as a 'serious' object of compassion; from his point of view, they have no serious grievances and are thus not to be considered as victims. Second, they only exist in the text as a group, and the narrator refrains from giving any information about their lives outside of this particular moment, which would suggest that they do not deserve this suffering. Thirdly, the repeated reference to these people as 'evildoers' and 'monsters' impedes by definition any identification between Shukri/the narrator and 'them'. On the contrary, these terms contribute to a process of 'othering' the deprived poor. Worse, as they are responsible for instilling fear into the hearts of the characters whom Shukri feels compassion towards, they become the origin or, in other terms, the *object* of fear. Rather than an individual reaction of withdrawal, fear expresses in this context a collective reaction towards the 'rabble'. It is an emotion that bonds the effendiyya and all the 'good people' against the threatening 'other', hereby excluding the underprivileged and the armed rebels from the realm of the nationalist movement. As articulated through Shukri's perspective, it serves the narrative's didactic purpose in terms of class. Fear is used to set the boundaries of class belonging.

At this point, it is interesting to refer again to al-Badawi's short story, in which fear is no less a central emotion, albeit one articulated very differently. In 'Dhata Layla', rather than being the object of fear, the armed rebel – who is also the short story's main character – is the one who experiences this emotion, as he is forced to hide after the British repression puts an end to the revolutionary struggle. The first-person narration and focalisation from the perspective of the armed man leads the reader to view him as worthy of compassion. Moreover, rather than dividing it, fear in 'Dhata layla' unites the nationalist front. It is experienced both by the armed rebel, a man from a well-known Bedouin tribe, and by the single woman from an underprivileged background who is hiding him. Fear thus becomes a strong incentive for inclusion beyond the boundaries of class and gender.

In contrast, the visceral fear of the looting poor is so central to the narrative in *al-Dahik al-Baki* that it becomes more essential than the original object of fear, namely the British troops. This is clear from the fact that, although *al-Dahik al-Baki* is one of the rare narratives that acknowledges the extent of the British repression in 1919, fear is not an emotion associated with that repression. Asyut is subjected to the British aviation's bombardments (68), while systematic arrests, multiple death sentences and cold-blooded assassinations become commonplace. The repression is so violent it returns the city to the Middle Ages (74). But all this ultimately leaves the protagonist with a sense of helplessness rather than fear.

Pashas and Nationalist Leadership

As I mentioned in the introduction to this chapter, *Al-Dahik al-Baki*'s virulent invective against the so-called 'rabble' is a recurrent pattern of the dominant narratives about 1919. However, Abaza's uncompromising depiction of the upper classes is less common. During the revolution in Asyut, the police, as well as the governmental institutions and the big landowners, are totally absent from the scene as Shukri and other young men try to protect the families terrorised by the looters. The narrator's words against the pashas are harsh: 'afraid of the revolution, the big houses closed their doors and placed guards in front of them, selected from among their peasants' (62). The 'big houses' refers to influential and wealthy land-owning families described as erecting a barrier between their protected space and the outside. By doing so, they are constructing themselves as outsiders to the revolutionary turmoil, and they thus lose their right to profess any leadership of it. When they do play a leading role, and are arrested for it, they are explicitly condemned by the narrator as being anti-revolutionary: 'the authorities arrested a huge number of leaders and celebrities whose mission in Asyut was to give moralising advice and restrain the energy of the revolution and the revolutionaries' (78). The only pasha who escapes the narrator's vindictive tone is Muhammad Mahmud Pasha (63).

As a group, the Upper Egyptian pashas are thus depicted as either hiding in a cowardly manner, or playing a counter revolutionary role, not contributing in any way to a positive outcome of the battle that is taking place. The absenteeism of the big landlords is elsewhere critiqued as a structural class behaviour[24] when, following his return to Cairo after the Asyut episode, a depressed Shukri takes a break in his native village. He finds the countryside devastated, in a state of extreme poverty; the women are mourning their sons who died in 'the deserts of Palestine' (132), in a reference to the conscription of Egyptian peasants in the British army starting in 1917, and the peasants complain about 'the period of investigations and trials' after the revolution (137). 'The good things are gone for good,' (135), because, as the narrator says, 'the masters emigrated to the capitals and rented the *diya'* to their peasants' (135), while 'politics kept the people in charge busy as of that date' (136), politics referring here to parliamentary elections and politicians' machinations.

This critical tone towards big landowners is paired with scepticism towards the Wafd policy, as becomes clear at the end of the narrative. In the narrator's comments on Saad Zaghlul's situation after the 1924 elections, he states that Zaghlul's dignity was affected during the negotiations with MacDonald (167), although he was able to form a cabinet/government 'from which emanated the scent of democracy and that did include some effendis' (165). The distrust the text expresses towards the self-appointed leaders of the movement, mostly important landowners, echoes the positions of the NP. While the Wafd's social basis belonged to the landowning class and the urban upper middle class, the NP had a social basis that was mainly composed of young effendiyya. According to Arthur Goldschmidt, 'the Watani Party's [NP] leadership and the mass of followers in the pre-First World War period was predominantly urban. Except for a few rural notables, the vast majority of the administrative committee probably belonged to the urban middle class or the effendiyyas' (Goldschmidt 1968: 333). This explains why the NP expressed a more radical position towards occupation than its more successful rival, or at least than its leadership.[25]

Gender and Anti-Colonial Struggle

The affiliation of its author to the NP might also explain why *Al-Dahik al-Baki* does not transmit the dominant narrative about women's participation in the revolution. Unlike canonical photographs, poems and novels about 1919, which focus on the demonstrations of March 1919 initiated by elite women belonging to Wafdist circles,[26] Abaza documents middle-class women's contribution to the organisation of the nationalist movement. This is achieved mainly through characterisation, especially the character of Mariam. Even though her relationship with Shukri is described in mawkish terms, with weak dialogues interrupted by tears and silences, Mariam is a strong character presented as independently involved in the revolutionary turmoil – that is, independently from Shukri or any other male character. She leads a girls' demonstration at an extremely delicate moment, as the colonial repression intensifies and the wafdist leaders remain absent, leaving the street to the students of the American School (76).[27] Moreover, she is extremely well-organised, with a sharp sense of initiative and opportunity: she makes use of her family connections in the prosecution office to warn Shukri of growing intelligence attention towards him and bids him to leave the city (79). She then embarks on an improbable search for the printer who published the anthem Shukri wrote, managing to find his name and address, and convinces him to destroy the manuscript in Shukri's handwriting. She also passes by the homes of her female friends and destroys all the copies they have in their possession (81). When Shukri finally gives in and announces he is ready to leave the city, she puts him in contact with a relative of hers who arranges for a military laissez-passer in order to get him on the only functioning train. In short, she is his saviour.

Mariam's character is emblematic of middle-class girls and women's involvement in the organisation of the nationalist movement. In his analysis of 'mosques and churches as revolutionary spaces', Ziad Fahmy notes that Egyptian women 'actively participated in and delivered important speeches at many of these mosque and church meetings' (147). He gives the example of 'a Muslim woman' who stood up and 'preached for a general strike' during a meeting in a Coptic church in Cairo on 3 May (148), and another example of 'several Egyptian ladies' walking 'into the Sayyida Zaynab Mosque in Cairo' to make 'speeches about the Egyptian revolution' (148). Women were also involved at various levels in Upper Egypt. In her article about 'the Revolutionary Gentlewomen in Egypt' Afaf Marsot mentions that, when Hidaya Hanim Barakat, an activist close to wafdist circles, took the train to Upper Egypt, her shopping baskets filled with clandestine leaflets, 'at every station female school teachers met her and received a basket with the pamphlets at the bottom' (271).[28]

Not only is Mariam a politically courageous character, but she is also a non-conventional one. She answers Shukri's question about whether they could possibly meet under the 'umbrella of a sacred contract' by 'religion is in my heart' (83), thus making clear she is ready to marry a man from a different religion,[29] an act which would put her at odds with her family and community.[30] Though her rape by British soldiers[31] in her native village would turn her into a victim, a 'noble and innocent prey that was ravished' (101), a Virgin Mary (al-Sayyida Maryam), and temporarily crushes her as an activist, Mariam manages to overcome its trauma. If during their meeting at the hospital in Asyut she wants to commit suicide and is this time saved by Shukri who convinces her not to, in yet another mawkish dialogue, she eventually becomes a happily married woman. In her last epistolary appearance in the narrative, she tells Shukri she is happy with her life as a wife and mother. While this ending brings her back to a traditional gender role, the free tone of the letter and the very fact she keeps a friendly relationship with an old lover is all but conventional. The many initiatives she takes on are those of a self-confident character, while the protagonist remains hesitant and unable to achieve marital or extra-marital happiness. Her character fits in neatly with the definition of the 'New Woman' as imagined by sections of the effendiyya: at once educated and equipped with a solid nationalist awareness on one hand, and on the other successfully fulfilling her traditional roles. It embodies both the political and sentimental didactic aims of the book, summarising *al-Dahik al-Baki*'s message.

As I said earlier, Abaza published *al-Dahik al-Baki* during a time of the nationalist struggle's recession, in which it had become clear that the anti-colonial movement had not yet fulfilled its aims, and in which the NP's figures were marginalised in the memory of the nationalist movement. This puts in context the urge Fikri Abaza felt to present in a didactic form a narrative about the 1919 revolution faithful to the NP's political values. By shaping a distinctive voice for the young effendi movement in an upper Egyptian city, *Al-Dahik al-Baki* distinguishes itself from the Cairo-centred dominant narrative about 1919, which insists on the leading role of the Wafdist elite. He urges his middle-class readers to learn from the past and not to rely on leaders who had been unable to lead the country to its independence. He provides them with the positive model of a young woman activist involved in the movement. Most importantly, he bids them to beware of the underprivileged's potentially harmful role.

In the struggle of narratives over the memory of 1919, Abaza's story of ruthless class tensions and disunity was soon to be defeated by the narrative that framed 1919 as the moment of birth of a new, modern nation. The dichotomy Abaza creates between a nationalist revolution and the poor people's rebellion is erased in subsequent representations, in which the elite is in total control of the movement, as is the case in the two canonical novels I analyse in Chapter 3, Tawfik al-Hakim's *'Awdat al-Ruh* and Naguib Mahfouz' *Bayn al-Qasrayn*.

Notes

1. The song, written by Mido Zuheir, is from the album Al-Ikhfa' (*Invisibility*), released by musicians Maryam Saleh, Tamer Abu Ghazaleh and Maurice Louca in 2017. It is available at <https://www.youtube.com/watch?v=4pvVjyntq70> (last accessed 5 June 2019).
2. The term used by al-Rafi'i is 'reports by the military authorities' (*balaghat al-sulta al-'askariyya*) (Rafi'i 1946: 189). He does not mention whether the reports were translated into Arabic, or if his analysis is based on his own translation.
3. *Ghawgha'* is defined in the medieval dictionary *Lisan al-'Arab* as *al-safala min*

al-nas wal mutasarri'in ila al-sharr (literally 'lowly people and those who hurry towards committing evil deeds). Though the term is sometimes used as a synonym of *ri'a'* and *'amma* (the common people), its pejorative connotations are stronger. *Lisan al-'Arab* notes that the term originally means 'locusts when they are ready to fly', that is, when they are about to inflict significant damage; it thus connotes an irresistible, destructive plague. The use of *al-ghawgha'* to designate crowds of people, implicitly describing them as violent and dangerous, is recurrent in classical Arabic literature. See for instance Taqi al-Din Ahmad ibn 'Ali al-Maqrizi (1936), *Kitab al-Suluk li-Ma'rifat Duwal al-Muluk*, edited by Muhammad Mustafa Ziyada, 4 vols. Cairo: Dar al-Kutub al-Mistiyya; 'Abd al-Rahman al-Jabarti (1997–8), *'Aja'ib al-Athar fil Tarajim wal Akhbar*, edited by 'Abd al-'Azim Ramadan, Cairo: Matba'at Dar al-Kutub al-Misriyya.
4. I first came across Fikri Abaza's text in Nathan Brown's *Peasant Politics* (1990), in which the author uses Abaza's novel to discuss the attacks on a wafdist landowner's estate in Asyut.
5. Among the autobiographies and memoirs that recall scenes of the 1919 revolution in Upper Egypt, see Fakhri 'Abd al-Nur (1992), *Mudhakkirat Fakhri Abd al-Nur*, Cairo: Dar al-Shuruq. He devotes several chapters to describe Saad Zaghlul's journey to Upper Egypt by ship in 1921, accompanied by Wafdist figures from the region. In his autobiography, Louis 'Awad recollects scenes of the revolutionary turmoil in 1920 and 1921 during his childhood in Minya (Luwis 'Awad (1989), *Awraq al-'Umr, Sanawat al-Takwin*, Cairo: Madbuli).
6. See Hoda Elsadda (2012), *Gender, Nation, and the Arabic Novel. Egypt 1892–2008*. New York: Syracuse University Press and Edinburgh University Press.
7. Qasim Amin is often presented as the pioneer of women emancipation in Egypt; however, feminist ideas were debated by many other intellectuals, and many women were actively involved in those debates. See Beth Baron (1994), *The Women's Awakening in Egypt: Culture, Society, and the Press*, New Haven, CT: Yale University Press. About the social context of the emergence of feminist thought in Egypt, see Juan Ricardo Cole (1981), 'Feminism, Class, and Islam in turn-of-the century Egypt', *International Journal of Middle East Studies* 13, pp. 387–407.
8. A member of the well-established land-owning Abaza family who was initially destined to a religious education, Fikri Abaza, the son of Husayn Abaza Bey, was educated as an effendi because he was 'unwilling to join al-Azhar' (Nessim 1951: 7) as a child. He was given an entirely secular education in the Giza primary school, the Sa'idiyya secondary school, and finally law school.

9. In contrast to its epigraph, which states that 'everything recorded in this book actually happened' and invites the reader to 'read it as the truth' (7), the author refuses to clearly acknowledge the text as his autobiography. Instead, he gives the main character a different first name than his own and the omniscient narrator, who presents himself as a close friend of the protagonist (65), repeatedly insists on differentiating himself from Shukri. He thus jeopardises what Lejeune calls the 'autobiographical pact' defined as 'the affirmation in the text of this identity [the 'identicalness' of the name (author-narrator-protagonist)]' (Lejeune 1989: 14).

10. The reviewer thereby links Abaza's text to the classical Arabic autobiographical tradition. In that tradition, the term 'tarjama nafsahu' 'signifies "to compile a titled work/entry on oneself" or "to translate/interpret oneself," in the sense of creating a written representation of oneself'. Dwight F. Reynolds (2001), *Interpreting the Self: Autobiography in the Arabic Literary Tradition*. Berkeley, CA: University of California Press, p. 3.

11. The narrator's discourse perfectly fits into what Marilyn Booth calls 'a gendered hierarchy of address, whereby it is assumed that the masculine subject is the first interlocutor and the feminine subject is addressed through his mediation and instruction' (Booth 2016: 347). Although the narrator of *al-Dahik al-Baki* includes females in his address to young people in one instance (70), his primary 'addressee' remains the male.

12. However, he had a good relationship with Zaghlul, who intervened in his favour as Minister of Education when he was expelled from school in 1909 (Abaza 2000: 240). He was often dispatched by his party, the National Party (NP) to confer with Zaghlul, as was the case in 1926, when the NP wished to negotiate a significant number of seats in the elections. The young Abaza failed to obtain from the aging leader more than fourteen 'closed districts', but he was granted by his party the opportunity to run in one of those districts and entered Parliament in 1926, successfully running in the elections until 1952. After the Free Officers' coup, he was marginalised by the new regime and prohibited from publishing until he 'signed a public apology letter in order to regain his position, though they had already appointed someone else in his place' (Filastin 2009: 413). Interpellations by Fikri Abaza in parliament are available in: Abaza, Fikri (1982), *al-Mawaqif al-Barlamaniyya lil-Marhum al-Ustadh Muhammad Fikri Abaza, 'Udw Majlis al-Nuwwab fil-Fatra min 'Am 1926 hatta 'Am 1949*. Cairo: al-Hay'a al-'Amma li-Shu'un al-Matabi' al-Amiriyya.

13. Abaza joined the NP in 1917. According to Tewfiq Nessim, he was elected a member of its administrative committee in 1921 (Nessim 1951: 8).

14. It is the narrator of the second part of his book, written in 1958, who gives these figures. That second part was published together with the first part in 1973 (Alexandria, al-Maktab al-Misri al-Hadith lil-Tiba'a wal-Nashr) and 2000 (Cairo, al-Hilal).
15. The British authority expropriated the hay to sustain its army, which explains why the spaces where the hay was stocked became, with many other authority buildings, the target of popular anger.
16. This anonymous testimony by a British official who nicknamed himself Tawwaf, titled *Egypt, 1919, Being a Narrative of Certain Incidents of the Rising in Upper Egypt* is kept in the Private Papers of F. M. Edwards in the Centre for Middle Eastern Studies, Saint Antony, Oxford University. It is translated into Arabic in *Thawrat 1919 fil-Aqalim* by 'Asim al-Dusuqi (1981).
17. See 'Abd al-Rahman al-Rafi'i (1999 [1946]), *Thawrat 1919*, vol. 2. Cairo: al-Hay'a al-Misriyya al-'Amma lil-Kitab.
18. The police chief (*ma'mur*), named Muhammad Kamil, was later sentenced to death by a military court for 'high treason'. His story is mentioned in several other sources, but not all of them concur as to his attitude towards the rebels. According to 'Abd al-Rahman al-Rafi'i, Kamil stated that he was advised by his superior to surrender (al-Rafi 'i 1999: 82). In *Egypt, 1919, Being a Narrative of Certain Incidents of the Rising in Upper Egypt*, the writer states that not only did Kamil let the insurgents in, but he also led their military actions. *Al-Dahik al-Baki*'s version is closer to that reported by al-Rafi'i as the narrator states that the police chief made many phone calls to make sure whether he was expected 'to use force' against the people (Abaza 1933: 78).
19. Originally written in Greek, the story is available in French and Arabic translations: Stratis Tsirkas (1983), *L'homme du Nil*. Paris: Le Seuil; Stratis Tsirkas (1994), *Nur al-Din Bumba*, translated by Yani Milakhrinudi, Cairo: Matba'at Atlas.
20. Berridge asserts that, although 'most sectors of Egyptian society participated in the nationalist movement', 'they certainly did not act according to the same agendas. Whilst those sectors of urban society that had been most disenfranchised under the protectorate were more likely to resort to anti-colonial violence, the affluent class of businessmen and lawyers that formed the political leadership of the nationalist movement were keen to prevent actions that posed a threat to the prevailigng social order in Egypt' (Berridge 2011).
21. Abaza was an active polemist against Marxism and published several articles against the socialist party in Egypt (Abaza 1925).

22. For the riots directed against Christians and European minorities in nineteenth century Egypt, see Juan R. I. Cole (1989), 'Of Crowds and Empires: Afro-Asian riots and European Expansion, 1857–1882', *Comparative Studies in Society and History* 31: 106–33.
23. These terms literally echo the definition of *ghawgha'* in *Lisan al-'Arab* as *'al-mutasarri'in ila al-sharr'* (see note 3, this chapter).
24. Several historical sources describe absenteeism as structural. See for instance Deeb: 'The class of large landowners which we define as those owning more than 200 feddans, and who were mainly absentee, living in Cairo and Alexandria' (Deeb 1979: 9)
25. Abaza himself is said to have twice refused to become a minister, as he was 'against serving in a cabinet while British troops occupied Egypt' ('Abaza', 2004).
26. About these demonstrations, see Introduction, note 21.
27. According to Badran, one of the founding members of the Egyptian Feminist Union, Bahiga Rashid, was educated in 'the American schools in Luxor and Asyut' (Badran 1995: 97).
28. Another woman from Upper Egypt follows Mariam's path in a novel published some eighty years later: in *1919* by Ahmad Murad (2014); Dawlat is actively involved in the underground organisation al-Yad al-Sawda'. Originally from a poor peasant family in a village close to Minya, she works as a teacher in Cairo (see Chapter 7).
29. The dialogue also symbolises the interfaith harmony often underlined as one of the characteristics of the 1919 revolution, already referred to in the text through the choice of a church as the space from which the first demonstration in Asyut takes off.
30. This short dialogue is immediately followed by a disclaimer in which the narrator tries to pre-empt the criticism it could provoke by stating his text does not aim at drawing 'the right model of the right experience' ('al-mathal al-sahih lil tajarib al-sahiha', 83).
31. Both Shukri's lovers, Tharwat and Mariam, are killed or raped by an Australian soldier or officer.

3

1919 and the Trope of the Modern Nation

> High-culture national literatures, both canonical and precanonical, are integrally bound up in the processes of national identity formation, maintenance, and change. Their development is promoted by elites with an interest in the unity, legitimacy, and prestige of the nation. (Corse 1995: 1299)

It is difficult to think of a better illustration for this quote than Tawfiq al-Hakim's novel *'Awdat al-Ruh* (*The Return of the Spirit*). Published in 1933, *'Awdat al-Ruh* is the coming-of-age story of a young adolescent from a landowning family. Sent to Cairo to finish his high school studies, by the end of the narrative Muhsin is a young man involved in the 1919 revolution. Articulating the revolution as the rebirth of a nation, the novel insists on both the unity and the pharaonic roots of the Egyptian people. According to a well-known anecdote, Nasser repeatedly declared that *'Awdat al-Ruh* was his favourite bedtime reading, one that nourished his ideological consciousness and inspired his political journey (Hafiz 2001: 775). The influence of al-Hakim's text on Nasser was such that he named the hero of the only novel he wrote, *Fi Sabil al-Hurriyya* (*For the Sake of Freedom*), after *'Awdat al-Ruh*'s Muhsin. Nasser's confession attests to the durable influence of al-Hakim's novel on the Egyptian imaginary, particularly that of its elites.[1] Several generations of scholars have further underlined the importance of *'Awdat al-Ruh* as a text that literally wrote the nation into being and 'contributed to shape what Benedict Anderson calls the National Imaginary' (Hafiz 2001: 775).

In this chapter, I analyse the novel's articulation of the 1919 revolution and its reception, along with that of Naguib Mahfouz' *Bayn al-Qasrayn* (*Palace Walk*, 1956). I argue that these two canonical novels have been central in shaping the dominant narrative about 1919. Both glorify 1919 as a major step towards the creation of a modern Egyptian nation. Rather than a chaotic disruptive revolutionary moment, 1919 is presented as a key moment for the upper middle-class elites to achieve their nation building project. Following Kirstin Ross in her work about May 1968 in France, I show that this is achieved by a set of 'dominant narrative configurations – mostly reductions or circumscriptions of the event – adopted by the official story': a 'temporal reduction' which produces 'an abbreviated chronology' and a 'geographic reduction' (Ross 2002: 8–9). Both al-Hakim and Mahfouz opt for a similar temporal and spatial framing, one which circumscribes the events of the revolution to March and April 1919 in Cairo. This specific articulation allows the narrator to focus on Zaghlul's exile as the main trigger for the protests. This postulate is further strengthened by a middle-class focalisation which establishes the effendi as the only legitimate storyteller of the revolution. Both narrators then impose the national over the social, the male over the female and the upper middle classes over the underprivileged in the memory of 1919, albeit each in different ways.

The critical reception of both novels as an objective rendition of reality played a pivotal role in carving out their central position in the Egyptian imaginary about 1919. Before proceeding to an analysis of this reception, I will present a brief reading of another literary work that operates as a 'glorification of the 1919 revolution' (Hafez 1993: 189), albeit from a different perspective. Written by 'Isa 'Ubayd in December 1921 and published one year before his premature death, 'Mudhakkirat Hikmat Hanim' is the last story in a collection titled *Ihsan Hanim* and dedicated to Saad Zaghlul. Unlike al-Hakim or Mahfouz' novels, this short story does not link 1919 to the formation of a modern Egyptian nation. Rather, it glorifies the revolution as an *extra-ordinary* moment of national unity. This is most prominently illustrated by the fact that, rather than restricting the revolution's actors to the would-be elite of the new nation, 'Mudhakkirat' offers an all-encompassing picture of the revolution, allowing for expressions of fraternisation beyond boundaries of class, gender, religion and even ethnicity.

The most interesting aspect of the short story is its female first-person narrator and focaliser. Written in the form of a diary, the text tells the story of a young and unconventional woman, Hikmat. Despite intense social pressure, as she is already twenty years old – a ripe age for marriage at the time – Hikmat is not really anxious to get engaged. At the end of the story however, she accepts the first serious marriage proposition she gets, to a man much older than herself, in order 'to satisfy' her mother ('Ubayd 1921: 89). This abruptly puts an end to what could have evolved into a more systematic revolt against the institution of arranged marriage. The writer nevertheless allows his heroine a significant escapade outside the domestic space through her participation in the 1919 revolution. Although the narrator and main character remain entirely silent about the political turmoil in the entries from 8 March till 8 April, she participates in the 8 April demonstration celebrating Zaghlul's release. Following her friends, who insist on joining the popular jubilation, she finds herself in the streets. Narrated by a woman, the 8 April march unfolds as one in which many other women from diverse cultural and social backgrounds participate. From the carriage in which she is seated with her friends, the narrator's attention is drawn to the women, 'nationalists and foreigners' (*wataniyyat wa ajnabiyyat*) waving from the balconies and throwing flowers to the demonstrators; the women from lower-class background welcoming them with their *zagharid* (83–4); the nationalist women from the lower class (*wataniyyat min al-tabaqa al-munhatta*) singing new nationalist songs and dancing *baladi* dances' (84).

The carnivalesque ambiance on the streets also captures her attention. Everybody is cheering as their carriage passes by, even the conservative imams. Villagers 'from the suburbs or the nearby villages' are chanting, accompanied by their decorated camels (84). The foreigners (*ajanib*) are saluting the demonstrators by taking off their hats. The description highlights the fact that this vast explosion of joy brings together people from all class, gender, religious and ethnic backgrounds. In addition to women from different social and ethnic belonging,[2] peasants, imams and non-Egyptians, the demonstration reunites Muslims and Christians. It intervenes in a context of confessional strife, only one day after a Muslim and a Christian shopkeeper of the narrator's neighbourhood had a fight. The march reunites them, and the narrator notices several flags in which the crescent and the cross are pictured together.

Finally, a striking element of the text is the comment the writer attributes to Mahabbat, the most revolutionary among the narrator's friends. Mahabbat, who is only fourteen, refers to the Irish struggle for independence as a model of sacrifice and steadfastness: 'Let Egypt become a second Ireland!' (81). The quote depicts the Egyptian struggle as similar and connected to that of other colonised peoples, even though they are neither Arab, Muslim, nor from the Third World. It mirrors a broad consciousness of the common interests between the Egyptian and the Irish anti-colonial struggles, echoing Elleke Boehmer's suggestion that Irish nationalism functioned as a frame of reference for a large number of anti-colonial movements (see Introduction). Moreover, the narrator's insistence on the participation of non-Egyptian women in the demonstration, and the cheerful welcoming gestures by non-Egyptian men, broadens the spectrum of political solidarities and sympathies beyond the frame of the nation. In combination with the reference to the Irish struggle, it depicts 1919 as an exceptional moment inscribed in a broad anti-imperialist balance of power.

However, this experience is short-lived, as the text ends with the narrator sadly accepting an arranged marriage. The structure of the plot thus displays the 1919 revolution as an *extra-ordinary* moment; before that, confessional strife divided Egyptian society; after that, the boundaries of gender challenged during the demonstration are reinstituted. The choice of narration and focalisation reinforces this message. The first-person narration assumes a subjective perspective to narrate the 1919 revolution from a point of view otherwise marginalised in the canonical narratives I analyse in this chapter. From that perspective, the 1919 revolution appears as the only moment of emancipation in the life of a middle-class Egyptian woman. Indeed, the narrator only overcomes gender oppression when she is actively contributing to the nationalist struggle. 1919 is thus framed as an *extra-ordinary* moment both in the life of the protagonist and that of Egypt. The fact that life resumes its ordinary course and gender dynamics remain unchallenged implicitly suggests that the revolution did not change the traditional organisation of society. It is interesting to note that 'Mudhakkirat Hikmat Hanim' was written while the revolutionary turmoil was ongoing. This might explain its vivid depiction of the joyful and chaotic scenes on the streets in 1919 and its fresh insight into the narrator's happiness as she witnesses social barriers being overthrown in the revolutionary momentum. Unlike this early expression of realism, which went mostly unnoticed by critics, al-Hakim and Mahfouz' novels were crowned as canonical nationalist narratives.

Realism as a Hegemonic Discourse

Although they were published more than twenty years apart, in 1933 and 1954 respectively, there are striking similarities in the reception of *'Awdat al-Ruh* and *Bayn al-Qasrayn*. Many reviewers praise the novels' convincing depiction of characters and environment and underline their rendition of Egyptian society as one very close to 'reality'. Although violent polemics were unleashed because of al-Hakim's daring use of colloquial in the dialogues,[3] *'Awdat al-Ruh* was immediately acclaimed for its 'Egyptianness'.[4] 'The work was greeted enthusiastically by Taha Husayn, and enjoyed unusual success, going through two editions in its year of publication' (Starkey 1987: 28). Muhammad 'Ali Hammad, one of al-Hakim's admirers, highlighted the fact al-Hakim wrote *'Awdat al-Ruh* 'about the persons you see every day or hear of every time the sun rises'. He insisted the writer presented those 'persons coming from the heart of society' 'in their true image' (Hammad 1933: 40).

Reviews of *Bayn al-Qasrayn* similarly insist on its faithful rendition of reality.[5] In a small box titled 'The Book of the Year', published in the weekly magazine *Akhir Sa'a*, Mahfouz is presented as 'one of the most prominent contemporary writers in his authenticity, realism, and his ability to describe with precision the environment in which he lives' (Ghurab 1957: 25). Yusuf al-Sharuni marvels at the fact that 'Naguib Mahfouz apprehended reality from all its angles' (Sharuni 1957: 565). Fawzi al-'Antabli presents *Bayn al-Qasrayn* as a 'panorama of Egyptian life in an important moment of our modern history', lauding 'its exhaustive artistic representation' and 'its precision in retaining the specificities of Egyptian society' (al-'Antabli 1958: 99). Other critics, including some on the left, described *Bayn al-Qasrayn*'s depiction of the 1919 revolution as an 'objective' one ('Awad 1989: 117).[6]

Objectivity has been associated with realism as a literary genre; more precisely, it has been perceived as one of the attributes of realism. But it could only be perceived as such because of the fact that realism 'instituted itself as a hegemonic discourse about the self and society' (Selim 2003: 111). In an article about 'realism and fiction in the Arabic canon' which is worth quoting at some length, Samah Selim ties realism as a literary genre to 'the rise of a secular, cosmopolitan bourgeoisie enmeshed in the economic and cultural web of world capitalism and nation-state ideologies' (Selim 2003: 112). She shows that literary realism, most prominently in the novel, was one of the ways through which the new elite imposed its hegemony. She explains that the novel, and new fiction generally, was systematically presented by the liberal elite as a genre that was in rupture with traditional narrative forms. Unlike the traditional *hakawati*, the new narrator, most often an omniscient, godlike narrator was not a transmitter of old stories. Rather, 'he was 'an individual standing "outside" the collectivity, observing it, describing it, narrating it, not as a communal historian, but from a position that embodied a subjective but nonetheless authoritative and hegemonic point of view' (Selim 2003: 112–13).

Both al-Hakim and Mahfouz were consecrated as 'objective' witnesses of modern history.[7] In that process, their class belonging, as well as their political and ideological affiliation, were erased as if they were non relevant. Although Mahfouz' belonging to the Cairene middle-class has often been underlined as an important element in his work, most critics did not seem bothered by the contradiction between identifying Mahfouz as a historian of the middle class and allegations of objectivity. Sharuni's review of *Bayn al-Qasrayn* is a case in point. Though he recognises Mahfouz produced 'a history of the middle-class social life', he insists, as I noted earlier, that the writer is 'apprehending reality from *all* its angles' (Sharuni 1957: 563–5). This astonishing conflation can be explained by the 'significance of realism in the Arab context', where it is 'not simply understood as a technique of representation built on simple verisimilitude'. Rather, '[w]hen Arab critics use the word "reality" to talk about Arabic fiction, they mean "national reality," a term that raises the specter of a whole set of specific historical and social issues such as colonialism and the anti-colonial struggle, the rise and hegemony of national bourgeoisies as well as the real and imagined social composition of the national community' (Selim 2003: 110).

Following Selim, I understand al-Hakim and Mahfouz' realism as an 'authoritative and hegemonic point of view'. That point of view was necessarily informed by class and gender biases. As Jeff Shalan argues in an article about Husayn Haikal's novel *Zaynab* and *'Awdat al Ruh*, 'the narrative articulation of the nation in each novel implicates a male intellectual elite as its primary agent while working to contain the potentially disruptive forces of class and gender that mark its context' (Shalan 2002: 211). Rather than a bird's eye-view or objective perspective, I contend that a class-specific perspective informs both novels' narration of the nationalist movement, and the 1919 revolution in particular, namely that of the rising Egyptian bourgeoisie.

The reception of al-Hakim and Mahfouz' works as an 'objective' discourse close to achieving absolute 'truth' can be attributed to the position they occupied in the literary field at the time of publication. They had both gained the legitimacy to utter an authoritative discourse about Egyptian reality. They had been able to impose innovative projects in their own field, drama for al-Hakim and the novel for Mahfouz. Both occupied a privileged position as liberal intellectuals entitled to give an opinion about a very wide range of issues and attributed with a role of 'conscience of the nation'.[8] Although he was still at the beginning of his career when he published *'Awdat al-Ruh*, Tawfiq al-Hakim (1898–1987) had already secured a solid position in the literary field; the success of his first 'intellectual' play, *Ahl al-Kahf* (*The People of the Cave*, 1933), had catapulted him to a respected position in the field of theatre. The play was a rupture with al-Hakim's earlier production, vaudevilles written in colloquial under a pseudonym (al-Ra'i 1992: 368). Its success might have encouraged him to finally publish *'Awdat al-Ruh*, a manuscript he had completed in 1927. Moreover, despite his revolt against his family's insistence that he enter the legal profession like his father, al-Hakim was forced to take over a position in the judiciary when he came back from Paris in 1928. Starting in 1930, he worked as a deputy public prosecutor (Starkey 1987: 26), a position that granted his voice the authority attributed to prominent figures in the judiciary.

Naguib Mahfouz (1911–2006) had been an established writer for a short while longer when he published *Bayn al-Qasrayn* serialised in 1954–6. After a series of historical novels which borrow their setting and main characters from Pharaonic history,[9] he chose the more difficult path of social realism, which exposed him to attacks from the establishment. In spite of the criticism, he was awarded the Arabic Language Symposium prize for his novel *Khan al-Khalili*, after interventions by 'Abbas al-'Aqqad (1889–1964) and Ibrahim al-Mazini (1889–1949), two leading figures in the literary establishment (al-Naqqash 2011: 161). However, Mahfouz's uncompromising portrayal of his characters, his corrosive depiction of the political elites' corruption and his choice of non-moralistic endings continued to expose him to criticism. According to Samia Mehrez, Mahfouz was interrogated twice about his early realist novels; the first time by the mufti of the Waqf Ministry about *al-Qahira al-Jadida* (*Cairo Modern*, 1946), as its plot appeared to echo a contemporary scandal involving a minister, and the second time by his peer, the writer Ibrahim al-Mazini about *Zuqaq al-Midaqq* (*Midaq Alley*, 1947). Al-Mazini told him in a friendly tone that realism was 'a bad thing' and that 'all the calamities in *Zuqaq al-Midaqq* [would] be dumped on [him]' (Mehrez 1993: 64). The two convocations denote their instigators implicitly recognised the possible impact of his novels. They establish Mahfouz as a writer who uses his novels to intervene in the ongoing political and social debates. By 1957–8, when reviews of *Bayn a-Qasrayn* first appeared, Mahfouz was already recognised as a leading figure in social realism.

The media where *Bayn al-Qasrayn* was published played an important role in establishing it as an authoritative narrative. Mahfouz was very cautious about 'how and when he circulate[d] what he ha[d] written' (Mehrez 1993: 63). *Bayn al-Qasrayn* is a case in point, as Mahfouz published its first volume serialised in a magazine close to the newly established Free officers' regime, *al-Risala al-Jadida*. The first episodes of the novel were published in April 1954, in a context in which the new postcolonial Egyptian state multiplied its expressions of independence vis-à-vis the imperialist system, in the period immediately preceding the nationalisation of the Suez Canal. The cultural field was reorganised by the Free Officers, in power since July 1952, in order to marginalise liberal intellectuals, who were perceived as potential supporters of the old regime (Jacquemond 2008: 15). It was the first time Mahfouz opted for serialisation, and what is more, in a new journal. April 1954 was *al-Risala al-Jadida*'s first edition. It was headed by Yusuf al-Siba'i, an officer nicknamed 'the general of the army of letters', whom Nasser had placed at the centre of the cultural apparatus. In addition to being directed by a figure of the new regime, *al-Risala al-Jadida* offered the advantage of being a prestigious journal, displaying in its table of contents some of the literary field's most prominent names. The first issue included contributions by Taha Husayn, the 'Dean of Arabic Literature', Louis Awad, the well-known Marxist intellectual who was dismissed from his university position a few months later and the critic Muhammad Mandur, who authored in the same issue an article about Mahfouz's *Khan al-Khalili*. Mahfouz' choice of the media to bring *Bayn al-Qasrayn* to public attention thus places him among the most prestigious pens of the time while putting him under the protective wing of the newly-established cultural authorities. Although the publication was the result of circumstance more than design or calculation,[10] it remains that it put an end to the relative marginalisation of his social realist works in the literary field. Displayed on the pages of the regime's literary magazine, *Bayn al-Qasrayn* enjoyed optimal conditions for its reception as an authoritative narrative.

Bayn al-Qasrayn

Considered as the peak of Mahfouz' social realism period, the *Trilogy* narrates the Caireen middle class' struggles with modernity and tradition from the end of the First World War till the end of the Second World War. Its first volume, *Bayn al-Qasrayn*[11] is set against the turmoil of the last years of the First World War and ends with the 1919 April demonstrations celebrating Zaghlul's return from exile. Told by an omniscient narrator, the novel revolves around the lives of a merchant from al-Gamaliyya, Ahmad 'Abd al-Gawwad, his wife Amina and their five children, Yasin, Khadija, 'A'isha, Fahmi, Kamal. It devotes many pages to a depiction of the family's life; 'Abd al-Gawwad is pictured as a despotic head of family, who allows himself a double life outside the house with his mistresses. Amina is a submissive housewife and the two daughters are more or less young replicas of their mother. Yasin, Ahmad's son from a first marriage, experiences tribulations similar to those of his father. Fahmi, the second son, a law student, participates in the 1919 revolution. Kamal, the youngest son and Mahfouz' alter ego, is too young to be involved in the political turmoil.

Mahfouz began writing *Bayn al-Qasrayn* in 1945[12] (El-Enany 2007: 67). Nearly thirty years had passed since the revolution, which Mahfouz witnessed as a little boy of eight 'from a small room on the roof' (El-Enany 2007: 3).[13] The mid-forties were a period of continuing political instability. After numerous popular mobilisations, and two Anglo-Egyptian treaties, in 1922 and 1936, full independence had still not been achieved. Led by Mustafa al-Nahhas, the Wafd governed several times, but the British as well as the palace systematically intervened in Egyptian politics, in particular during the Second World War. The beginning of the forties witnessed a drop in the Wafd's popularity and '[a]fter 1942, the Wafd no longer stood as the hegemonic nationalist power in the country' (Botman 1998: 300). Moreover, according to Joel Benin, the period between December 1945 and January 1952 witnessed an increase in the number of social protests and a process of radicalisation of the nationalist movement. People demanded no less than 'full British military evacuation', and 'an alternative leadership' emerged in the form of the National Committee of Workers and Students (Benin 1998: 329). Writers a decade or two younger than Mahfouz like Latifa al-Zayyat (1923–96) and Yusuf Idris (1927–91) played pivotal roles in this committee, which steered the anti-colonial student and working class demonstrations of 1946. Mahfouz was thus writing in a context of radical anti-colonial turmoil; he was pushed to the centre by a literary elite for which literature and political commitment were not to be dissociated. Although he confessed sympathies with Marxism (al-Naqqash 2011: 270), he positioned his literary discourse as non-ideological.[14] By doing so, he was seeking to provide his writing about the recent nationalist past with a stamp of neutrality and objectivity. However, Mahfouz' representation of the 1919 revolution in *Bayn al-Qasrayn* was faulted by leftist critics as one 'devoid of peasants and workers'.[15] Mahfouz answered these accusations by stating that he did not, with his *Trilogy*, 'aim at writing a history book' and that he was a novelist; had he 'transported the events to the countryside to highlight the peasants' role, there would have been many innacuracies in the sequence of events', he said (al-Naqqash 2011: 188).[16] My point here is not to add another voice to the concert of voices that have faulted Mahfouz for his representation of 1919. Rather, it is the reception of this representation as an objective one that I dispute. This representation, I argue, however masterful, mirrors the *specific* perspective of a male middle-class elite.

Spatial and Temporal Frame

According to Egyptian critics of the sixties who led the debate with Mahfouz from a leftist point of view,[17] *Bayn al-Qasrayn* fails to provide a convincing background for the 1919 revolution. As argued by Sami Khashaba, the way the historical events are narrated does not enable the reader to understand the actual reasons behind the 1919 revolution (Khashaba 1989: 88). The novel begins in October 1917 – as the reader understands from a conversation between Ahmad 'Abd al-Gawwad and his wife, mentioning the death of the Sultan Hussein Kamil, and the ascension of his brother Fuad 1 to the throne (Mahfouz 2014: 17). Though 1917 is an important date in the escalation that eventually led to the eruption of the 1919 revolution, the narrative partly empties it of its significance. 1917 witnessed an intensification of colonial pressure on Egyptian society, partly due to the extension of Egyptian peasants' conscription in the British army, which led to widespread peasant rebellions in 1918 (see Introduction). However, the life of the 'Abd al-Gawwad family remains nearly undisturbed until the British troops occupy the neighbourhoods of al-Husayn after the beginning of the demonstrations in March 1919. The narrative only briefly mentions 'the rise in prices and the scarcity of essential commodities caused by this war', through a remark by Ahmad 'Abd al-Gawwad. The 'Australian soldiers who had proliferated like locusts'[18] are presented mainly as hindering 'Abd al-Gawwad and Yassin's nightlife, in addition to a mention by sheikh Mitwalli of two Australian soldiers humiliating him (47).

More specifically, the revolution's chronology is demarcated by the news of Zaghlul's exile and release. In the third part of the narrative, the events build up after the armistice, as the family discusses news of Saad Zaghlul's visit to Sir Wingate in November 1918 to demand the implementation of the Wilson points. Matters escalate with Zaghlul's exile, announced through a conversation between 'Abd al-Gawwad and his friends (403–4). The popular explosion that follows is narrated according to a day-to-day schedule. It follows Fahmi from the first enthusiastic demonstrations in the Law School on Sunday, 9 March, to the bloodier marches on Monday, 10 March (414) and the two following days. The 16 March women's march is evoked through a conversation between Fahmi and Yasin. The novel ends with the 8 April demonstration celebrating Zaghlul's release. The choice of this date to end the narrative pushes into oblivion the protests and mobilisations that occurred after April 1919. The second volume of the Trilogy, *Qasr al-Shawq*, begins in 1924, effectively erasing from the narrative the post-1919 years during which the revolutionary turmoil continued.

Bayn al-Qasrayn hereby presents what Ross calls 'a temporal reduction' which in turn produces an 'abbreviated chronology' of the 1919 revolution, circumscribing it to the months of March and April 1919. This 'narrative configuration', to use Ross' terms, shapes the events of 1919 according to a calendar that ignores the important turbulences that happened starting in 1918, and all those of the years 1919–23. Moreover, in addition to a temporal reduction, the novel functions according to what Ross calls 'a geographic reduction of the sphere of activity' (9) to Cairo. In *Bayn al-Qasrayn*, the revolution is circumscribed to the Cairene demonstrations: a Giza tram, Fahmi's law school and the streets around it. The last demonstration, on 8 April, whose depiction is most detailed, starts from the square in front of Cairo's main railway station and is stopped by British forces near the Azbakiyya gardens. The events occurring outside of the capital are only briefly alluded to in conversations between Ahmad 'Abd al-Gawwad and his friends.

Through the Lens of the Rising Elite

As in all his realist novels, in *Bayn al-Qasrayn* Mahfouz uses the technique of the omniscient narrator, changing the focalisation according to the scene. The 1919 revolution is likewise narrated from the changing perspectives of his main characters. The news of Saad Zaghlul's arrest is announced from 'Abd al-Gawwad's point of view of (403–4). The occupation of the family's neighbourhood by British soldiers is first introduced through a meticulous depiction of Amina's worried senses as she hears unusual noises around the house at dawn (424–5). The colonial troops' use of live ammunition in repressing the demonstrations is described through the terrified ears of the young Kamal, in a chapter entirely devoted to the young boy's feelings as he finds himself caught in a demonstration heavily repressed by the British troops (416–24).

Most of the scenes narrating key moments of the 1919 revolution, however, are narrated from Fahmi's perspective. More specifically, it is the moments depicted as crucial to the nationalist movement that are described from the young man's point of view, such as the first demonstrations in the Law school (411–14), and the 8 April demonstration celebrating Zaghlul's release (567–74). This modern 'middle-class focalisation' renders the Mahfouzian narrative about 1919 a very specific account of the anti-colonial struggle, rather than the 'objective' one described by his contemporary critics.

A 'good boy' loyal to his family and a serious student, Fahmi,[19] unlike Yasin, is not inclined to any night life. There are no interesting events in his life before the revolution – except his love for the neighbours' daughter, Mariam, whom his father won't let him marry. What distinguishes him is his interest in politics; he repeatedly refers to the National Party leaders, Mustafa Kamil and Muhammad Farid, as heroes and engages in heated discussions with his family starting 13 November, the day Zaghlul, 'Ali Sha'rawi and 'Abd al-'Aziz Fahmi visit Wingate. Apart from this interest in politics, Fahmi's character is displayed as that of an average young man. He is no hero; on the contrary, he is shy and introvert. He lives with enduring feelings of guilt and sadness 'because he imagines he is not as brave as his peers' (568). Only slowly does he develop into a leader of the student movement, able to fully play his role as a nationalist militant.

One of the most significant elements of Fahmi's character construction is his identity as a law student. The fact that Mahfouz chose the law school for Fahmi is no coincidence. Indeed, among the schools leading the student movement in 1919,[20] the law school was the matrix of the nation's rising elite.[21] It is thus through the perspective of a member of this rising elite that Mahfouz describes the revolution.[22] His social belonging is decisive in Fahmi's construction as a character, more so than his political affiliation. This is confirmed by the fact that the narrative gives little detail about Fahmi's activities as a member of a students' committee. We only know that he distributes leaflets (which is an illegal activity), (400) and that, during the 8 April demonstration, he is assigned an organisational role as the 'representative of the Students' supreme committee' (*lajnat al-talaba al-'ulya*, 567). Spaces Fahmi visits as a nationalist activist are only rarely described[23] and not much information is given about the group he belongs to, nor about his colleagues in this group.

Moreover, the focalisation through Fahmi's perspective reinforces the postulate suggested by the restricted time and space frame, as it underlines Saad Zaghlul's exile as the sole factor behind the eruption of the revolution. Fahmi's emergence as an active character in the plot is linked to Saad Zaghlul's exile; his short political life is entirely defined and circumscribed by this event. The text frames it as central to Fahmi's nationalist motivation, more important – at least until the last, fateful, demonstration – than other factors, such as peer dynamics and emulation, or direct confrontation with colonial violence or injustice. Furthermore, Fahmi's imaginary is entirely dominated by the figure of Saad Zaghlul; the feelings he nurtures towards the old pasha are close to total adoration and the terminology he uses to describe them belongs to a sentimental register. The leader appears as someone who is both distant and intimate: 'When will you stand before Saad? When will you see him for the first time' (570). The focalisation through Fahmi's perspective thus contributes to articulating Zaghlul as an iconic figure.

The adoration he feels towards Zaghlul contrasts with his growing irritation with his family. He repeatedly expresses his annoyance with the members of his family who do not share his revolutionary enthusiasm. He is already living in an entirely 'new world, a new nation, a new house' with 'new family members' (376). Mahfouz masterfully opposes this new life Fahmi carries within, to the realm of tradition. He insists on the contrast between Fahmi's feverish inner life during the revolution and the daily rhythm of the house, metaphorically referred to by his mother's baking rituals (410 and 415). Fahmi explicitly expresses this contrast: 'death strolls on the streets of Cairo, it dances in its corners, and, what a mystery, what a strange thing, here is his mother, baking, as always' (410).

The Metaphor of the New Nation

This representation of the revolution as the irruption of the 'new' into the realm of the 'old' ties in with the main theme of the Trilogy as a conflict between modernity and tradition.[24] The text insists in several instances on the 1919 revolution as being a matrix for something new, a new state, a 'new country' (414), thereby literally echoing Fahmi's thoughts. Thus, Mahfouz is not so much concerned with the representation of 1919 as a revolutionary moment as he is with the representation of the revolution as a significant step towards the construction of a modern Egyptian nation. The irruption of national unity indeed carries off everything in its path; the human sea that swarms into the streets is described by Kamal and his young schoolmates as a flood (420). The metaphor of the sea Mahfouz repeatedly uses in his description of the demonstrations suggests that the march towards independence and modernity is irresistible, as it has the power to overflow everything in 'successive waves' (571).

Mahfouz' articulation of national unity is best encapsulated in his depiction of the 8 April demonstration. This scene is key to understanding how the trope of nationalism functions in the novel. A depiction of the march organised to celebrate the news of Zaghlul's release, the scene eloquently summarises the inclusions and exclusions of the nationalist discourse as embodied in Mahfouz' narrative. Unlike previous demonstrations, this one is presented as very well organised, supervised and led by the students. Its depiction is focalised through Fahmi's perspective as one of the organisers, who appears to be in full control of the situation: he knows of the timing and passage of the march, is recognised by others and recognises people as well. Instead of the joyful, carnivalesque scenes depicted by 'Isa 'Ubayd, to which I referred above, the narrator of *Bayn al-Qasrayn* insists on the disciplined aspect of the march. The demonstration is at least twice explicitly referred to as representing the entirety of Egyptian society: 'Egypt appeared to be one demonstration, one person, one slogan' (571). Many of the figures of speech used in these paragraphs concur to develop the image of unity; the demonstrators are personified as 'one person', shouting 'a single chant'. The narrator insists on the unity between the effendiyya and the imams: 'A hundred thousand people, *tarabish*, *'ama'im*' (570). The synecdoque *tarabish* and *'ama'im* underlines that those who wear the *tarbush*, namely the effendiyya and those who wear the *'amama*, headgear of the imams, in other terms modern and traditional elites are united in their fight for a 'new' Egypt.

This depiction of national unity brings together mainly social strata belonging to the middle class: 'students, workers, civil servants, the imams and the priests, the judges' (570). Apart from the workers, these people represent the male elite – or elite-to-be- of the country. Although it is concluded by the narrator's assertion that 'this is Egypt', this depiction is much less all-encompassing than it claims to be. Constructed to metaphorically represent Egypt, it excludes women, peasants, the urban underprivileged and the Jews, in addition to the non-Egyptians mentioned by 'Isa 'Ubayd. It is less a depiction of the people who were on the streets on 8 April than a depiction of the social strata who were, in Mahfouz' view, entitled to build the modern Egyptian nation. I will come back to Mahfouz' articulation of gender issues but it is worth mentioning here that unlike Mahfouz' 'objective' description, women's presence in the 8 April demonstration has been extensively documented. Among many other witnesses, one can mention the following:

> When Saad Zaghlul and other nationalists were released on April 8, 1919, women and men of all classes went out in a massive demonstration that was a stunning display of national unity but also of class and gender hierarchy. Men marched in front: members of the cabinet, then deputies from the Legislative Assembly, 'ulama, judges, lawyers, doctors, government employees, army officers, workers, and male secondary and primary school students. Women followed: upper class women in cars and finally lower-class women in carts. (Badran 1995: 77)

As for peasants and the urban underprivileged, their contribution is marginalised, both in the depiction of the 8 April demonstration and in the entire narrative. Peasants are nowhere referred to as actors of the revolutionary struggle, only as victims of colonial brutality.[25] The so-called 'rabble' who are the object of the author's vindictive prose in *al-Dahik al-Baki* are simply absent in *Bayn al-Qasrayn*. Unlike Abaza's, Mahfouz' representation of national unity thus denies the class tensions taking place at its heart.

Unlike in *al-Dahik al-Baki*, fear functions as a powerful unifying emotion cementing national unity. In Abaza's novel, the so-called 'rabble' are a main object of fear in addition to the British (see Chapter 2); in *Bayn al-Qasrayn* there is only one object of fear: the colonial troops. Fear of the British is experienced by several characters in the novel: Amina, when she discovers that the British soldiers are camping in front of their house (425); Kamal, when he hears 'for the first time in his short life the sound of bullets' (422) as he is hiding in a shop during a demonstration he found himself dragged into; and 'Abd-al-Gawwad himself, when he is arrested at night to fill up a trench dug by the resistance (512). In Fahmi's case, fear of death by British bullets is a structural emotion, at the centre of the inner life Mahfouz describes at length. Fear is what prevents Fahmi from being at the forefront of the battle during previous demonstrations, as he himself recalls: 'he had often answered an inner call prompting him to go forward and imitate the heroes. But his nerves always let him down at the decisive moment, as soon as the people retreated, he found himself at the rear, if not hiding or fleeing' (568). As the 1919 revolution is mainly apprehended through Fahmi's perspective, this fear designates the British troops as the sole enemy.

Gender Dynamics

Unlike narratives published earlier, such as the play *al-Intikhabat* by Amin Sidqi (see Chapter 1), the novel *al-Dahik al-Baki* (see Chapter 2) and the short story 'Mudhakkirat Hikmat Hanim', *Bayn al-Qasrayn* leaves nearly no space for women in this representation of national unity. This is particularly striking at the level of characterisation. Female characters in the first volume of the Trilogy are either submissive wives secluded to the realm of the domestic, or unprincipled *ghawani* (dancers and singers considered as licentious women) stigmatised by society as immoral.[26] None of them expresses any nationalist ideas, let alone indulges in nationalist activities. Even the younger women who are not brought up in 'Abd al-Gawwad's rigid household fit this pattern. Mariam, Fahmi's beloved, is cast in the role of a woman who is seduced by the British, flirting with one of the soldiers who occupies the neighbourhood.[27] Zaynab, Yassin's wife, is presented as politically naive; she is 'unable to understand the reasons behind this sentimental revolution'; she thinks that 'had Saad and his men lived as normal people do, nobody would have thought of exiling them' (408). The credulity Mahfouz insistently attributes to her (373–4 and 419) – thus putting her under the same umbrella as Amina – is unconvincing, given her characterisation as a more emancipated woman than her sisters-in-law. Zaynab's request to go to the theatre with her husband and her insistence on getting a divorce after she catches him trying to sleep with her maid puts her profile among those of the middle-class women who slowly forged a space for themselves in the public realm, many of whom were active members of the nationalist movement.

Women's participation in the 1919 revolution is only briefly referred to in a description of the spontaneous demonstrations that exploded after the news of Saad Zaghlul's release on 7 April. Mahfouz attests to the presence on the street of women from lower-class backgrounds, writing that '[t]ens of carts carried hundreds of women in *milaya laff* (black over-wrap) dancing and chanting nationalist songs' (556). In addition, the text refers to the 16 March demonstration (see Introduction) through an intertextual reference to Hafiz Ibrahim's poem, 'The Fair Ladies Went Out to Protest' (*Kharaja al-ghawani yahtajijna*). Fahmi quotes its four first verses, in response to Yassin's teasing remark about women's street marches (431). The verses salute and glorify the courage of the elite women who organised the 16 March demonstration, metaphorically describing them as 'stars in the darkness'. This intertextual reference to the poem attests to its lasting evocative power in the Egyptian imaginary and confirms that it contributed to 'fixing and reifying female participation in that particular moment' (see Introduction). It further extends in time this reductive understanding of female participation in the revolution.

Writing in a context of renewed battles against the colonial power, Mahfouz puts 1919 at the heart of the modern nation trope; his metaphor of national unity links it to the formation of a modern nation. The social strata that actively contributed to the revolutionary momentum but were not engaged in the process of nation formation, in particular the urban underprivileged, are erased from this metaphor. Class conflict has been entirely resolved to the advantage of the effendiyya, and women only serve as a photogenic element. This articulation of the 1919 revolution as the birth of a 'new' nation successfully polishes a metaphor introduced by Tawfiq al-Hakim some twenty years earlier.

'Awdat al-Ruh

'Awdat al-Ruh was written in 1927, in Paris, where al-Hakim was sent by his family in order to obtain a doctorate in law. Immersed in the Parisian theatrical and cultural scene, al-Hakim had acquired some distance from the ongoing events in Egypt, which had entered a period of instability after the assassination of the British Governor of the Sudan in November 1924 and the subsequent resignation of Zaghlul from his post as prime minister. Except for his contacts with the French family he lived with for some time, and his bohemian friends in Montmartre, al-Hakim was quite isolated, spending most of his days alone, reading, writing, or visiting the Louvre (Starkey 1987: 24–5). He was thus writing in a state of disconnection from the massive disillusion prevalent in the streets of Cairo (see Chapter 1).[28]

'Awdat al-Ruh is set between 1917 and 1919, mainly in Cairo in al-Sayyida Zaynab. A classical bildungsroman, it narrates the story of Muhsin, an adolescent from a wealthy family in Damanhur sent to the capital to

complete his high school studies. He stays with his three uncles and aunt: Salim, Hanafi, 'Abdu and Zannuba; the household also includes the servant Mabruk. Many pages of the novel are devoted to lengthy, often humourous depictions of the family life, including their quarrels. The most significant of these quarrels pits the men against each other when Muhsin and his uncles all fall in love with the same young woman, Saniyya, their beautiful neighbour. When the girl chooses to marry their neighbour Mustafa – whose love Zannuba was trying to win – their emotional disappointment leads them to get involved in the nationalist movement. At the end of the story Muhsin and the rest of the household – including Mabruk but excluding Zannuba – join the 1919 demonstrations. They get arrested together, and the novel ends with a scene metaphorically describing them as reunited, lined up as one people in the prison's hospital.

The spatial and temporal frame of the novel is very similar to the one Mahfouz chose twenty years later. *'Awdat al-Ruh* begins in 1917, as the First World War is still raging and ends in April 1919. Exactly as in *Bayn al-Qasrayn*, references to the ongoing turmoil are scarce: at the beginning of the text, Mabruk briefly tells the story of a cousin forcefully conscripted into the British army (al-Hakim 1998: 47). The novel thus similarly sketches an 'abbreviated chronology' of the revolution, framed by the arrest and release of Saad Zaghlul. The revolution irrupts at the end of the narrative, occupying only two of the novel's twenty-five chapters. As already noted by Jeff Shalan,

> the text provides the reader with no preparation for this narrative moment, remaining entirely mute on both the great historical events that precede it – World War I and the subsequent collapse of the Ottoman empire-and the obvious signs of social unrest in Egypt in the years leading up to 1919. The narrative effect, consequently, is one of a spontaneous, almost unconscious, awakening of nationalist fervor that seems to erupt exclusively in response to Zaghlul's forced exile' (Shalan 2002: 234).[29]

Although parts of the novel take place outside Cairo, more specifically in Damanhur, where Muhsin spends his summer vacation at his family's estate, the depiction of the 1919 revolution is centred on the capital, thereby operating a similar geographical reduction to that established in *Bayn al-Qasrayn*.

Narrated by an omniscient author, *'Awdat al-Ruh* is articulated through the perspective of Muhsin, a central character like *Bayn al-Qasrayn*'s Fahmi. Muhsin is younger than Fahmi and also less knowledgeable. His political awareness comes across as spontaneous; although he partakes with his uncles in printing and distributing leaflets, there is no information about his political affiliation. This leaves more space for other voices to describe the 1919 turmoil. Unlike *Bayn al-Qasrayn*, *'Awdat al-Ruh* gives a brief insight into the underprivileged's revolution, mainly through the character of Mabruk. The text does not condemn popular violence against the coloniser. On the contrary, it gives a laudatory account of the street battles in which Mabruk is involved with 'the butcher, his aid, the baker and the orange seller', smashing 'the gas lamps, the tree fences, armed with stones, sticks, batons and knives' (al-Hakim 1998: 532).[30] Similarly, the novel salutes – though briefly – the peasant action during the revolution, stating that 'the peasants express their anger more powerfully than the people of the city; they cut the railroads to prevent the military trains from arriving and burnt the police stations' (531).

Women are however totally absent from *'Awdat al-Ruh*'s representation of the revolution – both at the level of characterisation and of plot. There is not a single reference or allusion to the presence of women on the streets in 1919. On the level of characterisation, Zannuba is depicted as embodying the worst image of backwardness: she is illiterate and spends all the household's money on fortune tellers. Muhsin's mother shows only disdain for the Egyptian *fallah*. As for Saniyya, although she is educated and embodies the 'new woman' (see Chapter 2), she is not involved in any way in the 1919 revolution. She shows neither political interests nor nationalist feelings. Her character has often been read as an allegory for Egypt;[31] however, it is more convincing to describe her as a depositary for the love and desire of *al-sha'b*, or 'the people' as the household is referred to; 'she is both a catalyst for the novel's humorous portrayal of the male characters, and, more importantly, the one who generates the narrative's construction of, or movement towards, a national community' (Shalan 2002: 234).

The trope of national unity is articulated through the metaphor of 'the people' (*al-sha'b*, the term used by al-Hakim to designate the five men of the household) and their shifts from unity to conflict and back to unity. Al-Hakim's 'people' is a quite straightforward metaphorical representation of the Egyptian nation, and it has repeatedly been read as such. However, the metaphor is a reductive one, both in terms of class and gender: all of the people are men and four of them belong to the upper middle class: 'Abdu the engineer, Selim the police officer, Hanafi the schoolteacher and Muhsin. Exactly as in *Bayn al-Qasrayn*, these social strata are the ones endowed with building the modern Egyptian nation; they do not reflect the broad diversity of the social strata involved in the revolutionary momentum. However, the revolution abolished the class barriers between them: they are now lined up in the prison's hospital, all in the same beds, including Mabruk who used to sleep on a table. Indeed, unlike both 'Mudhakkirat Hikmat Hanim' and *Bayn al-Qasrayn*, *'Awdat al-Ruh*'s national unity story is one of success. At the beginning of the narrative, the men were united, but ill – in a metaphor representing the illness of the Egyptian nation; at the end they are united but are now in excellent health, joyful, after having overcome their sentimental conflicts.

Rather than a violent break with the past, the revolution that allowed this transformation is depicted as embodying continuity with the past. One of the most prominent aspects of *'Awdat al-Ruh* is its articulation of 1919 in romantic terms borrowing from pharaonic mythology.[32] The revolution marks the miraculous birth of a nation (*umma*) erroneously thought to have been dead (528). This birth is metaphorically referred to as a 'spring', a 'resurrection' (ba'th), intervening after a centuries-long sleep. It is a 'resurrection' of the 'spirit' of the Ancient Egyptian Nation – encapsulated in the title of the novel.

Zaghlul as a God-like Figure

Saad Zaghlul stands at the centre of this romantic imagery. He is Egypt's 'beloved son' and his identity is reaffirmed as that of a *fallah* deeply rooted in the Egyptian soil (528) – versus the alien elite represented by Muhsin's mother, who is of Turkish origin. This is reinforced through the use of pharaonic imagery, which endows Zaghlul with a god-like stature and places him above human conflicts. The leader of the Wafd is explicitly compared to the pharaonic god Osiris, 'one of the most important gods of ancient Egypt' whose name is 'the Latinized form of the Egyptian Usir which is interpreted as 'powerful' or 'mighty' (Mark 2016). Like Zaghlul, 'Osiris, who came down to reform the land of Egypt and give her life and light, was taken away, imprisoned in a box, and exiled in pieces in the depths of the seas' (531).

In addition to the similarities between the repression faced by Zaghlul and Osiris, the metaphor attributes to the leader the characteristics of the god. Osiris is 'the kind and just ruler, murdered by his resentful brother, who comes back to life' (Mark 2016). The metaphor of Osiris thus establishes the image of Zaghlul as an ideal ruler whose popularity, despite vindictive attempts, cannot be affected.

Zaghlul's class identity as a pasha and a member of the elite is hereby conveniently erased. This is further confirmed by the text's depiction of Zaghlul as the beloved of the people – rather than a political leader. Both *'Awdat al-Ruh's* Mushin and *Bayn al-Qasrayn's* Fahmi entertain an intimate relationship with the leader. Although he had never heard of Saad Zaghlul before 8 March, Muhsin 'felt in a moment that he had to give his life to this man' (529), expressing unconditional love and sacrifice. Likewise, Fahmi's emotions towards Zaghlul express adoration and are articulated in sentimental terms, as I showed above. It is interesting to note that the narrator and main character of 'Mudhakkirat Hikmat Hanim' does not show similar feelings towards Zaghlul, nor does his exile constitute a trigger for her nationalist motivation.[33] Similarly, Zaghlul is nowhere mentioned in *al-Dahik al-Baki*. This leads me to posit this god-like articulation of Zaghlul as a characteristic of those narratives that link 1919 to the modern nation trope. Although the metaphor of Zaghlul as the nation is used in poems about 1919 (see Introduction), both al-Hakim and Mahfouz significantly expanded it. The genre of the novel allowed them to link it to bourgeois consciousness as embodied by the characters of Muhsin and Fahmi.

Conclusion

In a talk about the 1881 Paris commune, Kirstin Ross notes that this radical episode of self-governance had either to be 'forgotten, or assimilated by the Republic'. She adds that 'in order to be well integrated, it had to be interpreted'.[34] I argue that the 1919 revolution offers a comparable example of a revolution that was interpreted in a certain manner to enable its integration into a dominant history. Both of the novels I have analysed in this chapter attest to the transformation of a story of revolution – with its potentially disruptive and threatening aspects – into one of nation building. The interpretation of the revolution al-Hakim and Mahfouz offer allowed its integration into the bourgeoisie's authoritative discourse about history. The canonical status of this interpretation was then rendered possible by the fact that, although it did not succeed in achieving 'complete independence', the Egyptian bourgeoisie emerged out of 1919 as a rising social class.

The many subsequent adaptations of both *'Awdat al-Ruh* and *Bayn al-Qasrayn* attest to the longevity of these canonical narratives. Both novels were adapted in the form of plays at the beginning of the 1960s, with little or no alterations to the original plot.³⁵ However, the later adaptations of both novels for the small screen, in 1977 for *'Awdat al-Ruh* and in 1987 for *Bayn al-Qasrayn*, present major alterations to the initial plots and characterisation. These changes allow women an important role as active actors in the revolutionary turmoil in the case of the first adaptation, and give the revolutionary struggle a significant armed dimension in the case of the second. These loose interpretations of al-Hakim and Mahfouz' novels have a predecessor: the cinematic adaptation of *Bayn al-Qasrayn* by Hassan al-Imam, which is the focus of the next chapter.

Notes

1. About the influence of al-Hakim on the Egyptian elite, see Israel Gershoni (1995). 'An Intellectual Source for the Revolution: Tawfik al Hakim's Influence on Nasser and His Generation', in Shimon Shamir (ed.), *Egypt from Monarchy to Republic: A Reassessment of Revolution and Change*, Westview Press, p. 230.
2. In addition, the narrator mentions the enthusiasm of underprivileged women from Upper Egypt, as she refers to a chant sung by one of her maids, Fattuma. She notes that she only understood from the song the terms 'istaglalna ya banat' ('we are now independent, girls'), in which the 'q' is replaced by the sound 'g', denoting a pronunciation from Upper Egypt.
3. See Ibrahim 'Abd al-Qadir al-Mazini (1933), "Awdat al-Ruh' *Al-Balagh*. Cairo, 25 June.
4. See Muhammad 'Ali Hammad (1933), "Awdat al-Ruh bayn al-'Amiyya wal 'Arabiyya' *Al-Risala*, Cairo, 15 September, p. 40.
5. See Taha Husayn's laudatory article, 'Bayn a-Qasrayn', in *Min Adabina al-Mu'asir*, Cairo, 1958.
6. 'Awad himself, however, does not share this point of view (see note 16, this chapter).
7. Some critics, however, did not share this point of view and articulated Mahfouz'

vision as one that was the product of his middle-class background. In an updated introduction to the third edition of his book devoted to Mahfouz, published after the polemic around his position on the Camp David treaty, Ghali Shukri writes that 'Naguib Mahfouz proves in that regard that the writer, regardless of his grandeur, does not escape the necessities of history . . . nor the vision of the class to which he belongs, both intellectually and socially' (Shukri 1982: ta').

8. The expression is from Richard Jacquemond (2008).
9. In *'Abath al-Aqdar* (1939), *Rhadubis* (1943) and *Kifah Tiba* (1944). Mahfouz won two literary prizes for these novels, the Qut al-Qulub prize for *Rhadubis* and the Wizarat al-Ma'arif (Ministry of Education) prize for *Kifah Tiba*.
10. Mahfouz later stated that it was al-Siba'i who approached him after his publisher, considering the text too long for publication, had refused the Trilogy. He states that he does not remember when exactly al-Siba'i approached him (al-Ghitani 2007: 97).
11. For a bibliography of the scholarship on *Bayn al-Qasrayn* see Hamdi al-Sakkut (2007), *Najib Mahfuz: Biblyughrafya Tajribiyya wa-Sirat Haya wa-Madkhal Naqdi*, Cairo: al-Hay'a al-Misriyya al-'Amma lil-Kitab.
12. It is interesting to note that historian 'Abd al-Rahman al-Rafi'i published the first volume of his history of the nationalist movement in 1946.
13. For more about Mahfouz' recollection of the 1919 revolution, see al-Naqqash (2011: 181). For his opinion about Saad Zaghlul and the accusations against him, see al-Naqqash (2011:188-190). Other works by Mahfouz include scenes of the 1919 revolution, like the stories 12–16, 18–19 and 23 in *Hikayat Haratina* (Cairo: al-Shuruq, 2017, 1st edition 1975, translated in English as *Fountain and Tomb*), (mentioned in El-Enany 2007: 4). Narrated by a first-person narrator, the stories dealing with the revolution mirror the feelings of a little boy in 1919 and include vivid depictions of the events. Story 12 describes the revolution as an earthquake and a flood. Story 14 tells the story of what the narrator calls a 'comic demonstration' (*muzahara hazliyya*), in which the crowd leads a donkey called Fu'ad I and shouts a slogan ridiculing the king. Story 18 describes the return of Saad as a moment of pure joy and mirrors the centrality of Saad in the little boy's imagination. Two of the stories contain references to the participation of women in the demonstration.
14. This does not mean that he thought of his literary work as non-political. On the contrary, Mahfouz repeatedly stated that his novels and short stories were a way for him to express his opinions, including critical opinions of the state and its intelligence services (see al-Naqqash 2011: 146).

15. See Yusuf al-Qa'id's testimony in the documentary *Naguib Mahfouz, The Passage of the Century* by Francka Mouloudi (1999).
16. Mahfouz repeats the same point of view ten pages further on, in a long answer to Louis 'Awad's discussion of *Bayn al-Qasrayn* in his autobiography *Awraq al-'Umr* (al-Naqqash 2011: 198–199). 'Awad refutes the description of *Bayn al-Qasrayn* as a narrative close to reality, repeatedly stating that he did not recognise that turbulent period, as he himself experienced it, in Mahfouz' novel. According to him, Ahmad 'Abd al-Gawwad's monumental character entirely dominates the narrative while the 1919 revolution remains in the background. 'Awad's discussion of the novel is unconvincing, as it is based on a vague and innacurate description of the plot – like for instance his claim that Fahmi is killed 'by chance' by British bullets. He attributes Mahfouz's vision to the fact that he belongs to the social strata of the merchants, which, according to him, remained a spectator of the 1919 revolution ('Awad 1989: 117–19).
17. See Ghali Shukri (1982), *al-Muntami*, Cairo (The name of the publisher is not indicated); Sami Khashaba (1989), 'Fahmi 'Abd al-Gawwad', in Ghali Shukri (ed.) *Naguib Mahfouz: Ibda' Nisf Qarn*, Beirut–Cairo: al-Shuruq; Mahmud Amin Al-'Alim (1970), *Ta'mmulat fi 'Alam Najib Mahfuz*, Cairo: al-Hay'a al-Misriyya al-'Amma lil-Ta'lif wal-Nashr.
18. Naguib Mahfouz (2014), *Bayn al-Qasrayn*, Cairo: Dar al-Shuruq, pp. 16–17. Unless otherwise stated, the translation is my own.
19. According to Rasheed El-Enany, 'the real life origin of the character of Fahmi 'Abd al-Gawwad' is Anwar al-Halawani, the son of a neighbouring family who was killed by British bullets in 1919 (see El-Enany 2007: 4 and Mahfouz (1977), *al-Maraya*, Cairo: Maktabat Misr, pp. 38–9).
20. Students of the school of medicine were also at the forefront of the struggle: – indeed many of the underground activists who participated in the armed struggle were medicine students, such as Ahmad Kira (see Chapter 7) and 'Iryan Yusuf Sa'd (see Chapter 5).
21. This remark about Fahmi's identity as a law student is inspired by a lecture by Amr Shalakany, '1919: A Revolution in Court Dress', given at the Annual History Seminar organised by the Department of Arab and Islamic Civilizations at the American University in Cairo: 5–6 April 2019.
22. The fact that Fahmi dies at the end of the novel does not invalidate the point about him embodying the rising elite of the nation. On the contrary; this brutal death highlights the deep ambivalence of the victory the people are celebrating on that day. By killing Fahmi, Mahfouz underlines that Zaghlul's return from

exile did not signify the revolution had been successful in its attempt at getting rid of British colonialism. In addition, he suggests that the elite which Fahmi represents had not yet been able to impose its nation building project.
23. An exception is Ahmad 'Abdu café in Khan al-Khalili (385).
24. 'The novel begins in the middle of a world war and terminates towards the end of another. The world is in the process of convulsive change and so is Egyptian society' (El-Enany 2007: 68).
25. The text mentions the attacks on the villages of Badrashin and al-'Aziziyya (543–4), including the rapes of women which are referred to in the following terms: 'they humiliated the women'(*ahanu*), 'they violently attacked (*i'tadu i'tida ijrami*) the women'. Beth Baron considers that 'Mahfouz's inclusion (...shows) that the village rapes . . . had become embedded in the collective memory' (Baron 2005: 48–9).
26. For a discussion of gender issues in Mahfouz' writings, see Latifa Al-Zayyat (1975), 'al-Mar'a fi Adab Naguib Mahfouz', *al-Tali'a*, April; Ibrahim El-Sheikh (1991), 'Egyptian Women as Portrayed in the Social Novels of Naguib Mahfouz', in *Critical Perspectives on Naguib Mahfouz*, ed. Trevor Le Gassick, Washington, DC: Three Continents; Miriam Cooke (1993), 'Men Constructed in the Mirror of Prostitution', in Michael Beard and Adnan Haydar (eds.), *Naguib Mahfouz: from Regional Fame to Global Recognition*, Syracuse, N.Y: Syracuse University Press; Michelle Hartman (1997), 'Re-Reading Women in/to Naguib Mahfouz's "al-Liss wal-Kilab (The Thief and the Dogs)"', *Research in African Literatures* 28, no. 3, Arabic Writing in Africa, pp. 5–16; Hoda Elsadda (2012), 'Naguib Mahfouz' Trilogy: A National Allegory' in *Gender, Nation and the Arabic Novel Egypt, 1892–2008*, Edinburgh: Edinburgh University Press and New York: Syracuse University Press.
27. The middle-class girl who participates actively in the organisation of the nationalist struggle in *al-Dahik al-Baki* is also named Mariam (see Chapter 2), and the cinematic adaptation of *Bayn al-Qasrayn* transforms her into a full-fledged nationalist activist (see Chapter 4).
28. Although he was briefly arrested during the 1919 revolution for composing patriotic songs (Starkey 1987: 21), al-Hakim was most probably not involved in the nationalist movement during the thirties.
29. 'Abd al-Muhsin Taha Badr expresses a similar opinion. He writes that 'the author did not not pave the way sufficiently for the revolution . . . which resembles, from his point of view, a miracle' (Badr 1977: 390).
30. In *Bayn al-Qasrayn*, the act of resistance of the *futuwwat* (tough men) who dug a

trench in order to halt British lorries is described through the ordeal of 'Abd al-Gawwad, forced to fill the trench with other inhabitants of the neighbourhood. He asks himself, fulminating: 'do they believe digging a trench will bring Saad back or kick the English out of Egypt?' (Mahfouz 2014: 519).

31. See Hilary Kilpatrick (1974), *The Modern Egyptian Novel: A Study in Social Criticism*, London: Ithaca Press. Kilpatrick notes however, that 'the characters unfortunately do not live up to their symbolic value: Saniya for example, is an ordinary girl with little thought of anything but teasing the neighbours and getting married' (Kilpatrick 1974: 42). Sabri Hafiz analyses the depiction of Saniyya's home as embodying the national imaginary (Hafiz 2001: 776). For a discussion of the symbolism in *'Awdat al-Ruh*, see Anshuman A Mondal, (2003), *Nationalism and Post-Colonial Identity: Culture and Ideology in India and Egypt*, New York: Routledge.

32. The pharaonic thematic in *'Awdat al-Ruh* reflects the fascination with pharaonic history in Europe at the time, which inspired an important literary trend in Egypt. About pharaonism in a colonial context, including phraonic themes in Egyptian literature, see Elliott Colla (2007), *Conflicted Antiquities: Egyptology, Egyptomania, Egyptian Modernity*, Durham, NC: Duke University Press. For an analysis of the reemergence of pharaonic imagery in post-colonial literature, see Samah Selim, 'New Pharaonism: Nationalist Thought and the Egyptian Village Novel, 1967–1977'. *The Arab Studies Journal* 8/9, no. 2/1 (Fall 2000/Spring2001), pp. 10–24.

33. The narrator only mentions the slogan 'Long live Saad pasha Zaghlul' (80). Moreover, she refers to the 'four exiled men of the Wafd' rather than Zaghlul alone, and notes that the crowds were heading to both 'Zaghlul and al-Basil's house to chant slogans for them' (82).

34. See 'Rencontre avec Kirstin Ross autour de "L'imaginaire de la commune"', available at <https://www.youtube.com/watch?v=c-rXTMzAZF4> (last accessed 30 May 2019).

35. *Bayn al-Qasrayn* was performed in 1960 at the Azbakiyya theatre. The play was directed by Salah Mansur, with performances by Muhammad Abaza, Amal Zayid, Mimi Gamal, Abu Bakr 'Izzat, 'Umar 'Afifi and Victoria Kuhin. Fatma Rushdi played the role of Zubayda (see Maha Sabri, *Akhir Sa'a* no. 1504 21.8.1963, pp. 44–5). *'Awdat al-Ruh* was performed in 1963. The play was directed by Galal al-Sharqawi, with performances by Salah Qabil, Sa'id Salih, Nur al-Dimirdash, Na'ima Wasfi, Sana' Mazhar and Salwa Husayn.

4

The Revolution on the Screen

Film, by its very nature, speaks to crowds; it speaks to them about crowds and about their destiny. (Sartre 1988: 216)

On 26 February 1964, one week before the release of Hassan al-Imam's *Bayn al-Qasrayn*, the weekly *Akhir Sa'a* launched its marketing campaign by casting the film as 'portraying an important moment in the nationalist struggle for freedom and unity'. Introduced by a short paragraph about 'the joy that lives in the hearts of more than 80 million Arabs after the success of the kings' and presidents' summit [the First Arab League Summit held in Cairo between 13 and 16 January 1964]', the article puts the film in the frame of contemporary anti-imperialist politics: 'Art reminds us that unity of purpose and ranks is the most powerful weapon in the struggle'.[1] It casts the film as the General Company for Arab Cinema's first project; the company, so goes the narrative, 'selected *Bayn al-Qasrayn* to start its journey in developing Arab Cinema, to be its messenger to the world in order to present 'our principles' and 'our victories'.

The importance that the state was giving to the film was such that when it was released, on 2 March 1964, 'Abd al-Qadir Hatim, minister of culture and national guidance, attended the first screening in cinema Rivoli, which was fully renovated for the occasion.[2] In the first week, *Bayn al-Qasrayn* played in Alexandria, Mansoura, Port-Said and Tanta,[3] then in Ismailiyah, Damietta and Minya. It became an immediate box-office success; tickets were routinely sold out, and it played at Cinema Rivoli for five weeks.[4] No wonder: the filmmaker, Hassan al-Imam (1919–88), was 'as commercial a director as there has ever been in the Egyptian cinema' (Armbrust 1995: 85).[5] Although contemporary critics were predominantly negative, turning it down as 'a weak police story' and lamenting the director's sensationalist style,[6] *Bayn al-Qasrayn* soon became a cult movie, repeatedly screened on television. The transition to the little screen secured a broader audience and guaranteed the transmission of the visual narrative, a landmark in 'public memory' (Bodnar qtd in Gordon 2002: 46) perpetuated from one generation to another. It was so successful that it gave a second life to the iconic characters of the novel in the popular imaginary,[7] with a particularly successful casting of Amal Zayid as Amina, the 'iconic traditional woman' (Elsadda 2012: 79) and Yahya Shahin as Ahmad 'Abd al-Gawwad, 'the icon of traditional manhood' (Elsadda 2012: 84).

Among the elements for which critics reproached al-Imam was the issue of fidelity[8] – or rather infidelity – underlining the fact that the director had been unfaithful to the spirit of the novel, transforming it into a 'belly dancers' film', a reference to the frequent dancing interludes, insistent close-ups on the dancers' bodies and erotic dialogues between 'Abd al-Gawwad, Yasin and their mistresses.[9] Rather than fidelity, I am concerned in this chapter with the way the film recontextualises the literary narrative in a very different political context. Mahfouz finished writing *Bayn al-Qasrayn* before the eruption of the Free Officers onto the political scene in 1952, when Egypt was a monarchy and still partially occupied by British troops. Al-Imam began working on the film in 1963, in a context in which, more than ten years after the coup that put an end to the monarchy, the Nasserist regime was fully engaged in building an independent, modern state. The regime had successfully ended the British rule after the nationalisation of the Suez Canal and the subsequent war in 1956. It had launched a broad policy of nationalisation and agricultural reform and tightened its control on all state institutions. The beginning of the sixties witnessed an acceleration of socialist inspired policies. A new wave of nationalisations took place in 1961, while the regime reaffirmed its socialist identity and confirmed its rapprochement with the Soviet Union, especially after the latter engaged in the financing of the Aswan Dam. But this period was also one of international and national tensions, and even internal dissensions among the former Free Officers, who were now ruling the country. The Unity with Syria (1958–61) had failed, and some of Nasser's closest colleagues expressed their dismay at what they perceived to be a Marxist conversion of Nasser and at the ongoing violations of freedom of expression, as fewer and fewer dissonant voices were allowed to speak out (Beattie 1994: 176). Nasser was indeed obsessed by 'the construction of a unique hegemonic order as an essential complement to his objective of socioeconomic change' (Beattie 1994: 198). That aim translated itself into the founding in 1962 of a mass political organisation, the Arab Socialist Union, and in the increased control of the political and cultural spheres.[10]

In his study of the state's role in the Egyptian literary field, Richard Jacquemond notes that 'the strengthening of the double link, political and professional, between the state and the intellectuals' during that period 'was also demonstrated in 1962 by the replacement of Tharwat 'Ukasha, judged too liberal, by 'Abd al-Qadir Hatim, another Free Officer, as Minister of Culture, who was also entrusted with the information sector' (Jacquemond 2008: 17).

The choice of Hatim indicated that Nasser wanted to expand the role of the media as a main actor of the hegemonic order he was seeking to establish. Hatim was much more active in the information sector than in the cultural sector, as he participated in founding the Middle East News Agency and the Maspero headquarters of the Egyptian Radio and Television Union. His presence at *Bayn al-Qasrayn*'s first screening confirms that the film was used as an element of his ministry's propaganda plan.

In this chapter, I analyse cinema as a genre that further 'defigurated', to use Ross's expression, the 1919 events, fitting it into the Free Officers' ideological reframing of the nationalist movement.[11] The trope of unity, central to the novel, is taken to another level, both in terms of form and content, through a number of compelling additions to the original plot presented in a melodramatic fashion. Unlike historian Joel Gordon, who claims that al-Imam accurately 'recreated the spirit of national unity in a way that does capture the political sub-text of Mahfouz's novel' (Gordon 2002: 82), I argue that al-Imam transformed Mahfouz's liberal representation of the revolution into Nasserist rhetoric. In his analysis of the film, Walter Armbrust states that 'it was in the depiction of violent nationalist struggle that the greatest departure from the spirit of the novel took place' (Armbrust 1995: 93). However, Fahmi's transformation from a nationalist student into an armed resister is only one of many plot changes that contributed to translating the literary narrative into the nationalist jargon of the sixties. In addition, the discourse about religious unity between Muslims and Copts is significantly radicalised, and women are granted a much more active role in the film than they are in the novel, as they are placed at the centre of the film's rhetoric about progress. Only references to class struggle remain absent from the cinematic narrative, as they are in the novel. Moreover, I show, through a detailed analysis of mise-en-scène elements – montage, music, style of acting – how al-Imam efficiently exploited the genre of the melodrama, playing with emotions of grief and joy in order to build a cathartic expression of unity. I contend that through a succession of referential images, the film contributed to imposing the state's official narrative about the 1919 revolution.

Cinema and the Film Industry in Egypt

Cinema is unique as an artistic genre in its mass popularity and its wide reach of audience. By the time *Bayn al-Qasrayn* was produced, cinema was a prosperous industry in Egypt, which was considered the Hollywood of the Middle East. Born in the mid-twenties with the establishment in 1925 of the Egyptian Company for Cinema and Performance, the Egyptian cinema industry was 'the oldest and largest film industry in the region' (Gaffney 1987: 53). Muhammad Bayyumi, who in 1923 had filmed Saad Zaghlul's return from exile, directed his first short feature film in 1923, *al-M'allim Barsum Yabhath 'an Wazifa* (*Master Barsum is Searching for a Job*). The first entirely Egyptian film (i.e. directed, produced and acted by Egyptians) was *Zaynab*, by Muhammad Karim (1930), an adaptation of the novel of the same title by Muhammad Husayn Haykal (Shafik 2001: 24). In 1934, the establishment of Studio Misr further consolidated the influence of Egyptian cinema in the Arab world. Between 1924 and 1999, 2,800 full-length films were produced in Egypt (Shafik 2001: 24); in the period between 1952 and 1975, the period of interest to us in this chapter, 1,100 films were produced (Gordon 2002: 35). The Nasser period witnessed direct state intervention in the cinema industry through the nationalisation of the major Egyptian studios, starting in 1960 (studio Masr, al-Nahhas, Galal, al-Ahram), and the major distributing companies and theatres. By 1963, all these institutions were 'placed under the auspices of the Egyptian Public Agency for the Support of the Film Industry, a part of the Ministry of Culture and National Guidance' (Gaffney 1987: 59).

Making and Reception: 'Beyond Fidelity'

When he made *Bayn al-Qasrayn*, Hassan al-Imam had already established himself as 'the master of Egyptian melodrama' (Shafik 2007: 25). Although most of his productions were romantic soaps, he had released a previous adaptation of a novel by Mahfouz, *Zuqaq al-Midaqq* (*Midaq Alley*, 1963), and he would later turn the two other parts of the trilogy into filmic adaptations (*Qasr al-Shawq*, 1966 and *al-Sukkariyya*, 1973).

Al-Imam began working on *Bayn al-Qasrayn* after the filmmaker Tawfiq Salih (1926–2013) refused the scenario written by Yusuf Gawhar (1912–2001), a prolific author of scripts and stories for the screen. Salih, who had at the time authored only two full length films, *Darb al-Mahabil* (*Alley of Fools*, 1955) and *Sira' al-Abtal* (*Struggle of the Heroes*, 1962), was a committed filmmaker who repeatedly suffered from censorship (Shafik 2007: 137). He had first been approached by Salah Abu Sayf (1915–96), then the head of the General Company for Arab Cinema, but they fell apart after Salih rejected Gawhar's scenario, and Abu Sayf ended up contacting al-Imam to direct the shooting, without taking into consideration the advice of a committee of specialists who had 'decided unanimously that [Gawhar's] scenario was not suitable'.[12] Mahfouz himself refused to take sides at the time, stating that 'Gawhar did the best a scenario writer could actually do in those circumstances' and that 'Tawfiq Salih offers a very precise and profound interpretation of the events, characters and aims of the story' (Kamil 1963b). However, in his conversations with Raga' al-Naqqash, Mahfouz clearly states that al-Imam, 'though he respected to a certain extent the spirit of the text', 'subjected it to his style, marked by sensual sensationalism and melodrama, to the point Ahmad 'Abd al-Gawwad seems to have no other interest than the *'awalim* and the pleasures of the flesh' (al-Naqqash 2011: 129).

The choice of al-Imam over Salih is indicative of the spirit that prevailed at the time in the leadership of the public sector: the priority was not to produce a high-quality cinematic rendering of Mahfouz' novel but to release, as soon as possible, a movie suitable for a large audience, a movie that 'speaks to crowds' (Sartre 1988: 216) . The film was indeed 'a big-budget affair', 'a joint public-private project: the public sector financed the project, but contracted the work out to a private-sector director and producer' (Armbrust 1995: 85),

Aflam Jabra'il Talhami, a company owned by a producer of Palestinian origins who had already produced, among a dozen other movies, *Sira' fil-Wadi* (1954) and *Bab al-Hadid* (1958), two films by Yusuf Chahine, and who was 'a self-professed specialist in large-scale epics' (Armbrust 1995: 85).

The unfavourable critical reception of the film among the 'legitimate' critics was informed by Hassan al-Imam's reputation as a commercial director, fond of long belly-dancing interludes.[13] His adaptation of Mahfouz's *Midaq Alley* had been badly received, as there was 'a broad consensus' among critics about the fact 'he took too much freedom with Mahfouz' text, to the point he was about to make it lose its artistic value' (al-Fishawi 1964). The prevailing perception about al-Imam was, therefore, that he was unable to understand all the subtleties of a novel by Mahfouz.

Most importantly, the negative reception of *Bayn al-Qasrayn* among critics of filmic adaptations is the result of the importance they gave to the notion of fidelity. The centrality of that notion has been widely questioned since then, and scholars in the field of adaptation studies now agree upon the need to move the debate 'beyond fidelity', according to Robert Stam. As Stam puts it,

> the shift from a single-track, uniquely verbal medium such as the novel, which 'has only words to play with', to a multitrack medium such as film, which can play not only with words (written and spoken), but also with theatrical performance, music, sound effects, and moving photographic images, explains the unlikelihood – and I would suggest even the undesirability – of literal fidelity. (Stam 2012: 76)

In his comparison of filmic adaptation to translation, Venuti states that while it likewise 'recontextualizes its prior materials . . . the process is much more extensive and complex because of the shift to a different, multidimensional medium with different traditions, practices and conditions of production' (Venuti 2012: 93).

The recontextualisation that the film's authors made in order to make it fit into the context of the mid-sixties went far beyond the needs of adaptation to a different medium. One could not think of a better illustration than *Bayn al-Qasrayn* for Stam's statement that 'many of the changes between novelistic source and film adaptation' have to do with ideology and social discourses' (qtd in Venuti 2012: 91). The main change made by al-Imam is not so much in his insistence on belly-dancer scenes for the sake of audience but in his total reshaping of the novel's discourse about the nationalist movement and the 1919 revolution in particular.

The 1919 Revolution at the Centre of the Narrative

The scenario of the film is built on numerous plot changes that place the 1919 revolution at the centre of the cinematic narrative, giving it much more importance than it has in the novel (see Chapter 3). The film starts and ends with scenes of nationalist militancy. In contrast to the novel, which begins inside the 'Abd al-Gawwad household as Amina waits for her husband to come home, the film begins with an exterior shot of a British parade filmed from the perspective of Fahmi (Salah Qabil) and his fellow students at the law school. This first image is accompanied by a statement Qabil recites in an emphatic tone: 'Only blood can water freedom's tree', which immediately establishes the ideological background for the film's representation of the 1919 revolution as a liberation struggle that requires a violent confrontation with the colonial power.

The images that follow show Fahmi joining an underground group fighting against British occupation. In this way, the filmmaker materialises on the screen the group Fahmi is a member of, while it is only alluded to in the literary narrative. The group then reappears at several pivotal moments of the plot, confirming that it is meant to embody the leadership of the anti-colonial struggle, while the historical Wafdist elite is absent from the screen, except for

Figure 4.1 Salah Qabil in the role of Fahmi (on the right) with 'Izzat al-'Alayli in the role of Ibrahim. In this scene, Qabil examines a gun. The still is taken from one of the YouTube versions available online.

Zaghlul's iconic figure. The choice of the location, the presence of a priest, the oath on the Qur'an, the picture of Saad Zaghlul next to that of Mustafa Kamil – all those elements of the mise-en scène further insist on the importance of religious and political unity among the organised, underground 'vanguard'. The scene anachronistically implies that in October 1917 – the date of the beginning of the novel and the film, before the formation of the Wafd – Fahmi is already an active member of an anti-colonialist group.[14] By placing him at the centre of the narrative, the screen writer credits him with a nationalist consciousness that is fully formed much earlier than it had been in the novel, in which he begins to get actively involved after Saad Zaghlul's exile (see Chapter 3). His nationalist feelings are framed as spontaneous, as shown in the opening scene referred to above, in which he expresses his opinions rather impulsively. The casting of Salah Qabil (1937–92) as Fahmi aptly participates in embodying Fahmi on the screen as the young idealist ready to sacrifice himself for the sake of the nation. Qabil had already been cast in a previous adaptation by al-Imam of a Mahfouz novel, as the well-intentioned and naive 'Abbas al-Hilw, overwhelmed by his ambitious fiancé, the heroine of *Zuqaq al-Midaqq* (*Midaq Alley*, 1963). He was thus the perfect incarnation of the middle-class, decent effendi,[15] of what Armbrust calls 'authentically Egyptian and modern' (129).

Interclassist Struggle, Anti-Colonial Violence and Religious Unity

Many plot elements have been added in the film to complete this initial image of a revolution led by a group of middle-class activists. Playing a much more important role than the one he is assigned in the novel, Fahmi soon manages to recruit Husni, the son of a poor man in his neighbourhood, making intelligent use of an incident in which the father has his wallet stolen by English soldiers. In contrast to Fahmi's exclusive student activism in the novel, in the film he displays an acute consciousness of the necessity of welcoming members from an underprivileged background in the nationalist organisation. In later scenes, basement shots of the group include several men wearing *galabiyyas* (indicating that they belong to popular strata of society) who actively participate, side by side with the effendiyya, in printing the leaflets. The scene is significant to the ideological apparatus of the film; the 'interclassist' dimension of the group directly echoes the populist ideology of

Nasser's regime, in which interclassist unity is presented as the condition for the success of any anti-colonial struggle. In his *Falsafat al-Thawra* (*Philosophy of the Revolution*, 1954), Nasser insists that the defeat of the 1919 Revolution came about as a result of the popular energy of the people being consumed by dissension among 'people and classes' (34–5).

Although the cinematic narrative adds actors from deprived social backgrounds in the group, it does so in a way that carefully avoids tackling class-conflict dynamics. The members of the clandestine organisation struggle for the same, exclusively nationalist, agenda and remain aligned behind their effendiyya leadership, in which Ibrahim ('Izzat al-'Alayli) plays a pivotal role. Except for having easier access to popular neighbourhoods in the capital, the new recruits do not add anything to the group; they are, in a sense, instrumentalised by the middle-class leadership, and both Qabil and al-'Alayli adopt a patronising acting style towards them.

Moreover, and although the city was the theatre of violent urban riots in March and April 1919, with barricades and bloody confrontations with colonial troops, these elements are absent from the cinematic narrative. The scriptwriter and filmmaker manage to avoid any allusion to the massive strikes that paralysed all cities in March 1919 and to the uprisings in the countryside where 'villagers looted grain stores and attacked British troops, railroads, and telegraph and telephone lines' (Brown 1990: 195). Addressing these events would have questioned the 'primary opposition . . . of Egyptians to foreigners'[16] (Armbrust 1995: 92), central to the film's construction. Indeed, popular revolutionary violence was not exclusively directed against symbols of colonial authority; *fellahin* also targeted police stations administered by local authorities and large estates owned by Egyptian landlords. Working-class strikers often had particular demands in addition to their rallying to the nationalist cause (see Introduction). However, portraying these movements on the screen would have led the audience to question the populist attitude of the Nasser regime. According to that populist ideology, the regime is in symbiosis with the people and distributes social benefits on its own initiative. The people are not expected to exert pressure on the regime to obtain these benefits; even more so, there is no space allowing them to exert this pressure. Hence, displaying massive demonstrations demanding more social rights could be interpreted as encouraging people to organise similar movements, which is something the regime was seeking at any cost to prevent.

In addition to the colonial repression, the only political violence displayed on the screen is the armed struggle of the underground organisation to which Fahmi belongs, which seems to be inspired by *al-yad al-sawda'* (the Black Hand), a secret group that organised assassinations of British officials and attacks against high-ranking Egyptians involved in the colonial system.[17] The young man's revolutionary fervour, as displayed in the first scene, indeed turns into a virulent defence of the necessity of armed resistance towards the end of the film. In contrast to the fear and vulnerability Fahmi displays in the novel, in the film he gives an impassioned discourse, stating that 'leaflets won't make the English leave Egypt' and that 'every Egyptian has to be armed'; although his friend and comrade, Ibrahim, tries to prevent him from taking an armed mission, he nevertheless ends up transporting guns and ammunition.[18] That the only violence allowed to exist on the screen is an organised one, led by middle-class activists, directly mirrors, again, one of the main pillars of Nasserist rhetoric.

The film similarly radicalises the novel's discourse about the unity between Muslims and Christians.[19] While Mahfouz refers to national unity only through slogans in demonstrations and a mention of the presence of priests in the streets, the film shows a priest at the centre of the first images of the underground group, as described earlier, and displays, towards the end, a priest preaching in al-Azhar and an imam giving an impassioned discourse in a church, in the midst of a crowd of welcoming Christian men of religion. These were quite common events in 1919, as 'Coptic Christians and Muslims regularly attended and participated in meetings held at each other's houses of worship' (Fahmy 2011: 147). Mahfouz' discourse, a liberal celebration of religious unity, is radicalised by images that show dignitaries from different confessions enthusiastically entering religious spaces in which their discourse suddenly gains an authoritarian position. During the mosque scene, the priest, magnified into a hero by the low angle shot, is made to speak from the *minbar*, the mosque's pulpit, a position normally restricted to Muslim clerics. This aptly translates the extra-ordinary authority he is given in a space that would otherwise never permit anything similar. Moreover, by subverting the normal, expected organisation of things, the shot fulfils a didactic purpose, forcing the viewer out of his or her familiar compartmentalisation of confessional spaces.

The Christian cleric on the screen is clearly an allusion to a historical figure, 'one of the leading and most subversive speakers at al-Azhar University . . . a Coptic priest named Murqus Sergius' (Fahmy 2011: 148).[20] However, al-Imam misses the spontaneous spirit inherent to the revolutionary momentum and fails to capture the profoundly subversive significance of that exceptional historical moment. Instead, he sets that moment in an emphatic, repetitive mode that is one of the trademarks of the Nasserist propaganda. The powerful image is followed by exterior shots of a mosque near a church with a background of bells mixed with the Islamic call to prayer, heavily insisting on the message of national unity. Moreover, al-Imam attributes to the priest and the imam a discourse that echoes the anti-imperialist rhetoric of his time. Both clerics use a stereotyped *langue de bois* and an emphatic acting style. The priest states that 'there is no place in the nation for the words Muslim and Copt anymore'. The imam takes a pompous attitude and announces: 'Here is the Muslim's hand, I put it in the hand of my Christian brother, so that we unite and become one soul, in a united nation'. As in the shot analysed above, the statement has a clear didactic aim, urging the sixties' audience to follow his example and to shout '*Yahya al-Hilal ma' al-Salib*', (Long live the crescent and the cross) as does the crowd of Muslims and Christians present in the church, a crowd that is astonishingly mixed, with women standing behind the *tarabish* of the first rows.

Gender Dynamics

At the core of its recontextualisation dynamic lies the film's bold adaptation of the literary narrative's gender politics. Indeed, the most striking plot and characterisation change in the movie remains the creation of a nationalist militant out of Mariam's character. Towards the end of the novel, Fahmi rejects the painful souvenir of his love story and subsequent separation from Mariam, whom he now considers a traitor because of her flirtatious exchanges with an English soldier (Mahfouz 2014: 572). In the film, the relationship between Fahmi and Mariam fully materialises, but only after she pays the price for flirting with the enemy, in a moralising scene that underlines the limits of gender emancipation as understood by Gawhar and al-Imam. Fahmi is made to confront Mariam and slaps her face; astonishingly, she acknowledges his right to do so, as he is her 'brother', 'and every brother beats his sister'. She recognises she was 'wrong' and promises 'not to do so anymore'. Once she has expiated her fault through Fahmi's vengeful gesture,[21] al-Imam launches her transformation into a nationalist militant.

Before becoming fully invested in the movement, Mariam, like her namesake in *al-Dahik al-Baki* (see Chapter 2), saves the young man from arrest by colonial troops by hiding him and the bag containing weapons during the search of the 'Abd al-Gawwad household – a plot element absent from the novel.[22] As in Abaza's novel, the trope of the woman as saviour subverts traditional gender roles in which it is the man who rescues his female counterpart. But unlike her namesake, Mariam saves her lover not so much through her tenacious character and organising skills as through her providential presence at this crucial moment. Moreover, it is under Fahmi's influence that she becomes an activist, after having read the leaflets she finds in his bag. He convinces her to participate in the demonstrations celebrating Saad Zaghlul's release. Her transformation from a passive and reclusive girl to a character fully participating in the socio-political life of her country is thereby achieved, as she becomes one of the leaders of the girls' marches. It secures the binary opposition between the 'good' Egyptian people and the 'bad' British colonisers. There was indeed no space in a film produced in a Nasserist context for an Egyptian woman cast by Mahfouz as a collaborator.[23]

The casting of Zizi Badrawi (1944–2014) as Mariam highlights the transformative potential of the character. Badrawi, one of many actors and actresses who were 'made' by al-Imam, who imagined her artist name, primarily played roles of innocent girls trapped in failed romantic stories.[24] As Mahmud Qasim puts it, she embodied the figure of the 'sinful virgin' (*al-'adhra' al-khati'a*) and was thus the perfect choice to personify a woman who manages to get rid of her 'sinful' past and to embrace a new beginning. That new life belongs not only to her, but also to the entire Egyptian nation.

The scene showing Mariam leading the demonstration is preceded by a shot in which she is filmed alone, on the roof, head raised, in a posture that evokes the statue by Mahmud Mukhtar (1891–1934), *Nahdat Misr*, also known as *The Awakening of Egypt*. Sculpted by Mukhtar in the wake of the 1919 revolution, the statue shows a woman standing next to a Sphinx with her hand lying on its head. 'Juxtaposing Egypt's ancient pharaonic glory with her modern awakening', the statue has been widely interpreted as depicting 'Modern Egypt as a woman' (Baron 2005: 1).[25] In the film, Mariam is standing alone, but the shot is immediately followed by shots of the female demonstrations with her as leader, a flag in her hand and a poster of Saad Zaghlul next to her; this transition thus encourages an allegorical interpretation of her character, embodying first the past – a hesitant Egyptian nation flirting with the enemy – and then the present – a proud nation fighting for its independence.

Female characters in Mahfouz's novels often lend themselves to an allegorical interpretation,[26] but that is not the case in *Bayn al-Qarayn*. On the screen, the allegory serves to transfer the dynamics of transformation from Mariam to the entire Egyptian nation. It also conveniently casts Fahmi's slap as a revenge for the sake of national honour, a notion that had taken root in Egyptian novels, poems, and plays during the first part of the twentieth century (Baron 2005: 50). Although there is often an 'inverse relationship between the prominence of female figures in the allegorisation of the nation and the degree of access granted women in the political apparatus of the state' (Pierson qtd by Baron 2005: 2), that is not the case in al-Imam's work. Demonstration shots in the last third of the film indeed display a massive presence of women and girls, in contrast to the literary narrative, in which their presence in the street is only mentioned *en passant*, as shown in Chapter 3.[27]

In the three demonstration scenes – first after Saad Zaghlul's exile, then during the spontaneous outbursts of joy at the news of his release, and finally during the pacific march that took place on 8 April – the female participation, mainly of middle-class girls and women, is shown to have been significant.[28] The wide shots insist on the large number of women, showing them at the front lines of the march, before the processions of male demonstrators; other shots show female and male demonstrators standing together on a tram. There is no mention of the women's demonstration of 16 March that gathered around '300 women from upper classes' (al-Rafi'i 1946: 137), led by two figures from the Egyptian aristocracy: Huda Sha'rawi, the well-known feminist figure and Safiyya Zaghlul (see Introduction). One of the shots instead replaces Sha'rawi by a school girl in the reproduction of a scene in which the elite-women's demonstration was stopped by British soldiers, 'who levelled their weapons at [them]'. According to the text of a petition quoted by Baron,

> Huda (left unnamed in some accounts) then challenged the soldiers with the words: 'We surrender to death, fire your rifle into my heart and make in Egypt a second Miss Cavell.' (Edith Cavell was a British nurse executed by the Germans in Belgium in 1915 for helping Allied prisoners of war escape). (Baron 2005: 110)

The choice of an anonymous school girl instead of Sha'rawi expresses a celebration of the *collective* mobilisation of women rather than the *individual* role played by a few famous women. The pupils of the Saniyya School for Girls, the oldest and most reputed school for girls in Egypt, founded in 1873, who form the majority of the female troops in al-Imam's representation of the revolution, are well known for having participated in the 1919 turmoil, as well as in the many nationalist movements. Al-Imam's articulation of the incident – which is not mentioned in Mahfouz' narrative – insists on the potential power of collective mobilisation: the massive women's demonstration, encouraged by the girl's stand, succeeds in forcing the soldiers to let them pass, while historically, the women ended up standing 'for two hours under a burning sun' (Baron 2005: 110).

Indeed, nothing seems to be able to stop the women, whose acting style expresses an ardent patriotism as they steadily advance to the rhythm of the national anthem; in the shots in which they are shown in the front lines of the march, the camera movement highlights their leading role in the nationalist movement. Their dress indicates that they belong to the middle classes; nearly all of them have removed their face veils, which suggests that they are discarding traditions in the wake of the anti-colonial struggle. As Laura Bier argued, 'it was the unveiled and active presence of women in an outer sphere of progress that marked the Nasserist public sphere as modern, secular, and socialist' (62). Nasser himself critiqued the veil and ridiculed the Muslim Brotherhood's Supreme Guide for suggesting that all Egyptian women should walk around with a (head) veil (*tarha*).[29] So the crowds of women *had* to be filmed without their face veils in order to better embody the film's message – anachronistically, as there is no evidence of upper middle class women taking off their veils en masse during the 1919 revolution, though documents of the time attest to the massive presence of women on the streets (see Introduction). Similarly to what he did with themes of armed struggle and unity between Christians and Muslims, al-Imam inserts into the narrative historical elements that Mahfouz had marginalised, albeit in a Nasserist fashion.

The issue of female emancipation was indeed at the core of the regime's rhetoric about progress, an issue for the sake of which the media apparatus of the state mobilised its most famous writers. More often than not, the debate would be translated in terms of progress and backwardness. In February 1964, the weekly *Akhir Sa'a* presented, under its rubric '*Qif*' an article titled 'Something Called Men's Supremacy', signed by S. J. In it, Salah Jahine (1930–86), at the time already a well-known poet and the author of numerous cult songs, violently attacks the writer 'Abbas al-'Aqqad (1889–1964), who had often been at the heart of heated polemics. 'No wonder', mocks Jahine, 'that al-'Aqqad preaches on television that women should return home; it would be no wonder either if he preached that men should return to the caves . . . Going backwards is, for 'Aqqad, the way things go' (Jahine 1964: 20).

Among the newspaper and magazine articles of the mid-sixties lauding the regime's achievements on multiple fronts, including the anti-imperialist struggle and workers and peasants' rights, are many that passionately advocate women's rights. Several papers salute the government's success in furthering girls' education in the countryside and encouraging female labour. As Laura Bier argued, 'the figure of "the working woman" was critical in mapping out the contours of a socialist, postcolonial public sphere' (62). Glorifying women's role in the nationalist struggle was naturally part of that narrative. *Al-Musawwar* of 13 April 1962, titled 'Jamila Buhrayd, hero of the Arabs', displays on its cover a picture of the famous Algerian nationalist militant. A week later, the same magazine featured an article titled 'Palestine's Army in a Defensive Experience', showing *fidayyin* in operation, including women.

Cinema also participated in glorifying the central role women played in anti-colonial struggles, and *Bayn al-Qasrayn* is only one example among many. *Jamila* (1958), by Yusuf Chahine (1926–2008), narrates the story of a well-known Algerian *mujahida* during the national liberation war. *Al-Bab al-Maftuh* (*The Open Door*, 1963), by Henri Barakat, an adaptation of Latifa al-Zayyat's novel of the same name and set between 1946 and 1956, narrates the coming of age of Layla, a young Cairene girl who decides to join the popular resistance in Port Said against the tripartite aggression. *La Waqt lil Hubb* (*No Time for Love*, 1963), by Salah Abu Sayf, an adaptation of a novel by Yusuf Idris, displays the central role that Fawziyya, a young teacher from Cairo, plays in the anti-British resistance in the early fifties.

Mariam and Fahmi's dialogues, supposedly taking place in 1919, astonishingly resemble those taking place between other iconic nationalist couples of the sixties. Fahmi's statement 'I have no right to personal happiness' echoes Hamza's life ethos in *La Waqt lil Hubb*, in which Hamza (Rushdi Abaza), an anti-colonial activist, is in love with Fawziyya, (Fatin Hamama), who is also involved in the nationalist struggle. Fahmi's acute awareness of his sacrifice, accepting the necessity of abandoning personal happiness for the sake of a public cause, is a concept alien to the novel. The fact that individual happiness can be truly realised only in the frame of collective wellbeing is instead at the core of Nasser's populist rhetoric; the individual owes himself/herself to the community, and Nasser 'forcefully attacked the "I" tendencies that imposed themselves on the behaviour of many leaders of the time' (before the 1952 revolution), as stated by the publisher in the preface to *Falsafat al-Thawra* ('Abd al-Nasser 1996: 6). Paradoxically, and while this life ethos is more often than not embraced by activists on the screen, the films nevertheless systematically link romantic and nationalist involvement. The way in which love and revolution are intertwined in *Bayn al-Qasrayn* is at the core of the film's melodramatic formula.

Unity in a Melodramatic Mode

The term 'melodrama', whose French coinage derives from the Greek terms *melos* (song) and *drâma* (theatrical act; drama), was used to describe a 'romantic drama characterized by sensational incident, music, and song' (Collins English Dictionary, 2012). In modern usage, it designates 'a play, film, etc., characterized by extravagant action and emotion' (Collins, Idem). 'Extravagant action and emotion' is obtained in this case by the sensationalist plot elements: Mariam's spectacular transformation from a woman flirting with the enemy to becoming a faithful lover actively involved in the struggle;

the risks related to the bag full of weapons; the subsequent search of 'Abd al-Gawwad's household; and, of course, Fahmi's death in Mariam's arms.

Though many of the 'emotional shock tactics' are secured by the addition of the plot elements mentioned above, what truly turns it into a melodramatic masterpiece is the 'orchestration' of it all. As Elsaesser puts it, 'this type of cinema depends on the ways "melos" is given to "drama" by means of lighting, montage, visual rhythm, decor, style of acting, music – that is, on the ways the mise-en-scène translates character into action . . . and action into gesture and dynamic space' (Elsaesser 2012: 446). Though Elsaesser works on American cinema, a cinema he describes as determined 'by an ideology of the spectacle and the spectacular', a cinema that 'is essentially dramatic (as opposed to lyrical – i.e., concerned with mood or the inner self) and not conceptual (dealing with ideas and the structures of cognition and perception)', what he says applies perfectly to Egyptian cinema, as noted by Joel Gordon (Gordon 2002: 12).

Montage and visual rhythm, as well as music, play a central role in al-Imam's pompous 'orchestration' of *Bayn al-Qasrayn*'s third part. The montage is based on systematic shifts from the private to the public, from romantic to nationalist love. All scenes of collective protests from the last third of the film are indeed introduced by shots bringing together Mariam and Fahmi. In these shots, the impact of emotions on the audience is increased by the systematic use of the close-up, a shot powerful 'in conveying and eliciting emotion', that has 'a certain affinity with the film melodrama' (Kuhn and Westwell 2012: 85). The camera's intimate close-up on Mariam and Fahmi's romantic exchange effectively conveys to the audience their ecstatic state of mind; the shift then literally *transfers* that state of mind to the nationalistic scenes, thus associating patriotic enthusiasm with pleasure and joy. In one of those striking transitions, the camera shifts from an extreme close-up on Mariam and Fahmi kissing after the news of Saad Zaghlul's release, to a close-up on a man kissing Zaghlul's picture and then to the outburst of popular joy in the streets of the capital. The montage hereby literally embeds the 1919 revolution in the film's melodramatic structure.

The way al-Imam translates 'action into gesture and dynamic space' in the demonstration scenes mainly aims at underlining the central motto of nationalist unity. The space is successively filled up with rows of demonstrators in order to underline their huge numbers. Coming in from different sides of the screen, lines of people meet at its middle, visually translating the idea that individuals from very diverse backgrounds all meet around a single objective. A succession of shots then further insists on the fact that all strata of society are represented: male students led by Ibrahim and Fahmi, female students, Azhar people, *galabiyya* wearers, priests and even children led by the secretary of their school, Yasin. The scene thus reunites the three 'Abd al-Gawwad sons and erases all political dissensions between them, minimising Yasin's nonchalance towards anything political and Kamal's friendship with one of the soldiers occupying their neighbourhood. In contrast to the novel, which displays no familial unity in nationalist situations, this scene is actually the natural outcome of previous similar shots. In an earlier scene, Fahmi, and even Yasin, rush to help their father, who has been arrested by the British, carrying packs of sand on his behalf with which to fill a trench dug by nationalist activists. While the event as presented in the novel is narrated from the patriarch's perspective, here it is shown through the eyes of his sons, a focalisation that melodramatically underlines the humiliating situation of the father. And at the end of the film, a melodramatic shot unites Mariam and 'Abd al-Gawwad in front of a huge portrait of Fahmi, definitively erasing all past conflicts – 'Abd al-Gawwad refused to marry his son to the daughter of the neighbours – and sealing the unity of the most conservative wing of the family with its less traditional one. Translated into the realm of the personal, nationalist unity is amplified.

As I noted earlier, music also plays a central role in securing the film's melodramatic accents. In her work on Arab cinema, Shafik devotes some twenty pages to the discussion of music, acknowledging the centrality of songs and dance in Arab films, as they often are 'a guarantee for box office hits' (Shafik 2007: 103). Though Shafik mainly discusses musicals in this part of her work, the insertion of singing and dancing interludes was considered a guarantee of success in general in films of other genres. The formula was a trademark of al-Imam's melodramas, which he also adopts in *Bayn al-Qasrayn*, with long interludes performed by actresses cast due to their careers as singers (Maha Sabri[30] as Zubayda) and dancers (Ni'mat Mukhtar as Zannuba). Shafik notes that 'a large part of traditional Arab music is connected to producing certain moods and emotions' (110), and she insists on 'the emotional functions of music', a function al-Imam fully exploits in the political and romantic scenes.

It is not by chance that *Bayn al-Qasrayn*'s soundtrack is nearly exclusively based on arrangements of famous songs by Sayyid Darwish, 'the single most important figure in early twentieth-century Egyptian musical production' (Fahmy 2011: 115). The choice appears as natural, because of the popularity of Darwish songs' in 1919, but in addition to that, it perfectly fits the film's discourse about modernity, progress and backwardness. Darwish was indeed 'instrumental in transforming traditional "oriental" music, with its stuffy Ottoman classicism, into a distinctly Egyptian and "modern" compositional style' (Fahmy 2011: 115). The demonstration scenes are backed by Darwish's national anthem, although anachronistically, as he composed it in 1923, right before his death, at the occasion of Saad Zaghlul's return from his second exile.[31] The choice of the song, the way it is inserted into the mise-en-scène, the theatrical mode on which the actors shout the accompanying slogans, heads up and fists risen, are all elements carefully orchestrated to arouse the audience's patriotism.

The romantic dialogues are also backed by a famous Darwish melody, 'Zuruni Kul Sana Marra' ('Visit Me Once Each Year').[32] The lyrics of the song are those of a dead person addressing his loved ones, asking them 'to visit him once each year', imploring them not to forget him. In the novel, Kamal is singing as Ahmad 'Abd al-Gawwad returns home after Fahmi's death; Mahfouz' choice of the song thus foreshadows the grief that is going to dominate the family's life for the coming years. In the film, al-Imam exploits it to the fullest, turning it into a leitmotiv. It backs the scene of the opening titles showing 'Abd al-Gawwad returning home after the news of Fahmi's death (which signals that the whole film is constructed as a flashback) and is then employed in most of the shots bringing the lovers together. Its insistent use makes death's ghost hover over the romantic scenes, foreshadowing Fahmi's tragic fate; in this way, the filmmaker plays with the audience's knowledge of both the sad song and the plot, giving the people that 'mixture of repetition and difference, of familiarity and novelty' that is one of 'the pleasures of adaptation' (Hutcheon 2012: 386). Moreover, its leitmotiv character embeds the sad melody in the cinematic narrative's structure, literally magnifying nostalgic grief.

The mise-en-scène of Fahmi's death is one of the central pieces of the melodramatic orchestration. Al-Imam secures the melodramatic accents of the scene mainly through focalisation. Fahmi's death occurs just after the beginning of the unexpected repression of the 8 April demonstration.[33] In contrast to Mahfouz' necessarily allusive depiction of Fahmi's death, as it is narrated from the character's own perspective, the scene in the film is shown through Mariam's eyes. The close-up on Mariam's face in the midst of the ongoing chaos highlights her feelings of fear and panic while she runs looking for her lover; when she finally finds him sitting on the pavement, his head bleeding, the camera, again, underlines her feelings of pain and shock. Her very presence and the presence of Fahmi's comrades at his sides while he passes away is a plot element that has been added in order to secure the film's melodramatic formula, as is the scene in which 'Abd al-Gawwad announces the terrible news to his wife, in contrast to the novel, which avoids showing the mother's pain. By its melodramatic magnifying orchestration of these feelings, the film allows a cathartic expression of pain and grief while at the same time inviting the audience to overcome such feelings. Pain and grief are filmed over such *familiar* tones that the audience cannot but connect to them. Furthermore, the didactic end of the film, which I will analyse presently, connects the family's grief to that of all people mourning a beloved who has passed away in the nationalist struggle.

The scenario indeed adds a final set of demonstration shots accompanied by a voice-over stating that 'Fahmi's death was not in vain; his pure blood gave the people the necessary strength to continue the struggle until all objectives were realized'.[34] With its awkward, didactic narrative, the film invites spectators to find consolation in the idea that those deaths have not been in vain and to seek satisfaction in participating in the nationalist struggle or, given the context, in actively engaging on the path of progress, with the aim of establishing a modern nation emancipated from the yoke of imperialism. *Bayn al-Qasrayn* is yet another example confirming that 'melodrama persists as a discursive strategy to organise and support power – or to contest power imbalances – in strife-torn societies', as noted by Susan Dever in her book about Mexican cinema (Dever 2003: 8). As in many other films from the same period, *Bayn al-Qasrayn* supported the regime in its attempt at imposing new power dynamics and in its efforts to impose its own narrative about the Egyptian nationalist movement.

All these struggles seem to constitute merely a single step in the march towards the realisation of 'all objectives', or the advent of the Nasser regime, which succeeded in putting an end to the British rule. In his analysis of the film, Gordon notes that 'the 1919 revolution is clearly posited as antecedent to the Free Officers coup' (Gordon 2002: 82). Nasser himself defined the 'revolution of the 23rd of July' as 'a realization of the hope that inhabited the people of Egypt since it began in modern times striving for self-governance' ('Abd al-Nasser 1996: 14). Historian Yoav Di-Capua defines the Nasserist discourse about the nationalist movement as one of 'historical determinism', a 'teleological' narrative that frames 1952 as the logical, inevitable outcome of decades of anti-colonial struggle (Di-Capua 2001: 93).

Di-Capua's work about Nasserist Egypt resonates with Kristin Ross's book about May 1968 in France. She argues that by asserting what she calls 'a teleology of the present', 'the official story erases those memories of past alternatives that sought or envisioned other outcomes than the one that came to pass' (Ross 2002: 6). The multiple struggles that took place during the years 1918–23, involving peasants, marginalised urban masses and impoverished women, were never really included in that official story, because their mobilisation, in addition to their potentially subversive inspiration, could not be framed in a teleological fashion. The official Nasserist story about 1919, made of a 'relatively systematic set of words, expressions, images, and narratives' (Ross 2002: 5), is literally enshrined in *Bayn al-Qasrayn*. Thanks to its success, the film actively contributed to the imposition of the state's 'official doxa' about the revolution, or, using Di Capua's term, the 'revolutionary master-narrative', the 'kind of master-narrative' that 'has the potential of transforming itself into the most influential type of history – the one that becomes part of the consciousness of ordinary people' (Di-Capua 2001: 88–9).[35]

Bayn al-Qasrayn contributed effectively to carving the Nasserist story about 1919 into the popular imaginary; it also contributed to the process of 'forgetting' all moments and actors of struggles that could not be accommodated in the frame of that story. Those past alternatives remained absent, not only from the screen but also from other media, until the door was opened in the post-Nasserist era to less-uniform narratives, as I will show in the next chapter.

Notes

1. *Akhir Sa'a* no. 1531, 26/2/1964, p. 54.
2. This information is mentioned in an anonymous advertorial for the film, dated 24 February 1964, available in the file '*Bayn al-Qasrayn*' at the Egyptian Catholic Center for Cinema. Many of the advertisements and articles in the file are not correctly referenced and are without date or title of publication.
3. *Akhir Sa'a* 4/3/1964, p. 39.
4. In his review of the film published in *Akhir Sa'a* on 18 March 1964, Sa'd Kamil recognises that 'it is very popular'. An advertisement published three weeks after the beginning of the release states that 'a million [*sic*] of viewers enjoyed the film *Bayn al-Qasrayn* in its first and second week'. The advertisement mentions that *Bayn al-Qasrayn* is playing in Cairo, Heliopolis, Alexandria, Ismailiyah and Damietta. A week later, a blank advertisement states that 'this space was booked for an advertisement about *Bayn al-Qasrayn* but the enthusiasm of the crowds convinced the General Company to give it up. The film plays at cinema Rivoli in Cairo and, from today, Cinema Palace and Miami in Minya'.
5. Hassan al-Imam is 'one of the most productive Egyptian directors, making a total of ninety full-length feature films between 1947 and 1986' (Shafik 2001: 99). Born in Mansoura in 1919, al-Imam 'was entirely oriented towards the mainstream and specialized in musical melodramas' (Shafik 2001: 27). Often 'dismissed as trivial, al-Imam focused on melodramatic plots that relied mainly on female seduction and moral vulnerability. His films featured dozens of fallen women and belly dancers. Al-Imam realized one of the biggest box-office hits in Egypt with his musical *Khalli Balak Min Zuzu* (*Take Care of Zuzu*, 1972), starring Su'ad Husni' (Shafik 2001: 99).
6. See for instance Kamil (1964a), and al-Fishawi (1964). Sa'd Kamil uses the expression '*qissa bulisiyya rakika*', noting that the film is nothing more than a succession of 'boring nationalist speeches' and underground meetings.
7. Among many other examples, there is the song 'Si Sayyid', by popular Lebanese singer Nancy Ajram, released in 2006, in which she addresses her lover, a stubborn and authoritarian man whom she calls 'Si Sayyid', asking him why he is so controlling (*mithakkim lih*). In the film *Bint min Dar al-Salam* (*A Girl from Dar al-Salam*), the singer and actress Shakira also performs a song titled 'Si Sayyid', in which she describes her lover as a man who 'has prestige from the outside'

but 'is from the inside a little schoolboy'. In the film *Snoop* (2013), the popular Egyptian singer Tamer Husni performs a song with the same title, in which he claims the 'Si Sayyid' identity, telling his beloved she shouldn't try to 'erase the differences between a man and a woman'; he remains the one 'who tells her what to wear'.

8. Walter Armbrust relates that 'some of the critics' contended that the film was an outrageous misrepresentation of the original story', quoting an article by Bakr al-Sharqawi stating that 'what Hasan al-Imam has shown is nothing but cheap sensation which comes at the expense of the entire society' (Armbrust 1995: 89–90).

9. In the report of the Egyptian Catholic Center for Cinema and Television about the film, written in French, the censor, ironically called 'Mary Ghadban', classifies the film as 'strictly for adults only', noting: 'Les danses sont sensuelles, gros plans sur les parties de la danseuse, attitudes, costumes, etc'.

10. Although political pluralism had already been abrogated, and most of the leaders of the communist organisations and the Muslim Brotherhood, as well as many intellectuals, had been in prison since the end of the fifties.

11. In addition to *Bayn al-Qasrayn*, two other fiction films – both biopics – display scenes of the 1919 revolution: *Mustapha Kamil* (1955) about the nationalist leader; and *Sayyid Darwish* (1966), about the well-known singer and composer, both directed by Ahmad Badrakhan (1909–69). *Mustafa Kamil* was made in 1951 but was censored under King Farouk and then screened only in 1953. For these films, see Joel Gordon (1999), 'Film, Fame, and Public Memory: Egyptian Biopics from Mustafa Kamil to Nasser 56', *International Journal of Middle East Studies* 31, no. 1, pp. 61–79.

12. This information is given in an article by Sa'd Kamil titled 'The Director Tawfiq Salih and the Conflict About the Film "Bayn al-Qasrayn"', based on Salih's version of the events (*Akhir Sa'a*, 29 May 1963, 34). Tawfiq Salih's critique of al-Imam's film is available in *Watha'iq al-Sinima'iyyin al-Misriyyin fil Kharij, Rasa'il Tawfiq Salih ila Samir Farid*, Malaffat al-Sinima 16, Cairo: Academy of Arts.

13. He expressed that obsession later in *Khalli Balak Min Zuzu* (*Take Care of Zuzu*, 1970), a cult movie giving a poignant description of a belly dancer's world and the social censure she faces.

14. In his review of the film, al-Fishawi underlines that the pictures of Saad Zaghlul on the wall in the first scene are anachronistic, since 'Saad Zaghlul was not yet popular at the time' (al-Fishawi 1964).

15. Twenty years later, Salah Qabil played the exact opposite role in *Laylat al-Qabd 'ala Fatma* (*The Night of Fatma's Arrest*, 1984), by Henri Barakat. He embodied on the screen the character of Galal, an opportunistic and corrupt man who pretends to have participated in the resistance against British occupation in Port-Said, taking advantage of this false heroism to enter parliament. Though the film goes back to events set in the fifties, it is released in a context of increased submission to a globalised economy, by both government and citizens. Barakat's choice suggests that Qabil was often cast to embody the spirit of the time: the revolutionary law student in 1919 and the corrupt businessman in the seventies.
16. That kind of opposition is recurrent in artistic and cultural productions of the time. Zeina al-Halabi, for instance, shows that 'My Beloved Nation' ('*Watani Habibi*'), a song produced in 1960 by the composer Muhammad 'Abd al-Wahab and the lyricist Ahmad Shafiq Kamil, 'is dominated by a binary opposition between the revolutionary and the oppressor, the good and the bad, the Arab and the colonizer'. That 'Arab unity' operetta was commanded by Nasser himself. Zayna al-Halabi (2013), 'Qatari Habibi, Malhat al-Ikhwan wa Ma'sat al-Nasiriyya', *Ma'azif*, 11 April, available at <http://bit.ly/2iqNXPK> (last accessed 30 November 2017).
17. There are many similarities between Fahmi's group and *al-Yad al-Sawda'* (The Black Hand): the meetings in a basement, the printing activities and of course the armed struggle. The novel *1919* by Ahmad Murad, which I analyse in Chapter 7, is inspired by *al-Yad al-Sawda'*.
18. The character of Ibrahim, who does not exist in the novel, is clearly inspired by a historical figure, Ibrahim 'Abd al-Hadi (1896–1981), a student leader and member of the Wafd's underground organisation. 'Abd al-Hadi was arrested and sentenced to imprisonment with forced labour. He was released in 1924, became involved in Wafdist politics, and was nominated prime minister at the end of the forties. His memoirs about his involvement in the armed struggle remain unpublished; parts of them are available in Muhammad al-Gawwadi (2009), *Mudhakkirat al-Shubban al-Wafdiyyin, al-'Amal al-Sirri fi Thawrat 1919, Mudhakkirat Ibrahim 'Abd-al-Hadi, Sayyid Basha, 'Iryan Yusuf Saad, Muhammad Mazhar Sa'id*, Cairo: al-Shuruq al-Dawliyya.
19. Although 'British reports confirmed that Jewish Egyptians participated in the nationalist celebrations' (Fahmy 2011: 141), neither the film nor the novel – nor any other literary narrative I came across in the course of my research about the 1919 revolution – mentions Jewish participation.

20. Sergius was an important figure of the 1919 revolution. He was arrested and exiled by the British authorities in April 1919, but he continued to act as a revolutionary agitator after his return. His political activism irritated the church and he was stripped of his clerical position in July 1920. See Magdi Girgis (2019), 'Ikhtitaf thawrat 1919 taht shi'ar al-hilal wal salib', *Kitab Maraya*, May and Muhammad 'Afifi (2019), 'Al-qummus Sergius: Khatib thawrat 1919', *Dhakirat Misr* 36, January.
21. It is worth noting that in a previous filmic adaptation by al-Imam of a Mahfouz novel, *Zuqaq al-Midaqq* (*Midaq Alley*, 1963), in which Salah Qabil plays a central role, the character he embodies, the young 'Abbas al-Hilw, similarly attempts to avenge the lost honor of the woman/Egyptian nation as he tries to kill his fiancé, Hamida, when he discovers that she became a prostitute.
22. Women play a prominent role in smuggling weapons in other films of the sixties, like *La Waqt lil-Hubb* (*No Time for Love*, 1963) by Salah Abu Sayf, in which Fawziyya hides the bag of dynamite (as she does in the novel by Yusuf Idris, *Qissat Hubb* [*Love Story*, 1957, translated into English as *City of Love and Ashes*, 2002], of which the film is an adaptation) and then organises its transport from Cairo to Ismailia (a scene that is not included in the novel).
23. Plots and characters were often modified in a moralistic direction in filmic adaptations of literary narratives. Among many other examples, one can mention the following two cases: in *Zuqaq al-Midaqq* (see note 21), a main plot element has been changed in the ending of the story. Unlike the novel, in which 'Abbas al-Hilw ends up lynched by British soldiers while Hamida survives and continues her life as a prostitute, both Hamida and her pimp are killed at the end of the film. In the cinematic adaptation of Fathi Ghanim's *al-Rajul alladhi Faqada Zilahu* (*The Man Who Lost His Shadow*, 1962), adapted in 1968 by Kamal al-Shaykh, Mabruka, the 'victimized peasant woman' who in the novel becomes a prostitute is transformed into 'an accomplice in anti-regime activity' (Gordon 2002: 214–15).
24. For instance, in *Shafiqa al-Qibtiyya* (*Shafiqa the Copt*, 1963) by al-Imam, she embodies the character of Su'ad, a girl from an influential aristocratic family who lives an impossible love affair with a student from a poor family.
25. Mukhtar made the statue after a popular fundraising campaign. It now stands in front of Cairo University. For Mukhtar and his work, see: Badr al-Din Abu Ghazi (2019), *Mukhtar Fannan Thawrat 1919*, Cairo: al-Markaz al-a'la lil-Thaqafa; Sobhi Sharouni (2007), *Memory of the Nation: Sculptor Mahmoud Mukhtar & his Museum, 1891–1934*, Cairo: al-Dar al-Misriyya al-Lubnaniyya;

Israel Gershoni and James Jankowski (2004), *Commemorating the Nation: Collective Memory, Public Commemoration, and National Identity in Twentieth Century Egypt*, Chicago: Center for Middle Eastern Studies.
26. For a discussion of gender issues in Mahfouz' novels, see Chapter 3, note 26.
27. In a television drama aired in 1977, adapted from *'Awdat al-Ruh* (*The Return of the Spirit*, 1933), the other canonical novel about the revolution, the plot is similarly changed to include women in the representation of the national community. In order to achieve this, the series, directed by the well-known filmmaker Husayn Kamal (1934–2003), operates a significant transformation of Zannuba's character in the last episode. Although she was until then, as she is in the novel, a self-interested superstitious woman (see Chapter 3), she suddenly becomes a nationalist militant participating in women demonstration. Similarly to *Bayn al-Qasrayn*'s Mariam, she gets rid of her reactionary past to embrace a modern future.
28. It is worth noting that in the other films of the Nasser period which display scenes from the 1919 revolution, *Mustapha Kamil* and *Sayyid Darwish*, by Ahmad Badrakhan (see note 8), the demonstration scenes feature only a few women. The shots mainly focus on middle-class men wearing *tarbouch* demonstrating on the streets, raising the flag and shouting slogans.
29. That part of Nasser's discourse is available at <https://www.youtube.com/watch?v=OWCJnFu9gF0> (last accessed 20 February 2018).
30. Maha Sabri was a very popular singer in the early sixties. She won the third place in a 'referendum' organised by the radio programme 'With the People', just behind Um Kulthum and Sabah (*Akhir Sa'a*, no. 1504, 8 August 1963, 44–5). In this interview, Sabri talks about the role in which she has just been cast in *Bayn al-Qasrayn*, wrongly presenting it as that of 'a young 'alma who participates in the 1919 revolution'.
31. Scenes of 1919 demonstrations in the film *Sayyid Darwish* by Ahmad Badrakhan are backed by the same music.
32. About the song, see Saadallah Agha Al-Kalaa, <http://www.agha-alkalaa.net/archives/4841> (last accessed 21 June 2019). According to Mustafa Sa'id, the song was written and composed by Sayyid Darwish in 1914 (see *Hawa al-Hurriyya* (*Whims of Freedom*, 2014), poster of the play).
33. The demonstration was authorised by the colonial authorities. Unlike the novel, the film displays the repression as extremely bloody, with dozens of corpses lying on the pavement.
34. These didactic, often documentary, images shown at the beginning or the ending

of films are recurrent in films of the period. See for instance *al-Bab al-Maftuh* (*The Open Door*, 1963), by Henri Barakat, which opens with images of armed women being trained to participate in the nationalist struggle.

35. Di Capua details his argumentation in an article dealing with what he calls the 'process of revolutionary symbolic formulation' (Di Capua 2001: 104) of the Nasserist regime, in which he analyses the commemoration of two important figures of the Egyptian nationalist movement, Mustafa Kamil (1874–1908) and Muhammad Farid (1868–1919). He explains that 'the new revolutionary regime was in need of a simple and logical historical narrative that would serve as a paradigm according to which it could organise historical facts in a new and meaningful fashion, building on the work of Pierre Nora about sites of memory, according to which "memory in the modern era requires some form of material support for symbolic representation" (88). 'The "commemorative narrative" necessary to achieve that, in the case of Kamil's mausoleum, assembles a "basic story-line": the revolutionary master-narrative"' (88–9). He also shows how key intellectual figures of the National Party provided help in doing so, among them 'Abd al-Rahman al-Rafi'i, who was also an important historian of the 1919 revolution, and Fikri Abaza, whose novel I analysed in Chapter 2.

5

The Politics of Rehabilitation

When he published *Min Wahid li-'Ashara* (*From One to Ten*) in 1977, Mustafa Amin (1914–97) had been out of prison for three years. A powerful journalist and a habitué of Nasser's intimate circle, Amin had suddenly seen his universe collapse when armed guards burst into his Alexandria villa on 21 July 1965. Charged with pro-American espionage, Amin was found guilty and condemned to life imprisonment by a military court.[1] It was only in 1974, after interventions by the diva Umm Kulthum and US Secretary of State Henry Kissinger, that he was finally released by president Anwar al-Sadat. A presidential decree soon returned him to his position as editor-in-chief of *Akhbar al-Yaum*, a daily he had founded with his brother 'Ali Amin in 1944, whom the same decree installed as chairman of the board after a ten-year exile in London. Both Mustafa and Ali wrote enthusiastic editorials supporting the slight democratic opening operated by Sadat, the 'war and peace hero' who had established his legitimacy with the October 1973 war against Israel.

While writing his editorials, Mustafa Amin simultaneously embarked on a more lasting project and plunged into his childhood and adolescence years. He became obsessed with the legacy of his illustrious grandfather, Saad Zaghlul – Amin's mother, Ratiba, was Saad's niece and was adopted by Saad and Safiyya after her parents' death. *Min Wahid li-'Ashara* is a recollection of Amin's childhood in the house of his grandparents. As its title indicates, the memoir narrates the first ten years of Mustafa Amin's life, from 1914 to 1924; it is the first volume of a coming-of-age narrative portraying the formation of Amin's vocation as a journalist. In this reconstruction of his childhood, Mustafa Amin gives a preponderant role to his education in *Bayt al-Umma* in the midst of the 1919 turmoil.

Figure 5.1 Saad Zaghlul with Safiyya Zaghlul and Ratiba Yusuf, leaving hospital on 17 July 1924. Rare Books and Special Collections Library, the American University in Cairo.

His first publication after his release, however, together with his prison memoirs, was a volume compiling documents belonging to Saad Zaghlul that were hitherto unknown to the public. Titled *Asrar Thawrat 1919* (*Secrets of the 1919 Revolution*), the book depicts 1919 as a revolution in which both popular and organised violence played a key role. It discusses the part played in this violence by the Wafd's underground organisation, which coordinated the demonstrations, financed an impressive network of informers and carried out a significant number of assassinations of British soldiers and officers in addition to attacks on high ranking Egyptian personalities collaborating with the colonial authorities.[2]

In his introduction to *Asrar Thawrat 1919*, Amin explains that the book was scheduled for publication in the early 1960s. However, although parts of it had been serialised in *Akhbar al-Yaum*, the publication was blocked in 1963 by 'a sudden order' from the authorities (Amin 1991: 4). While Amin had required permission from Nasser himself, the president let him know that 'he received reports from the different [intelligence] apparatuses' warning that 'the aim of this long reportage was to minimise the importance of the 23rd of July revolution', 'to prove the ability of an unarmed people to revolt against the army' and to 'encourage the people to attack the revolution' (Amin 1991: 3–4).[3]

As I have shown in Chapter 4, the Nasserist discourse framed the 1919 revolution in a teleological fashion, presenting the Free Officers' Coup of 1952 as the natural outcome of decades of nationalist struggle. The populist re-enactment of the 1919 revolution in the film *Bayn al-Qasrayn* was part of this rhetoric of progress and anonymous heroes, in which there was no space either for a figure as charismatic as that of Saad Zaghlul, that could have overshadowed Nasser, or for any reflection upon the subversive potential of the revolution. Sadat's era however was marked by a systematic 'revisionism' of the pillars of Nasserist ideology. The Arab socialist rhetoric was replaced by an Egyptian nationalist discourse lauding the advantages of 'freedom' and 'democracy'. The modernist terminology that was a trademark of the Nasser regime – and of other Arab socialist regimes – was replaced by a 'conservative orthodoxy that is well summarized in the famous "village morality" (*akhlaq al-qarya*) praised by Sadat' (Jacquemond 2008: 22).

Moreover, Sadat's rule was a period in which pro-government writers were prompted to criticise the wall of silence that prevailed during the Nasserist period; the slight democratic opening operated by the new establishment liberated pens that had been silenced for nearly two decades. Amin's enthusiastic editorials in which he proclaimed that 'after the October war there was no space anymore in [the] country for those who answered words with bullets' (Amin, 3.7.1974) fitted *l'air du temps*. Even his terrible prison experience, confined in a solitary cell, deprived of food and water for days and brutally tortured under the supervision of a man who had been an acquaintance (Amin 1975: 19), could now be made public. His personal anger at Nasser and his regime were now fashionable, as were his prison memoirs.[4] The period was thus favourable to revisiting the Nasserist discourse about 1919 and to questioning its silence on the figure of Saad Zaghlul, who had gone through a period of oblivion following 1952 (Clément 2005: 15). Shaped at once by the historical and personal moment in which he writes, Amin's narrative about 1919 functions as a conscious attempt at rehabilitating Zaghlul's charismatic figure in the public debate, albeit in a different fashion than that of the so-called 'liberal era' (1923–52).

Like *Asrar Thawrat 1919*, *Min Wahid li-'Ashara* unsettles dominant representations of the 1919 revolution and its leader. Instead of national unity, it is chaos, conflict and carnival that dominate the narrative. In lieu of a pasha who led the revolution in a strictly pacific manner, Saad Zaghlul emerges as the central brain of the Wafd's underground organisation. However, Amin does not dispute the dominant narrative from a committed or marginalised perspective. Rather, he attempts to inscribe this alternative representation in the dominant political landscape of his time. *Min Wahid li-'Ashara*'s autobiographical mode allows him to show how Zaghlul shaped him into adulthood and hence, to demonstrate the relevance of Zaghlul's values to the contemporary context. The reconstructed perspective of the little boy who looks up to his charismatic grandfather contributes to constructing an idealised, iconic image of the leader, albeit in terms different from those of the pre-1952 era. Zaghlul's character as a non-conservative man in his household and a pasha proud of his identity as a *fallah*, intuitively connected to the people, is articulated in a terminology that summons up the atmosphere of the Sadat era. Likewise, the image of the 1919 revolution takes advantage at once of the Nasserist legacy – which lifted the taboo of political violence as a means of resistance – and the slight democratic changes operated under Sadat, opening up a significant space to the voices of the revolution's anonymous actors.

Memoirs and Subjectivity

'Ali and Mustafa are only five years old when the revolution bursts into their life on 8 March as English officers enter *Bayt al-Umma* to arrest Saad Zaghlul. After the terror of the first night in a house emptied of its men, they plunge into a whirlwind of excitement, as they watch hundreds and thousands of people entering their home, youth 'who come bursting into the garden like arrows, their *tarbush* in their hands, sweat pouring from their faces' (Amin 1977: 167), leaders of the Wafd – who meet in the dining room – and those of the underground organisation – who meet in the cave. They witness huge gatherings in front of *Bayt al-Umma* that sometimes turn into bloody confrontations between demonstrators and police forces (277). They see bodies lying in the garden and watch their grandmother holding and kissing the head of a dead adolescent (170).

Min Wahid li-'Ashara is not Mustafa Amin's first memoir. He was an adept of the genre, as he produced, in addition to a number of novels and scripts,[5] uncountable journalistic writings and eight memoirs. Beside the two volumes narrating his childhood and adolescence years, *Min Wahid li-'Ashara* and *Min 'Ashara li-'Ishrin* (*From Ten to Twenty*), he wrote an account of his years as a student at Georgetown University titled *Amrika al-Dahika* (*Cheerful America*, 1944).[6] In addition, he wrote extensively about his years in prison in five autobiographical books, from *Sana Ula Sijn* (*First Year in Prison*) until *Sana Khamsa Sijn* (*Fifth Year in Prison*).

Like all autobiographical narratives, a memoir is a reconstruction of moments and events of the past. It does not necessarily constitute a faithful recollection of reality; rather, it is a personal, highly subjective recollection of events from the past. However, unlike autobiography, memoirs are not focused primarily on the author's self; instead, 'writers of memoir are usually persons who have played roles in, or have been close observers of, historical events and whose main purpose is to describe or interpret the events' (Memoir, 2017). According to Kathleen Waites, the focus of the memoir is on the external events or culture in which the writer lived, and the self is discussed, revealed, and explored relative to those events or that culture. Unlike the conventional autobiography, the memoir does not purport to tell the whole life story. Rather, the memoirist tends to focus on a slice of [his/] her life and the "others" that populate it.'

Memoirs thus aim at placing one's life in the context of given historical and political events. It is a genre that highlights 'an insider's subjective view of a historical moment' (Waites 2005: 379).

In the sub-genre of the coming-of-age memoirs, the narrator tells the story of a specific period of time that most often goes from childhood into early adulthood; it is a narrative about the formative years in the life of the narrator, in which he or she focuses on the decisive elements in his or her education: school and family background, social milieu and important political events. Childhood memoirs share many features with childhood autobiography, which is a genre of its own in modern Arabic literature. Many prominent intellectual figures of the twentieth century wrote accounts of their childhood; like Taha Husayn in *al-Ayyam* (*The Days*, 1929), Salama Musa (1887–1958) in *Tarbiyyat Salama Musa* (*The Education of Salama Musa*, 1947) and Ahmad Amin (1886–1954) in *Hayati* (*My Life*, 1950).

I have mentioned in Chapter 2 that Egyptian and Arab autobiographies from the first decades of the twentieth century were most often narratives of success and social mobility. This feature applies to Amin's memoirs as well; however, instead of a story of rupture, his success story is one of continuity. In many of the early twentieth century childhood autobiographies, the narrator relates his rupture to his native, most often rural, universe and his successful journey into the modern world of the capital, the typical example being Taha Husayn's *al-Ayyam*.⁷ Ryzova argues that 'the function of childhood narratives is to anchor the author's life in his *bi'a*, or "original environment", providing a necessary contrast to the transformation undergone, and distinguishing the past from the author's and reader's present' (Ryzova 2014: 145). In *Min Wahid li-'Ashara*, however, it is not in order to record his transformative self that the author devotes an entire volume to his childhood. Rather, it is to highlight the *continuity* between his contemporary self and his childhood self. The environment he lives in as an adult is indeed very similar to his childhood environment in terms of class and culture: it is an upper middle class, urban, multilingual, politically informed and cultivated environment. Most importantly, it is his education in *Bayt al-Umma*, partly by Saad and Safiyya Zaghlul, that allowed Amin to develop the values that shaped his journey into adulthood and his vocation as a journalist.

The centrality of Amin's vocation to the narrative is made clear in the introduction. Titled 'Umri Qissat Hub' ('My Life is a Love Story'), the introduction stands clearly apart from the text, as it is written in the first person in a more casual style; it functions as a metatextual reference which places journalism at the centre of Amin's life. The short text frames Amin's life as the success story of someone who was lucky to live his passion to the fullest and who remained in tune with his time, an intimate of famous and powerful personalities. Most importantly, he 'contributed to found great journalism' in his country (6). The introduction ends with the idea that it is difficult to dissociate Amin's story from Egypt's, for 'it is not my story . . . it is Egypt's story I lived' (6). Hereby the writer draws the reader's attention to the fact it is not merely a personal story he or she is about to read, but a story that provides a wealth of information about a whole period in Egypt's history.

The Little Boy and His Grandfather

In contrast to Amin's prison memoirs, in which he uses a first person narration, *Min Wahid li-'Ashara* is told by an omniscient narrator in the third person, a technique Amin also uses in his *Mudhakkirat Talib fi Amrika*. Third person narration in autobiographical narratives establishes a certain distance from the protagonist, which contributes to exposing his emotional evolution and social interactions during that period to a critical eye. In this case, the main aim is to highlight the upbringing of Mustafa Amin in *Bayt al-Umma*, or more accurately, the upbringing of the twins, as the little boy is seldom referred to in the singular; most often the narrator uses the dual and talks of the two children as one feeling and thinking entity.

Mustafa and 'Ali Amin were born on 21 February 1914. Although their father, the lawyer Amin Yusuf, refused Saad Zaghlul's request to let him adopt Mustafa – Saad and Safiyya were a childless couple – Mustafa and 'Ali

Amin had a sustained, very intimate, relationship with their grandfather. Saad Zaghlul spent many hours with them (81), going over lessons and telling bedtime stories – not the usual ogre stories, but 'stories about his life and adventures in which he was *al-Shatir Hassan* [a well-known hero in Egyptian popular tales] and his dreams about freedom and independence and democracy were *Sitt al-Husn wal Gamal*' [the beloved in Egyptian popular tales] (89). Important decisions about the children's education were left to Saad, who 'supervised their schooling in person' (243). Moreover, the narrative repeatedly underlines the role Zaghlul played in shaping values that would become cornerstones in the twins' personalities. He 'taught them to be independent' (371), 'encouraged them to be critical' (362) and helped them to formulate their own opinions and fight for them. These values are presented as formative in the boys' professional journey as journalists.

To the children, Saad was a 'legend' (*ustura*, 207), a 'hero' (*batal*, 207), a 'mountain' (*jabal*, 378). There was a special 'magic' to his presence:

> For millions of people, [he] was like a moon in the sky of nationalism.[8] . . . The boys felt that they were some of the few who had landed on the moon millions of people saw from afar. Saad's love for them and their mother was like a spaceship that allowed them this adventure. (378)

The godlike position Zaghlul occupies in the twins' life is mirrored in the narrative. Divided into twenty chapters, the text is not organised around the autobiographical self of its narrator, as Mustafa is not a protagonist of most of the scenes related in the book. Instead, it is structured around the persona of Saad Zaghlul, and, to a lesser extent, Safiyya. The opening scene, in October 1917 – 'Ali and Mustafa are then three and a half years old – sets the tone for the whole narrative. The family is seated for lunch, waiting for the 'head of the family' – unnamed until four pages later – as they are not allowed to begin eating in his absence. His presence is so central that 'the food has no taste unless he tries it first' (7). When he finally enters the room, he is so irascible he omits to kiss the twins and refuses to eat; later, it appears his fury is due to the nomination of Fuad I as Sultan of Egypt. As it establishes the time, space and characters of the story, this scene mainly uses the empty seat that halts the normal course of events to symbolically refer to Saad's central position – both in the family and in the narrative. Most of the chapters follow this pattern and long pages are devoted to Saad's dissensions with the king, his polemics with the Wafdist leaders and his relationships with family friends.

Focalisation is central to understanding the way the figure of Saad Zaghlul is constructed in the narrative. The perspective of the little boy, or more accurately, the perspective of the little boy as reconstructed by a grown-up narrator, gives the figure of Zaghlul oversized proportions. The boy looks up to his adoptive grandfather both literally and figuratively. Hence, every aspect of the 'hero's' personality is presented as an exceptional trait of character and the representation of Saad Zaghlul is built on a laudatory mode, as a godlike figure, on both political and personal levels.

A Godlike Figure

In *Min Wahid li-'Ashara*, Zaghlul appears as the main instigator and organiser of the 1919 revolution. According to Amin, ever since his imprisonment following his participation in the uprising against the British invasion led by Ahmad 'Urabi in 1882, Zaghlul had been silently preparing for the revolution. His entire life was devoted to preparing 'the zero hour' of the anti-colonial uprising (63). With extraordinary patience and endurance, he has been preparing for the 1919 revolution for thirty-seven years, Amin claims (34). Moreover, he is systematically presented as the brain of the revolution and its main initiator; he coordinated everything, from the codeword for the beginning of the demonstrations after his exile, to the names of Wafd leaders who would replace those arrested, exiled, or executed. He founded and led the Wafd's underground organisation behind the back of most of the Wafd leaders, who were not aware of its existence, let alone of the fact it was Saad himself who was leading it (231–2).

The narrator hammers home that Zaghlul was a truly liberal person at all levels and presents him as well ahead of his time. The fact that Zaghlul dealt with his family in a liberal way, specifically in matters related to gender roles, is presented as exceptional. Although 'it was unusual at the time', according to the narrator, 'for a man who was not a family member to be invited to sit at the same table with the ladies of the family, the previous azhari *fallah* Saad Zaghlul did not have any objection to his close friends sitting with his family for lunch or dinner' (119). Although this behaviour shocked some of Zaghlul's friends – the narrator for instance comically describes 'Abd al-Rahman Fahmi's manoeuvres in order to avoid looking into Safiyya's face as she is sitting unveiled in front of him during lunch (119) – it was not so uncommon in the upper middle classes of the time. In his article about 'Feminism, Class, and Islam in Turn-of-the-Century Egypt', Juan Cole classifies Zaghlul as a 'profeminist figure' among others, together with Qasim Amin, the famous author of *Tahrir al-Mar'a* (*The Emancipation of Women*, 1899) and Ahmad Lutfi al-Sayyid, who would later become the leader of the Wafd's rival party (Cole 1981: 392).

Saad's liberalism in matters political and religious is also presented as an exceptional trait which he has to fight for even against his closest friends and collaborators. According to the narrator, the integration of Copts in the Wafd's leadership is entirely due to his lucidity and his patient conversations with those leaders of the Wafd who were reluctant on that level, such as 'Ali Sha'rawi (127–32). However, other testimonies show that it is an initiative of the concerned themselves that built the momentum towards the integration of the Copts. In his memoirs, Fakhri 'Abd al-Nur (1881–1942) recalls how he and his brother Labib were delegated by a group of Coptic notables to meet Zaghlul in order to draw his attention to the fact that 'the names of the members of the Wafd mentioned on the petitions distributed in the country do not include a single Coptic name'; according to 'Abd al-Nur, the notables 'decided that this could not be allowed and that they had to remedy this deficiency' ('Abd al-Nur 1992: 45).[9] Coptic leaders thus did not wait for Zaghlul to include them in the leading organs of the Wafd. Rather, they imposed their presence on the Wafd and its leaders, including Zaghlul himself.

Moreover, the less glorious elements of Zaghlul's biography are either mitigated in *Min Wahid li-'Ashara*, or totally silenced. The fact that he served as minister of Education in 1907 under colonial rule is presented as part of his far-sighted strategy to fight British occupation. Commonly known facts about him, which he himself extensively talks about in his diaries, such as his gambling addiction,[10] are not alluded to by the narrator.[11] More fundamentally, the anti-democratic measures he took as prime minister are equally omitted, in particular 'his tight-fisted control of the chamber' (Botman 1998: 291) and the repression against unionists and communists (see Introduction).

Amin tries to justify Zaghlul's heightened control over the press by pretending that he was in fact extremely lenient towards the papers that were attacking him. According to the narrator, it is only under pressure that 'Saad accepted to use his right, like any other citizen, to present a court case against the paper *al-Siyasa* representing the Liberal Constitutionalists' (370).

Presented as intrinsically righteous and liberal, Zaghlul is not only elevated above power struggles, but also above class belonging and political affiliation. At once a pasha and a *fallah*, the narrator presents Zaghlul as a man proud of his peasant origins (104). This peasant identity is presented as key to Zaghlul's intuitive sense of connection with the people. Apart from the more radical leaders of the Wafd's secret organisation, he is the only one in his social milieu to be in tune with the people. Throughout the narrative, the narrator insistently highlights 'the *fallah* in Saad Zaghlul' as what allowed him to remain in tune with the immense majority of the people, a gift other politicians lacked: 'the peasant in Saad Zaghlul allowed him to feel . . . what the illiterate villager, who was planting his land with the hoe and the plough, was feeling' (101). What enabled him to do so is the fact that he does not share the dominant ideology of the time; he does 'not see in the worn-out faces of the peasants their weakness and thinness; as a peasant, he sees the spirit of determination and the ability to resist' (102).

Safiyya Zaghlul's Radicalism

Similarly to Saad's, Safiyya's character is romanticised through the little boy's perspective as a woman close to the people.[12] Although she is born to a pasha of Turkish descent who was prime minister for fourteen years under British rule, Safiyya is presented, like Saad, as a person naturally able to communicate with people from lower class backgrounds and understand their revolutionary mood. Immediately after Saad's arrest, Safiyya virulently expresses her dismay at the behaviour of her lady friends who adopt an attitude of lamentation, insult the people and display a lack of confidence in the very possibility of a revolution (163).

Amin's memoirs confirm that Safiyya Zaghlul was 'a formidable political actor in her own right' (Ramdani 2013: 47). He depicts her as the central brain of the struggle after her husband's exile. While tradition would require that she receives no male visitors in the absence of her husband, she decides to open *Bayt al-Umma* to the Wafdist activists. On the night of Saad's arrest, she calls 'Ali Sha'rawi and urges him to act as if 'Saad did not leave'; '*Bayt al-Umma* has to remain the house of the people', she insists.[13] Moreover, the narrator depicts Safiyya Zaghlul in radical terms, as a woman who put all her might into the battle against the Wafd's moderate wing. He repeatedly underlines her firm positioning in the revolution, presenting her as more radical than Saad and narrating a few anecdotes relating to their political disagreements. Safiyya for instance several times ostensibly left the house when Saad received political figures she considered as traitors to the revolution.[14]

The fact that people overwhelmingly welcomed her political engagement is an indicator of the flexibility of gender boundaries during the revolution. Indeed, while leaders of the Wafd opposed the idea that Safiyya should succeed Saad at the head of the party on account that this would be badly received by the people,[15] Safiyya appears in *Min Wahid li-'Ashara* as a popular leader. When she is finally allowed to join her husband during his second exile on 8 October 1922, 'inhabitants of villages on the train line from Cairo to Port Said came out' to greet her and her train 'was covered with bodies raising the flag' (285). From the windows of the train, she urged people to remain mobilised: 'if the revolution continues Saad will live and come back. If the revolution dies, he will die in exile and never come back' (285). Her engagement in the revolution is emblematic of that of hundreds of thousands of lesser known women, either as organisers or demonstrators. In *Min Wahid li-'Ashara*, women's participation in the anti-colonial struggle is not restricted to upper middle classes as in dominant narratives (see Introduction, Chapters 3 and 4). Rather, women from all social strata are involved, and the narrator gives several examples of women in popular neighbourhoods actively participating in the struggle.[16]

Intertextuality with the 'Text of the Revolution'

Amin's memoir is as much focused on the political events as it is on the characters of his grandparents. *Min Wahid li-'Ashara* carefully documents the revolution, including meticulous and detailed description of the settings, actors involved, clothing, slogans and songs. His vivid depiction of the struggle unsettles the canonical images I investigated in Chapters 3 and 4. The revolution is not evolving around a series of pacific Cairene demonstrations, nor is the trope of national unity central to its representation. Rather, it is an extraordinary event, chaotic, bloody and joyful; it is an outburst of popular violence in which women, underprivileged city dwellers and peasants play a key role.

The revolutionary scenes are either heard of by the two boys or personally witnessed by them inside *Bayt al-Umma*, from its balconies, or in the streets of Dumyat, their father's city where they would often spend a few months.[17] Many of the scenes are based on stories the little boys heard at *Bayt al-Umma*. In that case, they are identified as reported speech: 'the news began to flow' (168) or 'news was falling as rain' (168). Other scenes are based on events they personally witnessed, like those from the balcony, where they remain stationed for days and nights. A balcony is a space where one is in a sense 'already in the street', as it has 'more to do with public space than with private space' (Sansot 1994: 364). Their presence on that balcony is symbolic, first of all, of their situation as children; as they are not always allowed on the streets, the balcony becomes an ideal observatory. Moreover, it is symbolic of the blurring of boundaries between public and private that characterises their situation, as their home became a public space. Finally, it is symbolic of the narrator's situation as a writer of memoirs, a genre situated at the conjunction of the public and the private. More specifically, it metaphorically encapsulates Amin's narrative about the 1919 revolution, which is the product of both personal, private memories and a careful documenting of the public sphere.

Amin often inserts songs and slogans chanted by anonymous people on the streets into his narrative,[18] thereby achieving an intertextuality with 'the text of the revolution' (Mehrez 2012). He is not content with referring to the title or first verses of these songs; rather, he inserts entire stanzas in the text, thereby integrating parts and pieces of the revolution's actors' collective *parole* (Heshmat 2015: 71). Intertextuality in this context contributes to widening the scope of the actors whose memory he aims to preserve beyond those listed in the dominant historiography, and even beyond less well-known activists,[19] encompassing the anonymous voices on the streets. This allows him to document the revolution in a way alternative to the dominant narrative, on the level of both form and content.

Amin's narrative does not conform to the dominant trope of an idealised nationalist unity. Instead of glorifying national unity marches, it is chaos, conflict and carnival that prevails in *Min Wahid li-'Ashara*. The protests that erupt on 9 March 1919 are so big that they immediately turn into chaotic scenes. The situation is not at all under control of the Wafd leaders, who are 'terrified' by the students' statement that they will free Saad and his companions by force if need be (169). Nor is it framed as a series of demonstrations led by the effendiyya. Rather, it involves all social classes, with many actors of the turmoil coming from the ranks of the urban underprivileged and the peasantry. The dress metaphor Amin uses to describe the demonstrators illustrates the breadth of the mobilisations and their all-encompassing character, expanding the one used by Mahfouz in his depiction of the 8 April demonstration (see Chapter 3). '*Tarabish wa 'ama'im wa tawaqi wa lasat*' (169): to the effendiyya's *tarabish* and the imams' *'ama'im*, a metaphor for the unity between secularist and religious middle-class as occurs in Mahfouz' novel, Amin adds the *tawaqi* and the *lasat*, headgear of the popular classes – whether peasants or workers.

Instead of being led by student activists or even radical young women as in al-Imam's adaptation of *Bayn al-Qasrayn*, the crowds in *Min Wahid li-'Ashara* are an independent actor nearly impossible to tame, recalcitrant to negotiations. Frightening at times, the people are brave and tough. And they are 'mad' because they take unreasonable risks in facing the repression: 'some of the persons who call themselves reasonable were terrorised by these mad people! People who do not pay attention to bullets, who embrace canons and fight to obtain the honour of a death sentence by the English' (189). Popular revolutionary violence is presented in a positive light and the demonstrators' immediate, spontaneous violent reaction is depicted as a natural part of the struggle against the colonial power.

During the first days of the revolution, students attack British soldiers, knocking them off their horses (168); in the cities, people systematically destroy streetlamps and tram cars (169); women in popular neighbourhoods gather stones to provide the demonstrators with improvised weapons (169). Peasants cut the railway lines, put up barricades on the main roads and attack the British army's granaries (170). The people's radicalism does not merely materialise in their outburst of violence against colonial soldiers; rather, it pervades everything. Amin reports numerous acts of rebellion towards the authorities: Egyptian policemen refuse to open fire on the demonstrators (170) and the province of Minya declares its independence (170); on 11 March, working class strikes begin (173). Radicalism is also expressed in the people's sharp awareness of their interests and their refusal of negotiations, which necessarily triggers conflict, including inside the Wafd.

One of the scenes directly witnessed by the little boys from the balcony embodies this theme. One day, as the situation continued to escalate, 'the street suddenly split and three thousand *fallahin* in their blue *gallabiyas* appeared, carrying sticks, branches and hoes, shaking them in the air' (173); they came walking from Qalyub 'to avenge the innocent people killed by British bullets' (174). The twins stood behind 'Abd al-'Aziz Fahmi, one of the moderate Wafd leaders, as he gave a thirty-minute speech from the balcony, trying to 'calm' the masses and to convince them 'to let the Wafd strive for Egypt's good by legal means' (174). After the angry crowd standing in the street replied with a thundering shout of 'revolution, revolution, revolution', the kids saw 'Abd al-'Aziz throw his *tarbush* in fury while Safiyya laughed herself to tears (174). This episode illustrates the people's radical spontaneity, and the fact that the Wafd was largely overwhelmed by this revolutionary energy, which in turn triggered conflicts in the party that was leading the nationalist struggle. According to another testimony, it is Safiyya Zaghlul, representing the Wafd's more radical wing, depicted as sympathetic to the people – who finally managed to convince the angry crowd to return home.[20]

The revolution however is not reduced to revolutionary chaos or political conflict. It is depicted as a gigantic carnival which the two children enjoy to the utmost. Women are dancing on the streets, theatre troops perform on the sidewalk, and people are singing irreverent songs ridiculing the British, the King, and even the effandiyya's political naiveté.[21] Moreover, Amin depicts the revolution as an intoxicating, pleasurable event, likening it to 'wine': 'once you drink a glass you want more' (189). The metaphor aptly translates the *extraordinary* aspect of the revolution and underlines it as an interruption in the linear march of things, a disruption of the monotonous and dull daily lives. Instead of serious demonstrations imbued with a sense of duty and national unity, street protest is linked with joy and pleasure, in addition to anger and pain.

Autobiographical Recollections of the Revolution

This carnivalesque spirit Amin meticulously documents is exceptional among most autobiographical recollections of the revolution. This is partly due to the fact that this is a childhood memoir, attempting to capture the way a little boy experienced the revolution, often in a light, playful mode. More fundamentally, it is due to the fact that the memoirs are not written by well-known actors of the events. Memoirs by public figures are composed in an apologetic tone, as 'the narrator affirms and tries to justify his or her past actions' (Couser 2012: 40). They often focus on the protagonist's (the narrated I of the past)'s actions, decision-making processes and social relationships. Their authors are less concerned with documenting the outside than with justifying their past deeds.

Many leaders of the Wafd and of its secret organisation left autobiographical texts, most of which are 'memoirs of public office', as Lucie Ryzova calls them. These narratives are by definition more concerned with institutional politics than with what was going on in the streets; in addition, they most often avoid the personal in their treatment of the political. Typically, autobiographies 'by well-known men' are 'written for public consumption' (Omar 2014: 297).[22] The most extreme example is 'Abd al-Rahman Fahmi's (1870–1946) autobiography.

Writing in a pompous style, the secretary general of the Wafd and the leader of its secret organisation[23] gives a rich account of the political period, including hundreds of historical documents and detailed reports of the negotiations between the Wafd leaders and the British. Published more than forty years after his death, the three volumes of his autobiography contain some depictions of street protests but are devoid of personal stories. According to historian Yunan Labib Rizq, the text does not even deserve its autobiographical label and could easily be titled 'Egypt's political diary from 13 November 1918 till 23 August 1927' (22). Rizq further underlines that he finds it astonishing that the man he calls 'the Wafd's dynamo' does not write a word about what was arguably his central contribution to the anti-colonial struggle: his patient construction of the underground organisation of the Wafd (Rizq 1988: 24). Finally, 'Abd al-Rahman Fahmi frames his narrative with two dates that are less significant to his personal life than to Egypt's institutional politics: the text begins with the Wafd's visit to British High Commissioner Reginald Wingate and ends with Zaghlul's death.[24]

The personal tends to occupy a more significant space in autobiographical narratives by leaders of the Wafd's women's organisation and by lesser-known actors of the revolutionary uprising, although they display similarly apologetic dynamics. Among those texts, the most canonical remains Huda Sha'rawi's, who became famous as a leading figure of the Egyptian feminist movement.[25] Married at fourteen to her much older cousin 'Ali Sha'rawi, a leader of the Wafd, Huda became involved in the nationalist movement and recalls in her autobiography how she organised, with Safiyya Zaghlul and women from the upper middle class, the women's demonstration of March 1919.[26] Similarly, autobiographical narratives by lesser-known cadres of the Wafd contain detailed depictions of their personal militant experiences. 'Iryan Yusuf Sa'd's autobiography is one of the few available prison narratives about the 1919 revolution. Sa'd became famous after his (failed) assassination attempt against Yusuf Wahba Pasha, who had broken the nationalist consensus by accepting the offer of becoming prime minister in 1919. Published in 2007, the narrative is constructed around this central act and relates in great detail the years 'Iryan passed in prison.[27]

Paradoxically, among the Wafdist leaders' autobiographical narratives, it is Saad's diary, published in 1987 under the title *Mudhakkirat Saad Zaghlul (The Memoirs of Saad Zaghlul)*, that emerges as one of the most personal and least apologetic texts. As a genre, the diary indeed tends to be less apologetic. Unlike other autobiographical narratives, it conveys a sense of 'immediacy'; presumably, the diarist writes down all that goes through his or her head, without previous selection work (Sinor 2005: 191).[28] In addition to lengthy reports about his political conflicts and meticulous depictions of his daily life – especially during exile, the diaries reveal intimate ordeals and painful conflicts with Safiyya because of his gambling addiction, which probably explains why he did not wish to publish them.

Among the diaries of the 1919 revolution, a text by Shaykh 'Abd al-Wahab al-Naggar (1862–1941), *al-Ayyam al-Hamra' (The Red Days)*, serialised between March and May 1933 in *al-Balagh*, the Wafd's journal, and republished in 2010, is worth mentioning. The text is written in the form of daily entries in which the author, a recognised figure at al-Azhar well-connected in the political sphere, meticulously notes down all his observations about the turmoil between 15 March and 23 June 1919, providing in particular a detailed account of the civil servants' strike. The narrator gives ample space to the voices of the actors of the revolution themselves, as the text reproduces speeches by successive orators at al-Azhar and content of leaflets.

By its meticulous documenting, *Min Wahid li 'Ashara* shares many similarities with al-Naggar's diary. However, *Min Wahid li-'Ashara* is a text written nearly sixty years after the events, rearticulating them in the context of the post-Nasser years. It at once rehabilitates Saad Zaghlul as an icon of the anti-colonial struggle, and meticulously documents the revolution to address the fact that 'fifty years later, the names of the martyrs of the 1919 revolution [had] not yet been given to any *hara* or street in any village in Egypt' (278). In this way it resonates with the attempts at 'rewriting history' in narratives about the 1919 revolution published or screened in the decades following the 1967 defeat, which I will go on to analyse in the following chapter.

Notes

1. For Amin's arrest see Kirk J. Beattie (1994), *Egypt During the Nasser Years: Ideology, Politics and Civil Society*. Oxford: Westview. Beattie notes that the powerful journalist Muhammad Husayn Haykal deals at great length with Amin's case in his book *Bayna al-Sahafa wal-Siyasa* and 'implies that Amin did not deserve being labelled a CIA stooge' (note 145, p. 206). Beattie further notes that 'Amin had long maintained CIA contacts at Nasser's behest, as had Heikal, so the incident seems to have had more to do with signalling the United States and punishing Amin for his suggestion that cancellation of wheat shipments would bring Nasser to his knees, rather than with any broad attack on Rightist journalists, although a few others close to Amin were affected by this affair' (185).
2. According to Amin, it remains unclear whether or not Zaghlul had given his approval for a systematic assassination policy or was even aware of the role the underground organisation played in those assassinations. However, Amin states that Zaghlul repeatedly refused to condemn these acts (Amin 1991: 68–9).

3. *Asrar Thawrat 1919* is mainly based on the secret correspondence between Saad Zaghlul and the Wafd's secretary general, 'Abd al-Rahman Fahmi. This correspondence was also published by historian Muhammad Anis in a book titled *Dirasat fi Watha'iq Thawrat 1919, al-Murasalat al-Sirriyya bayn Saad Zaghlul wa 'Abd al-Rahman Fahmi*, Cairo: Maktabat al-Anglo al-Misriyya, 1963 and Dar al-Shuruq, 2019. It is interesting to note that it was published in 1963, the year *Asrar Thawrat 1919* was banned.
4. For prison narratives, see Isabella Camera D'Afflitto (1998), 'Prison Narratives: Autobiography and Fiction', in Robin Ostle Ed de Moor and Stefan Wild (eds), *Writing the Self: Autobiographical Writing in Modern Arabic Literature*, London: Saqi Books, pp. 148–56; Sha'ban Yusuf (2014), *Adab al-Sujun*. Cairo: al-Hay'a al-Misriyya al-'Amma lil-Kitab, and Banipal 50 (2014) *Prison Writing*, which contains extracts of Sun'alla Ibrahim's *Yaumiyyat al-Wahat* (*Diaries of Oasis Prison*) and Sherif Hetata's *Al-Nawafidh al-Maftuha* (*The Open Windows*) in English translation.
5. Among other titles: *al-Anisa Kaf* (*Miss K,* 1985), *al-Anisa Hayam* (*Miss Hayam,* 1989) and *Nijmat al-Jamahir* (*The Star of the People*, 1989). Some of these novels were written while in prison and serialised in *Akhbar al-Yawm* after Amin's release. In addition, Amin authored film and series scripts.
6. The book starts with an introduction provocatively titled 'this is not a book' in which Amin presents the text as a 'journalistic reportage about the cheerful life America was living before the war' (1). The trip, which he went on together with his father Amin Yusuf who was an attaché at the Egyptian embassy, had a lasting influence on Amin's personality. Amin published a second edition of this book under a slightly different title: *Amrika al-Dahika Zaman. Mudhakkirat Talib Muflis fil-Wilayat al-Muttahida* (*Cheerful America of the Past: Journal of a Penniless Student in the United States of America*), Jeddah: al-Dar al-Sa'udiyya lil-Nashr wal Tawzi', 1985). Memoirs of studying abroad are a prolific genre in Arabic Literature. See for instance: Louis Awad (1965), *Mudhakkirat Talib Bi'tha*, Cairo: Mu'assasat Ruz al-Yusuf, and Radwa 'Ashur (1983), *al-Rihla: Ayyam Taliba Misriyya fi Amrika*, Beirut, Dar al-Adab. For representations of America in Arabic narratives, see Kamal Abdel-Malek (2000), *America in an Arab Mirror: Images of America in Arabic Travel Literature: an Anthology, 1895–1995*. New York: St. Martin's Press; also Rasheed El-Enany's *Arab Representations of the Occident* (London: Routledge, 2006).
7. See Tetz Rooke (1998), 'The Arabic Autobiography of Childhood' in Robin

Ostle, Ed de Moor and Stefan Wild (eds) *Writing the Self Autobiographical Writing in Modern Arabic Literature*, London: Saqi Books, pp. 100–14.
8. In addition, the narrator provides many detailed descriptions of the way Saad Zaghlul was perceived. During one of their stays in the city of Dumyat, he relates that people on the street touched them as if for a blessing when they learnt they were Zaghlul's relatives. He writes that 'all the people in Dumyat want to hear about 'the venerated' (*al-ma'bud*) whom they had not got a chance to see. Some imagine he is a jinn (*marid*) . . ., some insist that he is a prophet (*nabi*) . . . and others say he is a saint (*qiddis*)' (206).
9. This reference is cited in an article by Gabir 'Usfur (2009), 'Thawrat 1919 ba'd 90 'Aman: al-Aqbat wal Thawra', *al-Shuruq*, Cairo, 18 June.
10. The gambling addiction of Zaghlul is commonly dealt with by historians and journalists and also referred to in contemporary narratives addressing larger audiences. See for instance Muhsin (2009) and the episode about the 1919 revolution in *Madrasat al-Mushaghibin*, a programme presented by the journalist Ibrahim 'Isa.
11. One could however argue that the years between 1919 and 1923, the years of revolution, were a period in which Zaghlul ceased gambling. In addition, Amin alludes several times to this gambling addiction in the second volume of his memoirs, *Min 'Ashara li-'Ishrin*.
12. For Safiyya Zaghlul, see Beth Baron (2005), *Egypt as a Woman: Nationalism, Gender, and Politics*, Berkeley, CA: University of California Press. Chapter 6 is titled 'Umm al-Misriyyin' and is entirely devoted to Safiyya Zaghlul, and Fina Gued Vidal, *Safia Zagloul*, Cairo: Schindler (no publication date available).
13. See also Huda Sha'arawi's autobiography (Sha'rawi 2013: 119).
14. Naguib Mahfouz relates the same incident (al-Naqqash 2011: 190)
15. Amin relates the debates in the Wafd after Saad Zaghlul's death in 1927 in the second volume of his autobiography.
16. Amin devotes part of a chapter in *Asrar Thawrat 1919* to 'the role of women in the secret organisation' (Amin 1991: 327).
17. Amin rarely cites sources for his reporting. Sometimes, the narrative functions as a 'family narrative' probably transmitted to Mustafa by Safiyya.
18. The students' song, '*ya 'am Hamza, ahna al-talamdha*' (O 'Am Hamza, We Are the Students',169), later sung by poet Ahmad Fu'ad Nijm and Sheikh Imam and the song 'Pardon Wingate' (187), among other songs.
19. Throughout the narrative, Amin makes a conscious effort to relate acts of bravery

and militancy by lesser-known figures – like the worker Ahmad Gadallah, a member of the secret organisation who carried out a number of assassinations on British soldiers.
20. See note 2, p. 52.
21. Like this song: '*khud al-bizza wa-skut, khud al-bizza wa nam, ya wad ya illi bi ti'ra gurnal al-ahram*' (take the tit and shut up, take the tit and sleep, you lad! you who read Al-Ahram, 189).
22. Hussein Omar cites memoirs by 'Isma'il Sidqi Pasha, Muhammad Farid Bey, Ahmad 'Urabi Pasha, Ahmad Shafiq Pasha and Muhammad Husayn Haykal' (Omar 2014: 311).
23. 'Abd al-Rahman Fahmi was an officer in the Egyptian army. For more about his military education and other elements of his biography, see Anis (2019), Introduction.
24. A recurrent feature of autobiographical narratives by Wafdist leaders is to put Zaghlul at the centre of the narrative as they reconstruct their narrated selves around their relationship with him. Mustafa al-Nahhas (1879–1965), head of the Wafd after Zaghlul, goes so far as to make his autobiography begin in 1927, after the mythical leader's death. Similarly, the subtitle of Fakhri 'Abd al-Nur's memoirs, which depicts the author's contribution to the political struggle between 1919 and 1924, is telling in that regard: 'The 1919 Revolution, the Role of Saad Zaghlul and the Wafd in the Nationalist Movement'. A Wafdist leader from a big landowning family in Suhag, 'Abd al-Nur begins his text with a chapter titled 'How and When I met Saad'. The figure of Saad Zaghlul thus systematically overshadows the autobiographical selves of his closest companions, obliterating many personal elements.
25. Another autobiography by a female public figure who took part in the 1919 revolution is that of Ruz al-Yusuf (1897–1958), a pioneer in the fields of theatre and journalism, who devotes a short passage to the artists' demonstration in 1919. See Fatima al-Yusuf (2010), *Dhikrayat*, Cairo: Ruz al-Yusuf, pp. 61–2. A special edition of *al-Musawwar*, published on the occasion of the revolution's fiftieth anniversary, contains testimonies by ten women who participated in the revolution, including Ceiza Nabarawi (1897–1985), a feminist figure and close friend of Huda Sha'rawi, Hidiya Barakat (1898–1969) and Esther Wisa (1895–1990) (*al-Musawwar*, 7/3/1969, pp. 44–7).
26. About Huda Sha'rawi's autobiography, see Introduction, note 20.
27. 'Iryan's text is one of the few prison narratives currently available about the

1919 revolution. Many documents, in addition to Zaghlul's diaries, are available about the Wafdist leader's life in exile, but not much about the life of the hundreds and thousands of activists who spent months and years in prison, many of them awaiting death sentences.

28. There are a few exceptions to this. Hussein Omar provides an interesting insight into Fathallah Barakat's autobiography, astonishingly much more personal than his diaries, which 'were a detached record of things as he had seen them, with little space for emotion or internality' (Omar 2014: 297).

6

Rewriting History in the 1990s

In January 1998, Salah Tawfiq, Zifta deputy in the People's Assembly, deposed an early-day motion to the then-Information Minister, Safwat al-Sharif. The deputy was angered by the television series *Gumhuriyyat Zifta* ('The Republic of Zifta'). Screened during Ramadan 1998, the series narrates a well-known episode of the anti-colonial struggle in 1919, during which the Delta city of Zifta issued a declaration of independence from the occupied monarchic Egypt, established a self-governance system and nominated Yusuf al-Gindi, a lawyer from the village, as its president.[1] The deputy wished to bring to the attention of the Assembly what he deemed to be 'historical mistakes' in the series. 'The character of Hishmat Basha, the Turkish pasha who, according to the series, represses and humiliates the peasants, never existed', the deputy protested. On the contrary, there were '22 pashas at the time in Zifta, and they played an important role in the national movement'.[2]

The figure of the evil pasha, however, did not bother all inhabitants of Zifta. Muhammad al-Gindi, the son of Yusuf al-Gindi, lauded 'the positive values embedded in the series' (al-Gindi 1998: 70). *Gumhuriyyat Zifta* was further welcomed in the media as 'a truly nationalist work' (Fadl 1998). Interestingly, many articles interpreted the series as a commentary on the contemporary situation. 'I do not consider it a historical work', Bilal Fadl argued. 'Rather, I see it as a contemporary work that deals with the heroism of the Egyptian citizen who remains capable of endurance in the face of oppression, despotism and occupation', he added (Fadl 1998). Under the title '*Gumhuriyyat Zifta* Confronts the New World Order', another columnist found the Britain of the past to be very similar to the 'new international order' controlling 'our present through the one force represented by the US' (Abu Bakr 1998). The scriptwriter of the series, Yusri al-Gindi, stated that his work was 'an expression of a real necessity to awaken patriotism', as well as likening the US to Britain (Gabir 1998: 25).

Fadl further commented on the social problematic of the series, noting that it 'came as an indirect tribute to the sacrifices of the Egyptian peasants, faced with a law seeking to expel them' (Fadl 1998). The year 1997 had witnessed broad peasant mobilisations against the implementation of a new law for land rent that 'abolished hitherto secure tenancies, and allowed for market forces to be the sole determinant of rent value' (Saad 2016: 4).[3] The implementation of the law left one million families (almost 10 per cent of the population then) 'without their main source of livelihood' (Saad 2016: 5). Peasants who refused to leave land plots they had in some cases been planting for decades were heavily repressed. The Land Centre, an NGO concerned with agrarian laws, brought together hundreds of testimonies and complaints by peasants about the violence to which they had been subjected. The following complaint, from a village falling under the Zifta administrative centre, is a good illustration:

> on 12 October 1997 Hassan Anwar, landowner, beat six women to force them to leave their land and sign a declaration in that sense. Mirvat Mardani, Nafisa Hassan and Alya Mitwalli then went to the police station in Zifta [to file a complaint] . . . but the police chief refused to write an official report about the facts and interned them for 48 hours, forcing them to sign a statement asserting they would leave the land.[4]

In *Gumhuriyyat Zifta*, Salim Abul Nur is arrested and tortured when he refuses to sell his cotton to the pasha at lower than market rate. In the same manner as the police chief of the same town did in 1997, in 1918 the police chief sought to force Abul Nur to submit to the landowners' law. The series tells the story of Abul Nur and the Zifta peasants' resistance to this complex network of colonial and feudal power. Shying away from the narrative of nationalist unity as previously recounted, it presents the peasants as the real heroes of the 1919 revolution. I argue that the series rewrites the history of 1919 in the context of a systematic erosion of the social benefits acquired by the working and rural underprivileged classes under the Nasser regime. Annihilating the Nasserist experience, the neoliberal violence of the present allows for a new understanding of the colonial feudal violence of the past.

With its exacerbated class struggle in the countryside, the present permits a re-articulation of the class struggles of the past.

In this chapter, I examine narratives about 1919 published, performed or screened after the 1967 defeat. In addition to *Gumhuriyyat Zifta*, I analyse a play by Sa'd al-Din Wahba, *al-Masamir* (*The Nails*, 1967), a novel by Mustafa Musharrafa, *Qantara al-Ladhi Kafara* (*Qantara the Infidel*, 1966) and a novel by Amin 'Izz al-Din, *al-Faylaq* (*The Legion*, 1999). I argue that these works, though belonging to different genres, can all be read as sites for rewriting the history of 1919. Furthermore, I show that, although published, performed and aired three decades apart, they each articulate the revolution in a similar way, most prominently by questioning the leading role of the upper middle class in the nationalist movement. The play and both novels rewrite history in a militant mode, and identify resistance, including armed resistance, as the only way to induce change. In contrast, the television series *Gumhuriyyat Zifta* presents the 1919 history in a moralistic and emotional mode, which narrates the revolution in a nostalgic tone characteristic of the post-*Infitah* committed culture.

Rewriting History in the Context of the Post-Nasser Dream

The new tenancy law was implemented exactly three decades after the *Naksa*, the 1967 defeat. The 1967 war, which led to the destruction of most of 'the infrastructure of the Egyptian armed forces, especially the grounded air force' (Roussillon 1998: 357), the occupation of the Sinai, the West Bank, Eastern Jerusalem, Gaza and the Golan Heights, came as a painful surprise. It laid bare the deficiencies of the Nasser regime and the lies of its propaganda system as to its invincible military forces. This had

> contradictory consequences on the relationship between the intellectuals and the state. On the one hand, it 'reinforced their adhesion to the objectives of the 1952 revolution', but on the other, it weakened the regime's legitimacy and led intellectuals to demand the right to be consulted on how the crisis should be managed. (Jacquemond 2008: 21)

The defeat delegitimised the state's ambition to present itself as embodying the nationalist struggles of the past (see Chapter 4). The credibility of the state in leading a social project in addition to the nationalist one was further weakened by the *Infitah*, the open-door policy initiated by Sadat in 1971, which consisted of encouraging foreign investments and ending public-sector monopoly on a series of activities, and was the cornerstone of the regime's 'project to dismantle the system of redistribution set up by the Nasserist state' (Roussillon 1998: 363). It also had drastic consequences for the living conditions of large parts of the population, mainly because of the concomitant inflation, which led to an impoverishment of the middle classes and threw large sections of society into marginality. The eighties and nineties witnessed an acceleration of this liberalisation policy, which the Mubarak regime further implemented through a series of agreements with the International Monetary Fund (IMF) and the World Bank.

Although these post-Nasserist policies provoked a popular revolt on 17 and 18 January 1977 against the price rise of first necessity products, the years after that remained mostly quiet in terms of social dissent. This was due in part to the government implementing its liberal policies 'more tactfully and progressively, avoiding the shock effect that had done much to unleash people's anger' in 1977 (Roussillon 1998: 363), but also because the rise of the Islamist movement and the armed confrontation between such forces and the regime had muted other dissident voices. At the end of the nineties, however, the broad peasant mobilisation of 1997 marked a new rise in social movements. Moreover, a significant number of opposition writers took advantage of the relative opening in the freedom of the press made by the Mubarak regime starting in 1981 (Jacquemond 2008: 25). This allowed opposition voices to emerge, most of them critical of the regime's alignment with global neo-liberal and geo-strategic policies dictated by the US. Some of these voices were previously close to the Nasser regime, or had even occupied key positions, but were now relegated to the margins of the system after the systematic purges led by Sadat.

The post-1967 period is also a period that witnessed systematic questioning of the state's narrative about history. This project was first shouldered by the sixties generation, 'a new generation fed on a new ideology, a new rhetoric, and a new self-image' (Mehrez 1994: 98), whose political consciousness and aesthetics were shaped both by the ideology and failures of the Nasserist project. Brought up in the realm of the Nasser regime, that generation was the one most marked by the shock of the defeat. Its members were in their twenties during the student demonstrations of February 1968, which demanded the judgement of 'those responsible for the Six Days defeat', in addition to 'the reestablishment of political freedoms' (Roussillon 1998: 358).

As I noted in the introduction of this book, this generation systematically invested in literature's potential space to express an alternative view to the state's totalitarian narrative about history. Samia Mehrez shows how the novel provided a forum for producing an alternative history (Mehrez 1994: 7). Other scholars studying Arabic literature underline the potential of literature as a depositary of 'truth'. In her study of three fictional accounts of Nixon's visit to Egypt, Noha Radwan contends for 'a place for fiction in the historical archive' – as she states in the title of her article. These novellas, she argues, are 'part of a counter-discourse to the hegemonic narrative of Egypt's socio-economic and political development' (Radwan 2008: 81). A congress of the European Association for Modern Arabic Literature, focusing on 'History and Fiction,' held in Naples in 2018, featured several contributions about novels presented as effectively contributing to write an alternative history.[5]

Other genres have also been invested with historical ambitions. According to Joel Gordon, television series began to be increasingly devoted to historical topics towards the end of the 1980s: 'the 1990s arguably marked a moment in Egyptian television when the country turned its attention increasingly (although never monolithically) toward historical serials as a means of recreating and reinterpreting modern Egyptian history' (Gordon 2018: 76). Lila Abu-Lughod confirms that this interest was not monolithic. Rather, 'the 1990s signify a particular complex political moment in Egypt's national history when the hegemony of one vision, of which state media was to be an instrument, was seriously eroding' (Abu-Lughod 2005: 15). Television drama became a privileged site for the expression of often 'revisionist' – to use Gordon's terms- readings of history. This space was particularly invested by writers who were ideologically close to the Nasserist project, like Usama Anwar 'Ukasha (1942–2010). One of 'Ukasha's most acclaimed works, *Layali al-Hilmiyya* (*Hilmiyya Nights*) attempts to rewrite Egypt's modern history starting in the 1940s. This ambition caused the series staff problems with the official censors, whose 'requests focused on removing lines in which President Nasser was praised or defended by sympathetic characters' and objecting to 'scenes suggesting criticism of President Sadat and his policies'

(Abu-Lughod 2005 17).⁶ *Gumhuriyyat Zifta*'s scriptwriter, Yusri al-Gindi, can be credited with an ideological background similar to 'Ukasha's. In addition to *Gumhuriyyat Zifta*, al-Gindi authored a number of historical series, many of which denote a particular interest in the themes of social justice and anti-colonial struggle, like *'Abdalla al-Nadim* (1982), a leading figure of the 'Urabi revolt in 1881, or *'Ali al-Zaybaq* (1985), a Robin Hood-like character in an Arabic popular story. Before examining al-Gindi's historical adaptation of 1919 on the small screen, however, I will discuss a play rewriting the 1919 revolution some three decades earlier, in addition to two novels respectively published in 1966 and 1999.

Al-Masamir (*The Nails*) or the Cathartic Defeat of Resistance

On 12 June 1967, only days after the defeat in the war against Israel, playwright Sa'd al-Din Wahba sat at his desk and wrote *al-Masamir* (*The Nails*).⁷ A reenactment of some dark moments of the 1919 revolution in the Egyptian countryside, the play was performed on the stage of the National Theatre during the 1967–8 season. Directed by Saad Ardash, the casting brought together several theatre stars from the period. Staged fifty-two times and seen by 12,512 viewers ('Ashri 1973: 10), the play became a fair success.⁸ Witnesses recall Nasser attending the performance several times, with the audience applauding enthusiastically, more specifically at a passage of the end of the first act, in which actress Samiha Ayyub addresses the hero in a weeping voice: 'Stay strong, 'Abdalla, the people want you, all the people are with you' (*islub tulak ya Abdallah, al-nas bitnadik ya 'Abdalla*).⁹ As underlined by Marxist critic Mahmud Amin al-'Alim (1922–2009) in his preface to the published script, the play had a cathartic quality: 'it carried the pulse of the disaster that releases all powerful emotions in the soul' (al-'Alim 1967:ta'). *Al-Masamir* portrays the 1919 revolution as a painful defeat, literally echoing the events of June 1967.¹⁰ Most importantly, it shifts the perspective from which the revolution is most often narrated. It replaces the efendiyya perspective by that of disenfranchised peasants, identifying the peasants as the revolution's main actors and celebrating the importance of resistance.

Sa'd al-Din Wahba (1925–97) is considered an important figure of the 1960s theatre, and a well-known scriptwriter.¹¹ Wahba was close to the Nasser regime; he served as a police officer from 1949 to 1956 and occupied several

Figure 6.1 Samiha Ayyub in the role of Fatima and 'Abdalla Ghayth in the role of 'Abdalla on her left. From the Archives of the Centre for Theatre and Music, Cairo.

official positions after his resignation. He pursued a degree in philosophy at the beginning of the fifties, was the director of publication of *al-Jumhuriyya* between 1961 and 1964 and then occupied several leading posts in the Ministry of Culture. Before *al-Masamir*, he had written a few plays that can be interpreted as interventions in the ongoing debates during the Nasser era: *Kafr al-Battikh* (1962) and *al-Sibinsa* (*The Guard's Van*, 1962). One of his most famous plays, *Sikkat al-Salama* (*The Road of Safety*, 1965), is considered to have raised the alarm about the future *Naksa*.

Despite Wahba's close relationship to the regime, the government censors attempted to stop the performances of *al-Masamir*. In a preface to the play published in his collected works (1997), Wahba recalls that the censor, Mustafa Darwish, saw in *al-Masamir* an attack on the president and the regime. However, the minister of culture in charge at the time, Tharwat 'Ukasha[12] did not heed the censor's concerns and issued orders to the National theatre to go on with the performance.[13] A day before the curtain was lifted on *al-Masamir*, the newspaper *Akhbar al-Yaum* published an article stating that 'the director of censorship' announced he would 'request the police to stop the performance of *al-Masamir* despite the approval of the Minister' (Wahba 1997: 138). The threatening declarations notwithstanding, the performance went on for several months.

The reception of *al-Masamir* shows that it was understood as a play in which the events of the 1919 revolution were used to comment on, and interact with, the contemporary defeat, 'with the objective of feeding the spirit of resistance' ('Ukasha 2004: 741). In the words of 'Ukasha, Saad al-Din Wahba 'courageously dealt with the defeat through another catastrophe that took place in a village of our countryside during the 1919 revolution' ('Ukasha 2004: 741). Al-'Alim's preface paved the way for this reading, as he described the play as 'a symbolic expression . . . of the reality of our current lives' (al-'Alim 1967: ya').[14]

Al-Masamir's rewriting of the past is at once a mirror of the disillusion of the present, and a tool with which to counter such disillusion. I argue that Wahba uses the 1919 revolution to comment on the contemporary context in an agitprop mode, appropriating the voices of the past in order to allow a cathartic experience for the audience and to encourage people not to lose hope, urging them to resist. In order to do so, Wahba changes the focalisation from which the revolution is most often narrated, by setting the events in a small Delta village and narrating them through the perspective of the villagers; this allows him to read the 1919 revolution as a defeat. He furthermore identifies the main actors of the 1919 revolution as underprivileged peasants, questioning the leading role most often attributed to *beys* and effendiyya by casting the village's bey in the role of a feudal figure collaborating with the British and its effendi as a late-comer to the struggle. Though the village community is defeated in its attempt to resist the British soldiers, it does not lose faith. The musical structure of the play, through the use of a popular anti-British slogan, is central, I contend, to its agitprop dynamics. By countering the mode of triumphant nationalism in which the 1919 revolution was previously narrated, *Al-Masamir* displays an original understanding of that event and questions the teleological narrative of the Nasser period, which portrayed it as merely a step in the march towards the achievements of the regime (see Chapter 4).

The historical ambitions of the play are contained in its epigraph, two paragraphs from 'Abd al-Rahman al-Rafi'i's *Thawrat Sanat 1919* (*The 1919 Revolution*, 1946). By quoting a detail from a famous history book about

1919, Wahba's objective is twofold: first, he states that what he is going to write has a 'referential' value, as it contends 'for a place within the discourse about what 'really' happened in Egypt' in 1919 (Radwan 2008: 79). Second, he states that what he is going to put at the very centre of his play is exactly what had previously been considered a 'detail', hence confined to the margins of the dominant narrative about 1919. What is of interest to him is not what happened in the capital, during its photogenic demonstrations, whose leaders have since been attributed street names, but rather what happened in two small villages of the Delta to unnamed people. The first paragraph narrates that on 26 March 1919, 'nearly 400 British soldiers came to the village of Kafr al-Shaykh' and settled in the school of the village with men and horses. Then, they proceeded to plunder the village and ordered 75 villagers to be flogged everyday' (Wahba 1967: 3). The second paragraph narrates how British soldiers, on 30 March 1919, arrested four men from the village of Nazlit al-Shubak, buried them to the waist and then shot them dead.

Al-Masamir is set during March and April 1919, in a small Delta village near Itay al-Barud simply named *al-kafr*, 'the hamlet'. Most of the play involves a discussion among a group of villagers about the strategies to follow in order to confront the British troops that settled on parts of their land. The main character, 'Abdalla, who is constructed as a peasant hero in the tradition of folk heroes, advocates the necessity to resist and attempts to organise his fellow peasants in order to do so. In the first act, he is isolated, supported only by his wife Fatima, her uncle Salim, and sheikh 'Abd al-Samad. In that first scene, the teacher Ramzi effendi is represented as someone who seeks peace with the coloniser, inviting 'Abdalla 'to think with reason' (30). The character of the bey, Zaydan, is portrayed as a collaborator with the colonial authorities, as well as his intendant Rashwan. But when Ramzi effendi announces that twenty-five men from the village will be flogged every day, ('land owners, civil servants and those who have done primary school are excepted' 34), the balance of power changes. George, the British chief of police forces Rashwan as well as Zaydan into the queue of men led to the flogging.

In the second act, set in the military shack, Zaydan is saved by Georges. Rashwan, however, is not spared, and gets flogged just like the rest of the men, which revives his nationalist consciousness. All of this encourages the peasants to act and attack the British troops. In the third act, which depicts the aftermath of that attack, some of the peasants begin quarrelling, while others accuse 'Abdalla of being responsible for the defeat.[15] As they leave the meeting infuriated, 'Ilwan and Mansur are arrested by the British, along with Salim. They are forced to dig a hole, are buried in it to the chest and sentenced to death. The play ends as the peasants are standing by helplessly while their loved ones are killed in the cruellest way.

The village is represented as totally isolated from the rest of the country. This element, in addition to the generic name of the place, *al-kafr*, highlights the allegorical quality of the play. The small village functions as an allegory of the nation, and the characters refer to the different social classes and strata involved in the Nasser regime – the *bey* embodying what was called 'the remnants of the old regime'. The play is entirely focalised through a small peasant community; from that perspective, upper middle-class characters appear devoid of nationalist sense. The *bey* is represented as a traitor to the nation, consistently identified as the source of all ills (73). He collaborates with the colonial authorities throughout the play and is therefore ostracised from the text's representation of the peasant community, symbolically sitting away from the peasants while waiting to be whipped, even though he is about to share their destiny.

The members of the middle-class eventually acquire a nationalist consciousness, however only through a transformational process triggered by a personal confrontation with colonial violence. In the first act, Ramzi effendi praises British civilisation and calls for a peaceful solution with the occupying soldiers. He begins to protest only when the soldiers use the school as a stable for their horses (75). He is then arrested and his stay in prison has a transformational value, as he meets other effendiyyas and a *bey* arrested for having resisted the orders of the colonial administration (an irrigation engineer and a representative of the local prosecution), or for having participated in an anti-colonial demonstration (a teacher) (90). As for Ramzi, with his stay in prison, for Rashwan it is the flogging that has a similar transformational value; he later confesses: 'I returned to my right mind when the first whip fell on my body' (103). The flogging in this case therefore acquires a purifying value, delivering the men from their illusions and weakness.

Paradoxically, despite its painful end, the play is not only a narrative of defeat; it also functions as a narrative of empowerment. The peasants do not give up resistance; more specifically, 'Abdalla manages, over the course of events, to gain over to his point of view those who were hesitant or even active at the other side of the divide. While some of *al-Masamir*'s heroes lose their life at the end of the play, they have gained their 'truth', their 'true ideology' to use Greimas' terms. This applies in particular to 'Ilwan and Mansur, at the beginning vehement opponents of 'Abdalla, who consistently state their opposition to his choice of resistance. Similar to what happens to Ramzi and Rashwan, it is when they are buried to the chest, waiting for the death sentence to be carried out, that their transformation takes place and that they gain their ideological truth. 'Ilwan expresses this most clearly, confessing to Salim that he 'was wrong' (158).

The popular anti-colonial slogan '*ya 'aziz ya 'aziz kubba takhud al-ingliz*' (O Aziz, o Aziz, may an epidemic befall the English'),[16] central to the play's structure, plays an important role in that agitprop dynamic. It is first shouted by Sab'awi (pp. 19 and 26), presented as 'the simple minded of the village', then by another peasant, Zaqzuq, at the end of Act 1 (68). The stage directions indicate that it is to be repeated by 'all the peasants', 'in a thunderous voice as they hurry to follow the line of men' who are led to the flogging. At the end of the first scene of Act 2, after the flogging (95), the first half of the slogan is chanted in a weeping voice by Fatima, the second half by the peasants, 'weakly but wilfully', according to the stage directions, before the curtain falls. At the end of the play, 'voices' are heard shouting it after Salim, Mansur and 'Ilwan are killed. The slogan thus functions as a structuring refrain, chanted collectively three times, before or after moments of colonial violence. Moreover, chanted at a moment that has much to share with the one the audience is experiencing – a dark, depressing moment in which the prospect of defeat seems insurmountable – the slogan acquires an agitprop dimension. The actors invite the audience not to lose faith in the importance of resistance.

In his first long monologue, 'Abadallah uses the metaphor of the nails as a sharp, harmful body, alien to the soil, to describe the internal conflicts in the village:

> Nails have been planted in our land, O men. When we walk, we walk on nails, when we eat, we eat nails, when we breathe, the nails remain stuck in the throat of each one of us, strangling him, killing him.

At the end of this monologue, he calls upon his fellow villagers to remain united (24). Only when this unity is realised, at the end of the text, do the nails disappear: they melt into the ground. In the conclusion of the play, Fatima stands alone on stage, hysterically mourning her uncle, addressing him as if he were still alive, in a scene that constitutes the apex of the play's cathartic construction. As she hears the sound of bullets, wondering where 'Abdallah is, she recites:

> I know. You are over there. You are avenging us. You and the men. I can see you, I can see the men. They are all there, their heads rising to the sky. Nobody has his head to the ground. The land carries them, the land is happy. There are no thorns in the land, no nails . . . You are paying our debt. The debt of the whips, of the guns, of the cannons. The nails in the land have melted . . . the blood that streamed on them made them melt… the blood of the poor who want to live. (176–7)

The play ends on Fatima's pressing injunction to the men:

> Hit, Salim, hit, Mansur, hit, 'Ilwan, hit, all of you! The land is as smooth as silk, there are no nails. The sky is protecting you, there are no crows. Your hands are made of iron, your hearts are steel. Hit, the whole world is looking at you. (178)

Now that the land has been purified of its nails, resistance is possible and is underlined as the only meaningful choice.

Two Novels 'Rewriting History' in a Militant Mode

Resistance is also articulated as a central value in the two novels I analyse in this chapter, *Qantara al-Ladhi Kafara* by Mustafa Musharrafa and *al-Faylaq* by Amin 'Izz al-Din. Mustafa Mustafa Musharrafa's life was overshadowed by that of his famous elder brother, 'Ali Mustafa Musharrafa, nicknamed 'the Arab Einstein'. Not much information is available about the younger Musharrafa, and what little there is is based on a testimony written by Muhammad 'Uda, 'Qantara wal Ayyam al-Khawali' ('Qantara and the Old Days', 1991). Born in a wealthy family of Dumyat at the beginning of the 1920s, Mustafa studied literature. He is said to have 'killed for the sake of Egypt' during the 1919 revolution ('Uda 1991: 24), an allusion to the fact he was probably a member of the Wafd's secret organisation.[17] Later on, having failed to find a publisher for one of his short stories, he emigrated to England, where he studied and taught English language, wrote in English and sought to distance himself as much as possible from his mother tongue and country. Then, in yet another volte-face, he decided to return to Egypt, where he obtained a post at Cairo University.

It took Mustafa Musharrafa around twenty years to write *Qantara al-Ladhi Kafara* ('Ayyad 1991: 15).[18] The short story writer Yusuf Idris declared it the most outstanding text written about the 1919 revolution, after *'Awdat al-Ruh* by Tawfiq al-Hakim and *Bayn al-Qasrayn* by Naguib Mahfouz (Idris 1991: 9).[19] Set in Cairo, more precisely in a *rab*[20] in the popular neighbourhood of 'Abdin, the novel evolves around the life of its main character, al-sheikh Qantara, an unemployed Dar al-'Ulum graduate, and a young woman, Sayyida, his neighbour and occasional housekeeper. At the beginning of the narrative, several hilarious pages show Qantara writing a *qasidat madh* (a panegyric) to a pasha, Naguib 'Asim, in order to get it published in *al-Ahram*. He hopes the pasha, who is a vague acquaintance, will soon be nominated prime minister and help secure him a job. He even hopes that what he calls 'the Wafdist' government[21] will fall and Naguib Basha will be nominated to negotiate with the British. But his opportunistic endeavour fails, and he becomes so desperate for an income that he sends Sayyida to work at a wealthy bey's household, in fact prostituting her.

The novel's chronology implicitly questions that of the dominant narrative about the 1919 revolution (see Chapter 3). At the beginning, the Spring 1919 demonstrations are already going on, but they serve only as the background to the life of these impoverished marginalised characters. Qantara has no real interest in those demonstrations. On the contrary, he is eagerly waiting for the Wafdist government to fall. It is only during Saad Zaghlul's second exile to the Seychelles Islands in October 1921 that Qantara, still without a job, becomes involved in the protests and turns into an armed revolutionary. He joins an underground group, led by one of the *rab*'s inhabitants, Si Muhammad, and takes part in assassinating British soldiers and officers. His life becomes totally linked to the movement, to the point of committing suicide in 1924, when he and all his comrades suffer from depression after Zaghlul's resignation from his post as prime minister. The novel ends in

1927, after Saad Zaghlul's death. Si Muhammad and his wife Huda, a nurse at the Qasr al-'Ayni hospital who participated in organising the demonstrations with him, are mourning the leader. The last grandiloquent sentence, totally different from the caustic humour of the beginning, states that 'it is necessary for the present generation to die in order to leave room for a better one' (Musharrafa 1991: 187). [22]

Unlike the narratives I analysed in Chapters 3 and 4, this novel frames the Cairene underprivileged as the true heroes of the revolution. Their action is not presented as a reaction exclusively to Saad Zaghlul's exile. Rather, the colonial arbitrary is tangible from the beginning of the narrative, when Qantara remembers having seen a drunken Australian soldier terrorising women in the tram, lifting their skirts with a stick (Musharrafa 1991: 77). Marginalised by the system, the unemployed sheikh, who is constantly told that 'there are too many Arabic teachers', is in a way pushed to take arms against the colonial oppressor. The reasons for revolt are thus sketched out as socio-economic as much as political, and the class dynamics in the 1919 revolution are as important as its nationalist impetus.

Musharrafa's narrative can be considered as one of the earliest attempts at rewriting the history of the 1919 revolution against the grain of dominant historiography in the mid-sixties. More than three decades later, in the context of the growing contestation of the end of the nineties, Amin 'Izz al-Din (1921–99) published *al-Faylaq*, a novel whose plot shares many similarities with that of *Qantara al-Ladhi Kafara*. Both *Qantara al-Ladhi Kafara* and *al-Faylaq* seek to present alternative discourses about 1919, as they give voice to actors often silenced or objectified in canonical narratives. Both texts stand out by their narrative strategies, empowering working class and peasant characters as actors of revolutionary violence through plot, focalisation and language.

'Izz al-Din is the author of a two-volume history of the Egyptian working class, focusing on its development before and after the 1919 revolution. He is also the author of an article about the Egyptian Labour Corps, published in *al-Musawwar* in March 1969. *Al-Faylaq* is his only novel, and was published two years after the 1997 peasant movement protesting against the new tenancy law which I refer to at the beginning of this chapter. Thus far, it has gone nearly unnoticed by both literary critics and the public.[23] Set between

1917 and 1919, it narrates the stories of villagers forced into the British Army in 1917,[24] focusing on their resistance strategies and highlighting the subsequent formation of a collective subject. From the very start of their journey, as they are packed in a cattle train heading North, the villagers find comfort in their presence together, in their jokes and discreet solidarity. This camaraderie grows stronger when they finally arrive at the Qatiyya camp in Sinai where they will pass nearly two years in forced labour, cleaning sand off the railways. They discover various tricks to pretend they are working, find ways to send letters to their relatives and manage to get extra food through one of their number who works in the kitchen. While building these adaptation strategies, the men overcome their divergences – between Muslims and Christians ('Izz al-Din 1997: 63), families and tribes who used to fight in the village and between inhabitants from different villages. Among them, Mursi 'Attallah stands out as a hero; he is their *rayyis*, the head of their unit and their leader. He is the one who advises them to overcome their conflicts whenever they are fighting, as well as the one who sets fire to the tanks of the camp (113), after one of them is killed by British bullets while trying to escape. Nuh's death is a turning point in the narrative, as it leads to an acute consciousness among the villagers of their potential fate and leads them to abandon their individual adaptation strategies and adopt collective resistance strategies, while they still carefully avoid any direct confrontation with the colonial power, fearing possible retaliation. This resistance strategy appears to have totally matured by the end of the novel, when they are shown back in their village as Mursi 'Attallah is standing with the Qatiyya men near the railways in 1919, waiting for the signal to blow up a military train.

The structure of the narrative, I argue, frames the violence of the end as the natural outcome of the plot. Very similar to that of *Qantara*, this ending underlines revolutionary violence as a necessary, inescapable consequence of oppression; rather than a spontaneous, chaotic outburst, violence is represented as a consequence of years of deprivation and suffering. Its actors have first-hand experience of colonial brutality; they have witnessed it with their own eyes, experienced it with their own bodies; they have seen their brothers and friends fall under British bullets; they have suffered in their flesh, have been whipped, have endured hunger. Thus, their reaction appears as a *natural* one. Violence is no longer described as the reaction of the so-called 'rabble' (see Chapter 2). Rather, it is narrated in a laudatory mode, framed as the choice of the heroes, masculine heroes in this case. It is important to note indeed that women appear only briefly in the course of the resistance, as they physically resist the men's conscription, shouting, beating and scratching soldiers (46).

As I have just shown, both *Qantara* and *al-Faylaq* use plot as a central element in their strategy to rewrite history from a subaltern perspective. Focalisation and language are other essential elements in that narrative strategy. *Qantara* is entirely focalised through the perspective of the inhabitants of a popular neighbourhood: the sheikh, his young neighbour Sayyida and a peasant from Upper-Egypt, Kamil al-Sa'idi; *al-Faylaq* is exclusively narrated through the perspective of the villagers.

Moreover, both novels attempt to narrate the subaltern's story in their *own* language. In *Qantara*, both the narration and the dialogues are rendered in the colloquial of Cairo's underprivileged,[25] thus mirroring the authors' acute consciousness of class dynamics. Although that particular brand of colloquial was not Musharrafa's own, as he came from a wealthy peasant background in Dumyat (Idris 1991: 11), he successfully turns it into a poetic language, most prominently in the first part of the novel, in which he sketches out his characters and delves into their thoughts in a stream of consciousness style. With its carefully crafted structure, vocabulary and expressions, Musharraffa's colloquial is indeed so well rendered that it efficiently expresses the spirit of a specific, popular, way of speaking. In *al-Faylaq*, most of the dialogues are in fact 'group conversations' embodying the ritual of 'rural chat' identified by several Egyptian novelists and critics 'as a central feature of Egyptian peasant culture' (Selim 2004: 173). This strategy is quite similar to that analysed by Samah Selim in *al-Ard*: 'this rural chat is written as a contrapuntal subaltern dialogue that both exemplifies peasant culture and challenges the efficacy of centralized narration' (Selim 2004: 173). Although there is no centralised narration to be challenged in *al-Faylaq*, as there are no narrative voices coming from outside the peasant community like in *al-Ard*, the result is the same: the collective narrative voice that emerges from the text mirrors the formation of a collective subject (Selim 2004: 161).

The choice of a colloquial brand specific to the underprivileged reflects these two authors' attempt at producing a class-conscious narrative about

1919. Instead of the Cairene law students or the pashas, or even the middle-class women, it is the peasants and urban underprivileged who are framed as the actors of the revolution, collectively shaping its course and building the power struggle. Both novels are narratives of empowerment, narrating the story of men who managed to rid themselves of the chains of oppression so as to become active actors of their own destinies. Like *al-Masamir*, those narratives highlight resistance against the occupier as the right choice to follow. This laudatory articulation of the underprivileged's resistance in the wake of the 1919 revolution soon enjoyed a much broader audience, through a drama series about a famous episode of the revolution.

A Television Story of Peasant Resistance

Based on a scenario by Yusri al-Gindi (b. 1942) and directed by Isma'il 'Abd al-Hafiz (1941–2012), the television drama *Gumhuriyyat Zifta*[26] was aired in January 1998, during Ramadan. Shot in different settings, with large numbers of participants in scenes sometimes featuring hundreds of peasants, it necessitated a 'huge budget'[27] and was produced by the state television.

Drama series differ from cinema in that they are diffused at home, and 'the medium has a potential for intimacy, that arises from its domestic setting and its consequent role within our everyday lives' (Cardwell 2012: 172). A drama series aired during the month of Ramadan could count on a wide cross-class audience, as most Egyptian households possessed a television set at the end of the nineties, nearly thirty years after television had been introduced in the country. Ramadan is mostly a familial moment in which television functions as a social gatherer. In addition, drama series differ from film mainly by their serialised form and shooting methods. Serialisation, one of the key features of television drama, contributes to rendering the events closer to the audience, creating a special bond between the audience and the characters. Margrethe Vaage has shown

> how the extended narrative that is characteristic of TV benefits from an emotional standpoint and a stronger familiarity with the characters, which in turn influences the degree of sympathy that spectators feel towards them; this can even affect the moral judgments placed upon their actions. (Garcia 2016: 7)

Shooting methods, in particular the systematic use of the close-up and over acting, contribute to injecting high doses of emotionality, thus allowing for a strong identification with the characters.

Like the other texts examined in this chapter, the series' representation of the 1919 revolution shies away from a triumphalist celebration of nationalist unity. Instead of focusing exclusively on the figure of Yusuf al-Gindi, presented as a member of the Wafd's underground organisation who had personal contacts with Saad Zaghlul, the series highlights the role of the village's peasant community in the events leading to that experience. As in *al-Masamir*, both plot elements and focalisation through the peasants contribute to shedding a critical light on the effendiyya's contribution to the struggle. As in Wahba's play, *Gumhuriyyat Zifta* mostly differentiates between fundamentally 'good' and 'bad' characters along class lines, in a fashion reminiscent of a Nasserist ideology that, although relegated by the 1990s to the opposition, was still very popular, particularily among script writers. As in *al-Faylaq*, special attention is given to language through the use of the specific colloquial of the Delta.

However, it is the emotional mode in which it rewrites the history of 1919 that distinguishes *Gumhuriyyat Zifta*. In her analysis of television melodrama in an Egyptian context, Lila Abu-Lughod posits that television serials in Egypt triggered what she calls a 'melodramatization of consciousness'. She argues that 'it is a technology for staging interiorities (through heightened emotionalism) and thus constructing and encouraging the individuality of ordinary people' (Abu-Lughod 2001: 112–13). Through my analysis of *Gumhuriyyat Zifta* I show that, firstly, the serialisation specific to television series efficiently builds close bonds between the peasant characters and the audience. Second, the shooting methods specific to television melodrama are used to highlight human, ordinary emotions – such as romantic and paternal love – thus contributing to bringing the peasants of 1919 closer to a 1998 audience. Finally, the musical interludes of the series, poems by 'Abd al-Rahman al-Abnudi sung by Muhammad Munir, contribute to that emotionality, at once celebrating the virtues of peasant and nationalist resistance, and lamenting its defeat in a nostalgic mode.

Gumhuriyyat Zifta is set between 1918 and April 1919. Most of its twenty-five episodes constantly shift focus between Cairo, Zifta and the surrounding villages. Although it contains scenes displaying important episodes from the nationalist struggle – Zaghlul, Sha'rawi and Fahmi's visit to Sir Wingate on 13 November 1918, Zaghlul's arrest on 8 March 1919 and his exile – the series focuses primarily on the events as they unfold in Zifta. At the beginning, in episode 4, we see peasants running away for fear of being conscripted into the British army and parents weeping over sons gone to war. The main dramatic tension during the first twenty episodes lies in the struggle between the peasants and Hishmat Pasha, an influential landowner supported by the colonial administration.[28] This struggle revolves around social issues and starts when one of the peasants, Salim Abul Nur,[29] refuses to sell his cotton to the pasha at a price below market rate. Salim's arrest and torture in the police station, which I referred to at the beginning of this chapter, is the spark that leads to the escalation of the conflict, during which emerges a peasant hero who leads an armed struggle against the pasha and his allies. Originally a gardener working at the palace, who had been placed there by his father in the hope that he would thereby be saved from forced conscription, Ibrahim is heavily punished because he refuses to reveal the name of the young effendi who is dating the pasha's daughter. This brutal experience turns him into an armed Robin Hood. He repeatedly introduces himself in the palace to threaten the pasha and forces him to order the release of the villagers who were arrested while they were protesting the treatment received by Salim. He recruits the men of the Dahbi gang, that previously worked for the pasha, and with their help, steals the pasha's entire cattle, sells it on the market and distributes the money to the families of the ginnery workers, arrested by the chief of police as they attempted to organise a sit-in. At that point, Ibrahim becomes a legendary character in the village, living in hiding, operating his good deeds in darkness. He comes to embody on the screen a folk hero, comparable to the figure of Adham al-Sharqawi (1898–1921), a good-hearted brigand known for his armed actions against colonial troops and rich landowners.

Scenario writers often 'attribute good and evil to different social classes' (Abu-Lughod 2001: 115). Al-Gindi, a playwright known for his Nasserist ideas, attributes good in *Gumhuriyyat Zifta* to the underprivileged and evil to the wealthy, although there is an attempt to escape this Manichean division by representing one of the pasha's daughters in the role of an ardent supporter of the *fellahin*. Ibrahim is a living incarnation of 'good': he has a strong sense of justice, is attached to the land, the village and its people and is ready to sacrifice his personal comfort for the public fate – as he gives up his dream of a calm life with his beloved Budur. The series places the peasants among the 'good' characters: most prominently Ibrahim, Salim who possesses an innate sense of resistance, his daughter Budur, the simple-minded Mus'ad, the singer Rabi' and even the men belonging to the gang who appear to have been forced onto that path. The effendiyya belong to that fundamentally 'good' category, although they several times inflict harm on the peasants. Sabir, the young law student, unwillingly provokes Ibrahim's ordeal when the latter refuses to reveal his name to the pasha. Yusuf al-Gindi's absenteeism, because of his repeated trips to Cairo to meet the Wafd leadership, leads to dramatic consequences and is several times angrily and sarcastically underlined by the peasants.

Most importantly, similarly to Ramzi effendi in *al-Masamir*, Zifta's effendiyya appear to be joining an already-ongoing struggle, not as initiating it. The battle against the landowning pasha backed up by the colonial administration has already been going on for more than a year when al-Gindi finally decides to devote all his time to Zifta – doing so only after the shock of Ibrahim's murder, killed while he was attempting to release Salim and the other prisoners. The death of Zifta's providential Robin Hood constitutes a trigger that reveals to al-Gindi the full extent of his responsibilities towards his native village. The epilogue of the series, filmed in a dream-like mode, clearly indicates that it is al-Gindi who is inspired by Ibrahim, and not the other way around. It shows al-Gindi in a white suit, seemingly lost on the Zifta tracks. Suddenly, Ibrahim appears to him in a white *gallabiyya*, with a comforting smile: 'why are you confused? Here is the path to follow, come with me'. It is thus the peasant who guides the effendi; it is the peasant who embodies 'good' on the screen, at once in its moral and political sense.

Among the 'bad' people, the British characters do not occupy a significant space on the screen. Rather, it is the pasha of Turkish descent, alien to Egypt and to its 'good' people, who occupies that position, seconded by *al-khawaga* Kiryaku, whose character is constructed according to the anti-Semitic stereotype of the Jewish usurer.[30] Only two men in the village consistently collaborate with this evil front: al-Dahbi and, after his death, Ghatata. The pasha's other acolyte, the corrupt and weak police chief, does not belong to the village; nor does the Egyptian policeman who kills Ibrahim. They represent state officials who collaborate with the colonial occupation.

As mentioned above, serialisation is a feature that favours 'long-term engagement' with the characters; moreover, 'following a character closely is a powerful way to create sympathy for a character' (Vaage: 20 and 27). In the case of *Gumhuriyyat Zifta*, this feature works in favour of the peasant characters, Ibrahim, his beloved Budur and her father. At the beginning a man with little will of his own, Ibrahim turns into a hero and most of the suspense is linked to his daring deeds. The viewer follows this transformation step by step. And as Ibrahim systematically resorts to illegal practices, such as stealing and threatening, the viewer is made to sympathise with him because these practices are put at the service of the peasant community. The viewer is also made to sympathise with him through the systematic highlight of his home and beloved ones. The frequent change of focalisation through which the character is approached, from the perspective of his father or Budur, emphasises the solid family ties between them. This in turn allows for a strong identification with the character.

Figure 6.2 Fu'ad Ahmad in the role of Ibrahim's father with Sabrine on his left in the role of Budur and Kamal Abu Rayya on his right in the role of Yusuf al-Gindi ©Al-Ahram Archives.

Furthermore, in accordance with the genre of the television melodrama, the series systematically uses over-acting as well as insistent close-ups on the faces of the actors,[31] in order to more efficiently convey emotions. In combination with the dichotomy between 'good' and 'bad' characters, this technique allows for a strong degree of compassion with members of the peasant community in their ordeal. One of the main emotional leitmotivs of the series is the pain of Ahmad's father, who has gone mad waiting for his son to come back from the First World War, and that of Ibrahim's blind father, Nu'man, who untiringly laments his decision to send him to work as a gardener at the palace. The over-acting and close-ups on the faces of the two actors highlight this paternal pain and anxiety, aiming at triggering feelings of compassion among the audience. As the television drama singles out the men as figures deserving of the audience's compassion, it builds on the assumption of a common identity between the audience and the characters. In this case all the three requirements of compassion I discussed in Chapter 2 are reunited:

> a belief or appraisal that the suffering is serious rather than trivial; . . . the belief that the person does not deserve the suffering; and . . . the belief that the possibilities of the person who experiences the emotion are similar to those of the sufferer. (Nussbaum 2001: 306)

The television drama hereby allows the audience to identify with the characters. The romantic aspect in the peasant hero's life story is similarly articulated in a manner that renders it close to the lives of the 1990s audience. Indeed, unlike Fatima in *al-Masamir* and the heroines of anti-colonial struggle in the 1960s, Budur is an ordinary woman who longs for a calm life with her beloved, trying to prevent him from taking any dangerous risks. Similarly, unlike the armed fighters recurrently depicted on the 1960s screens (see Chapter 4), Ibrahim does not take pride in the fact he has no time to devote to his beloved but laments it exactly as she does.

The songs further contribute to rendering the Zifta people's struggle emotionally closer to a 1990s' audience, by rooting it in the protest culture of the end 1990s.[32] The choice of the poet 'Abd al-Rahman al-Abnudi (1938–2015) to write the lyrics, and the casting of Muhammad Munir (1954) in the role of Rabi', the landless singer, are both significant in that regard. Al-Abnudi was an outspoken opponent of Sadat's politics and faced systematic hinderance from the regime.³³ He wrote in colloquial and presented his work as echoing the voice of the underprivileged. Munir had an audience of young people looking for an alternative to the commercial hits of the eighties. He was regularly cast in plays, series and films which shared a committed agenda, among which are *al-Malik huwa al-Malik* (*The King is the King*), a play by Saʿdallah Wannus directed by Murad Munir in 1988, and *Hadduta Masriyya* (*An Egyptian Story*, 1982), a film by Youssef Chahine.

The songs' articulation of patriotism as an innate feeling of the underprivileged, in a context in which the regime was operating a rapprochement with Israel, is a trademark of Abnudi's work. The hit that accompanies the opening and closing titles, 'Habibti' ('O My Love') is a celebration of the values of attachment to the land and the country, depicting patriotism as a feeling beyond control. The songs further celebrate the people's resistance in terms that belong to the political idiolect of the sixties and which were later used by groups opposing Sadat's politics. The song accompanying the scene of gathering the *tawkilat* (powers of attorney) for the Wafd at the beginning of episode 12 in *Bayt al-Umma* is entitled 'al-Gamahir' ('The Masses'), a term whose use to indicate the people as a potential actor of change is characteristic of the politically committed culture of the 1960s. In 'Ighdabi ya dunya' ('Get Angry You People'), the poet uses a phraseology praising working class and peasant anger, predicting its overwhelming victory, as 'the martyr's blood will come back to destroy the wall/and free the prisoners/from the houses and the farms, from the churches and the mosques, . . . from the schools and the factories'.

As it articulates the past in the cultural terminology of the present, the television drama enables the audience to relate to the emotions of the past. I contend that the drama thereby establishes a continuity in the suffering of the peasants, from 1917 to 1997. Those two moments witnessed widespread rural hardships, touching hundreds of thousands of people. In 1917, nearly one million peasants endured forced conscription in the British army. Eighty years later, in 1997, the implementation of the tenancy law affected a similar number of people – one million families (Saad 2016: 5) – as I noted at the beginning of this chapter. Moreover, the series connects the resistance of the present to that of the past. As in *al-Masamir*, the series' ending celebrates resistance as a value. Although the brief experience of self-governance in Zifta is defeated, as the British siege puts an end to it,[34] the voice-off at the end comfortingly states that 'regardless of its results, what happened was in itself a great thing'. The series thus articulates the Zifta experience – including the important contribution of the peasantry – as a possible inspiration for the present. By rewriting the history of 1919 in a way that resonates with contemporary stakes, the series constitutes both a mirror of the peasant resistance and a militant intervention in a context of growing social contestation. It is a rewriting of history that deeply connects the present to the past. These links between past and present would become more fertile in the aftermath of the 2011 revolution, as young creators attempted to rewrite their revolutionary past.

Notes

1. For this experience, see Chapter 1, note 8.
2. *Al-Akhbar* 31.1.1998.
3. See also Reem Saad (1999) and Saqr Al-Nur, 'Al-Falahhun wal-Thawra fi Misr: Fa'ilun Mansiyyun' (publication date not available).
4. In 'Malaff lam Yughlaq: al-Awda' al-Rahina fi Rif Misr, September 97-Mai 98', prepared by Markaz al-Ard li-Huquq al-Insan, Mai 1998, p. 44.
5. See Ada Barbaro, (UNIOR, Napoli), 'I Will Tell You My (Hi)Story: Re-write to Revolt in the Process of al Ta'rīkh al-Badīl' and Maria Avino (UNIOR, Napoli), 'Khayri Shalabi, a Writer Versus History'.
6. For an analysis of the reception of the series and more details about the conflict with the censors, see Abu-Lughod 2005: 14–18.
7. This analysis is based on the written text of the play. As far as I know, there is no available recording of the performance.
8. It was the fifth most successful play out of nineteen that played during the season. The first one, *al-Harafish*, was seen by 44,805 people (al-'Ashri 1973: 8).
9. See 'al-Masrah al-'Arabi wal Naksa', available at <http://www.startimes.com/?t=30825303> (last accessed 18 September 2019).
10. The months following the Naksa would witness the production of another Arab play addressing the 1967 defeat: *Haflat Samar min Ajl Khamsat Huzayran* (*Soirée for the 5th of June*) by the Syrian playwright Sa'dallah Wannus. According to Roger Allen, this 'violently critical play struck a responsive chord in the questioning, recriminative and sobering atmosphere of Arab society after June 1967'

(Allen 1984: 101). It was 'seen in performance by some 25,000 people during its run in Damascus in 1971' (Allen 1984: 99). See See Roger Allen (1984), 'Arabic Drama in Theory & Practice: The Writings of Saʿdallah Wannus', *Journal of Arabic Literature* 15, pp. 94–113.
11. He wrote the scenario of a number of landmark films, including *Al-Zawja 13* (*Wife No.13*, 1962) by Fatin ʿAbd al-Wahab and *Zuqaq al-Midaqq* (*Midaqq Alley*, 1960) by Hasan al-Imam.
12. For Tharwat ʿUkasha and his role under the Nasser regime, see Chapter 4.
13. ʿUkasha described the play as a 'heroic exploit on his [Wahba's] side and a political adventure on our side' ('Ukasha 2004: 741).
14. Interestingly, despite the cathartic quality that might explain its relative success when it was staged, the play remained marginal in the work of Wahba. It is most often only briefly referred to by critics when they expose Wahba's work.
15. ʿAbdallah responds that accountability will happen later, and that he is ready to step off if need be. This is one of many instances in the play in which his character could be read as an allegory of Nasser. The scene can also be interpreted as a reference to the accusations Nasser had to face, and most importantly to his resignation speech.
16. About the word *kubba*, see Abdallah Ghunaym, 'Taʾkhudhak kubba aw kubba taʾkhudhak: kayfa tataharrak al-lugha bayna al-gamaʿat al-thaqafiyya?'. Available at <https://manshoor.com/life/origin-history-of-arabic-words/> (last accessed 17 March 2019).
17. See Sana' al-Bisi (2007), 'Huwa wa Hiyya, ʿAmid al-ʿIlm: ʿAli Mustafa Musharrafa', *Al-Ahram*, 2 June. Al-Bissi writes that al-Musharrafa told Muhammad ʿUda about this in 1957. Available at <http://www.ahram.org.eg/Archive/2007/6/2/WRIT1.HTM> (last accessed 1 April 2019).
18. Towards the end of the novel, its main character, 'Qantara al-ladhi kafara' explains to a curious interlocutor that his name is that of an alley in Darb al-Gamamiz, the Cairo neighbourhood Musharrafa is writing about. Originally named Qantarat Cafarelli, after one of the savants who accompanied the French expedition in 1798, the name of the alley was soon changed by the people into Qantara illi kafar or Qantara al-ladhi kafara.
19. The 1991 edition of the novel (Cairo: Majallat Adab wa Naqd), which I use here, contains seven critical articles about the novel, authored by Yusuf Idris, Shukri ʿAyyad, Muhammad ʿUda, Muhammad Rumish, Ibrahim Aslan, ʿAbdallah Khayrat and Farida al-Naqqash. The more recent edition of the novel (Cairo, Dar Battana, 2019), edited and prefaced by Shaʿban Yusuf, contains all these

articles, in addition to an article by Taha Husayn about writing in colloquial, and short stories and articles by Mustafa Musharrafa himself.
20. A large building divided into small apartments overlooking a common courtyard.
21. This ministry is most probably a reference to 'Adli Yakan's brief role at the head of the government, from March to December 1921.
22. According to several testimonies, the writer Muhammad 'Uda, a close friend of Musharrafa, contributed to the writing process of the novel. 'Uda states that its idea was born during conversations between himself and Musharrafa and that the inspiration for the novel came from the neighbourhood he inhabited. He then uses the first-person plural to talk about the beginning of the writing process: 'we began [writing] the story' ('Uda 1991: 28). In his preface, Musharrafa thanks 'Uda and states that he was his source of inspiration, as 'one of the true heroes of the story and an inhabitant of the *rab*'' (Musharrafa 1991: 71).
23. Sha'ban Yusuf gives a possible explanation to this marginalisation, noting that 'Izz al-Din passed away a few months after the publication' of the novel (Yusuf 2017: 14).
24. For conscription during the First World War and resistance to forced conscription see the Introduction, note 28.
25. Writing in colloquial was not new, but this choice remained unwelcome among the literary establishment. The rejection of Musharrafa's short story I referred to earlier is a telling example thereof. For more about narratives in colloquial, see Madiha Doss and Humphrey Davies (2013), *al-'Ammiyya al-Masriyya al-Maktuba*, Cairo: al-Hay'a al-Misriyya al-'Amma lil Kitab. For the position of the literary establishment about literary narratives in colloquial, see extracts from an article by Taha Husayn quoted by Sha'ban Yusuf: 'the colloquial language did not succeed to become a literary language' (Husayn qtd in Yusuf 2019: 19).
26. As is often the case in television series of the 1990s, the music, the sets and the actor's clothes do not accurately render the ambience of the 1910s. For instance, when meeting Sabir in Cairo, the pasha's daughter appears without either a face or a head veil, wearing black trousers and a blouse belonging to the style of the end of the 1980s.
27. The series was produced by Sawt al-Qahira lil Sawtiyyat wal Mar'iyyat, a subsidiary company of state television (*Majallat Fan* no. 416 19.1.1998).
28. The pasha can be read as embodying the comeback of a landowning class enjoying privileged links with foreign capital.
29. Some commentators have noted that the character of Salim Abul Nur was

similar in many ways to that of Muhammad Abu Suwaylam in the novel *al-Ard* by 'Abd al-Rahman al-Sharqawi (see for instance Fadl 1998).
30. Kiryaku's main role in the village is that he pressures the peasants to pledge their lands. He is presented as a greedy character and a miser.
31. This technique is also used in film melodrama (see Chapter 4).
32. This culture is heir to the protest culture of the seventies, embodied, among others, by poet Ahmad Fu'ad Nigm (1929–2013) and singer Sheikh Imam (1918–95). For 'The Poetry of Revolt', see Elliot Colla (2011), Jadaliyya, 31 January, available at <http://www.jadaliyya.com/Details/23638/The-Poetry-of-Revolt> (last accessed 14 April 2019).
33. He was prevented from leaving the country until an intervention by star singer 'Abdel Halim Hafiz – for whom he had written several patriotic songs – loosened the grip on him. See Muhammad Shu'ayr (2009), "'Abd al-Rahman al-Abnudi: fil Shi'r... Laysa Nadiman 'ala Shay", *Jaridat al-Akhbar al-Lubnaniyya*, Beirut, 23 March.
34. The committee in charge of the city manages to avoid a bloodbath by fraternising with the besieging Australian soldiers, sending them leaflets underlining their common status as victims of the British. As the colonial troops ask for twenty men to be arrested and flogged, the besieged deliver them the 'traitors' to the national cause, including the pasha and his accomplices.

7

Rewriting History in the Wake of 2011

> Appeals to the past are among the commonest strategies in interpretations of the present. What animates such appeals is not only disagreement about what happened in the past and what the past was, but uncertainty about whether the past really is past, over and concluded, or whether it continues, albeit in different forms, perhaps. (Said 1993: 1)

In these first lines of *Culture and Imperialism*, Edward Said insists on the porosity between past and present, on their irremediable connectedness,

> even as we must fully comprehend the pastness of the past', he writes, 'there is no just way in which the past can be quarantined from the present. Past and present inform each other, each implies the other and [. . .] each co-exists with the other. (Said 1993: 4)

Throughout this book, I have been arguing that representations of the past are ultimately a function of our present. In my introduction, I insisted on Walter Benjamin's argument that the images of the past that survive are those that the present could recognise as ones 'of its own concerns' (Benjamin 1969: 255). Following Benjamin, I have tried to show in the preceding chapters that what remains, and what is lost, of those 'flashes' of memory, is ultimately a function of the present, of the power struggles of each historical period, between the 'victor' and the 'oppressed.' In this chapter, I show that this porosity between past and present is nowhere as striking as in the connection between 1919 and 2011. Although those two revolutionary moments obviously have many dissimilarities, there are striking resemblances in the energies and emotions unleashed by both revolutions. The successive anger, joy, fear and disillusion experienced in 2011 enabled writers and artists to connect in new modes with century-old emotions. The defeat, with its deep bitterness, brought to life 'flashes' of memory hitherto lost in successive presents where they could not be recognised as meaningful.

In this chapter, I focus on two narratives about 1919 written and produced in 2014: a play by Laila Soliman (1981), *Hawa al-Hurriyya*,[1] translated as *Whims of Freedom*, and a novel by Ahmed Mourad (1978), titled *1919*. Both narratives attempt to 'rewrite history', by offering alternative representations of 1919 to those hitherto dominant about that key moment in the anti-colonial struggle. I argue that these attempts both benefit from and engage in the cultural dynamics that accompanied the 2011 revolution. Furthermore, I contend that their different articulations of 1919 can be explained by the specific ways both authors engaged in those dynamics, from two different positions in the post-revolutionary cultural field.

Soliman and Mourad both began writing after the initial enthusiasm of the eighteen days in Tahrir had cooled down, in a context where broadly shared feelings of disillusion and bitterness prevailed. Despite sustained mobilisations, and the deaths of thousands of people, nothing much had changed. Trials of figures of the 'old regime', including Mubarak and his sons, did not yield any concrete results. The social demands articulated during the revolution were also not met, despite hundreds of strikes organised during and after the eighteen days.[2] Constitutional changes, introduced in March 2012, did not bring the hoped-for change, despite massive popular participation in the successive parliamentary, constitutional and presidential elections. The election of Muhammad Mursi, a figure of the Muslim Brotherhood, as president in June 2012 accentuated the polarisation of the political and cultural fields that began to appear in the aftermath of the revolution. However, after Mursi's overthrow in July 2013, the military definitively tightened its grip on society, and the revolutionary impetus was lost.

Nevertheless, 'as sweeping as the counter-revolution may be, it cannot erase the experience lived during those two years, an experience that has been especially decisive for the young generation whose political socialisation took place in this context' (Jacquemond 2016b: 366). This manifested in what Jacquemond calls 'the expansion of public space' between January 2011 and June 2013, which in turn allowed for a relatively large diffusion of many forms of art, such as street art, but also other visual arts, pop music, theatre and literature.³ The revolution of 2011 provided both a large audience and an inspiration for artists in these diverse fields.

However, the blossoming artistic creation that had emerged in concomitance with or in reaction to the political battles of the years 2011–13 now echoed prevailing feelings of bitterness and disillusion. Richard Jacquemond reads the 'black humour' recurrent in Egyptian satiric narratives and dystopian novels as 'the literary expression of the state of mind of large sections of the Egyptian youth' in the post-revolutionary context (Jacquemond 2016b: 366). Elena Chiti describes how fictional and non-fictional narratives merge into a similar dystopian discourse about post-2011 Egypt. She notes that dystopia has gained a 'realistic dimension' (Chiti 2016: 279), observing that Egyptian receptions of Muhammad Rabie's *Utarid* (2014) underline the 'perfect plausibility' of a text otherwise categorised as a dystopian science fictional novel. She similarly highlights 'the commercial success and wide availability, in Egypt, of several editions of the classic dystopian novel *1984* by George Orwell' and analyses the shift 'from supernatural to realistic' in the presentation of a new edition in 2016 of a book by Ahmad Khalid Tawfiq originally published in 2009 (Chiti 2016: 279–80).⁴

Similarly, the walls of the city, that had hitherto functioned as revolutionary media, its frescoes depicting heroic battles throughout the country,⁵ now displayed, instead of highbrow militant slogans and celebrations of the mobilisations, a sad, laconic incantation above the pictures of martyrs: *iftikruhum*, remember them. As they faced the regime's frenzy to erase all traces of the revolution, most prominently embodied in the attempts at removing grafitti from the country's walls (see Introduction), groups of political and cultural activists appropriated the memory of the struggle that had been going on for the past years. The urge not to forget was taken over by activist groups like *Mosireen*, who gathered an archive of the revolution, posting online pictures, interviews and videos of successive demonstrations, sit-ins and confrontations with the police.⁶

It is in that context, marked by a haunting possibility of erasure and distortion of the struggles and sacrifices of the preceding two years, that Laila Soliman and Ahmed Mourad began reflecting on the 1919 revolution. In addition to their role as 'underground historians', I argue in this chapter that the revolutionary context, and its immediate aftermath, in which Mourad and Soliman were working, entrusted them with a unique relationship to their revolutionary past.

An Intimate Bond with the Past

Both *Hawa al-Hurriyya* by Laila Soliman and *1919* by Ahmad Mourad are pervaded by a sense of defeat and an aftertaste of bitterness quite similar to that of the post-1919 plays I analysed in Chapter 1, and both attempt to write an alternative history of 1919. However, despite these similarities, they ultimately propose very dissimilar articulations of 1919. As I said earlier, my contention is that these differences can be explained by the specific ways both authors engaged in the 2011 revolutionary dynamics, from two different positions in the cultural field. While Mourad comes from the 'commercial pole', where arts and politics are often dissociated, Soliman's work is emblematic of 'an art (or culture) of the revolution' – to use Jacquemond's terms – committed to both the aesthetic value of art and its potential as vector of political and social change. I will first present Soliman's background and an analysis of *Hawa al-Hurriyya*, before turning to Ahmed Mourad's work.

Soliman's work belongs to an independent theatre scene which, beginning in the 1990s, developed as playwrights sought an alternative to commercial theatre.[7] Her performances are most often privately produced and performed for small audiences in Cairo or at international festivals. She operates from the margins of the cultural field, with little to no access to the venues of the Ministry of Culture or Broadcasting. Her work is both informed by and productive of this marginal position. One of her early plays, *Ghurba* (*Images of Alienation*, 2006) performed at the Falaki theatre of the American University in Cairo, metaphorically expresses feelings of estrangement and marginalisation in social spaces, constructs and social bodies. Although it does not focus on her own experience as a theatre director, the play can be read as a powerful metaphor of Soliman's alienation in the Egyptian cultural field.

Nevertheless, her creative work is consistently connected to, and inspired by the contemporary social and political context in which she is working. She often conducts field work in diverse socio-economical milieus while preparing for her plays. Moreover, as I mentioned earlier, her works systematically offer a committed perspective on the themes she deals with. *The Retreating World* (2004), her first play, was performed in the aftermath of the US-led invasion of Iraq and subtitled 'An Ode to Iraq'. In *Fil Khidma* (*At Your Service*), performed in 2009 at the Hanager theatre, a woman narrates her relationship with her imprisoned son, an Islamist engaged in armed struggle. Focusing on the woman's painful experience of motherhood, the play also displays her leftist past in addition to the political oppression faced by her son, including arbitrary detention and torture. Finally, Soliman's work explores the empowering aspect of theatre, both on the collective and individual levels, as is the case of *Sahwat Rabi' fil Tuktuk* (*Spring Awakening in the Tuktuk*, 2010), an adaptation of German playwright Frank Wedekind's work which deals with gender relations and sexual frustration, seeking to encourage both boys and girls to overcome traditional relationships.

When she started reflecting on *Hawa al-Hurriyya* in the winter of 2012, Soliman had already produced two performances about the 2011 revolution, *Durus fil Thawra* (*Lessons in Revolting*, 2011) and *La Waqt lil Fan* (*No Time for Art*, 2012).[8] Both deal with the main events and slogans of the revolution from the perspective of its actors, and can be considered as militant interventions in the then-ongoing revolutionary turmoil. Performed in August 2011, after the dispersal of the July sit-in by the military police, during which one of the performers of the play had been arrested and tortured, *Durus fil Thawra* was conceived as a kind of 'active resistance', as Soliman puts it, in a context in which despondency was becoming widespread among activists (Stuhr-Rommereim 2011).

Though focusing on the 1919 revolution, *Hawa al-Hurriyya* operates a similar intervention in a context marked by the post-revolutionary 'urge to remember'. Soliman's attempt at rewriting history, I argue, is based on the dynamic relationship between past and present, as it goes back and forth between moments in 1917, 1919, 2011 and 2013. By exploring the past, while systematically linking it to the present, it triggers a reflection upon the post-revolutionary reality of the spectator, inviting him or her to become aware of processes of remembering and forgetting, and of their implication for the future. Written in a fragmentary mode, the play's use of archival documents – some hitherto unseen – can be read as an empowering source of knowledge for the present; its use of old songs further provides an emotional connection with a disturbingly familiar past.

Hawa al-Hurriyya is born from a commission by the London International

Festival of Theatre (LIFT) to address the First World War.⁹ Soliman recalls that she early on realised that the First World War was inseparable from the revolution that erupted a few months after the November 1918 armistice in Egypt. Her work then unfolded as an attempt at capturing voices that had been lost in the dominant narrative about 1919: 'no records are available to the public about individuals or about small people so to speak', she said.¹⁰ The parallels the play draws between 1919 and 2011 were inspired by a recurrent feeling of déjà-vu she had to cope with while delving through the 1919 documents, including 'political events, photos' and 'parallel jargons of past and present' (ibid.).

The performance re-enacts the research process the team went through, with references to the post-revolutionary context of 2013–14. Forty-six minutes long, it is based on a text written collectively by the director Laila Soliman, performers Zeinab Magdy and Nanda Mohammad, and the historian Alia Mossallam, who undertook the historical research for the play. In Cairo, the performance was held in a small space situated exactly in front of Saad Zaghlul's mausoleum. The opening scene directly tackles its main theme, as Nanda Muhammad plays an old song on a phonograph, attempting to re-connect with lost voices of the past;¹¹ despite the bad quality of the recording the audience can still make out the famous song 'Salma ya Salama' ('O Safe and Sound') as originally sung by singer and composer Sayyid Darwish.¹² It then jumps to an introduction by performer Zeinab Magdy who tells the audience about a letter she sent to a friend imprisoned in Tura in the aftermath of the 2011 revolution.

The performance continues in a fragmentary mode, as the narrative is organised according to the contingencies of memory and associations of ideas, constantly going back and forth between moments of the past and the present. In his discussion of archival art, Hal Foster interprets this will 'to connect what cannot be connected' as 'a will to relate – to probe a misplaced past, to collate its different signs . . . to ascertain what might remain for the present' (Foster 2006: 145). *Hawa al-Hurriyya* can be read as a tangible illustration thereof, as it aims at making the forgotten archive available in the present, not only in itself, but also as a source of potentially empowering knowledge in the post-2011 context.

Soliman's use of archival documents functions as a 'gesture of alternative knowledge or counter-memory' (Foster 2006: 144), a 'counter-archive' to that of the state.[13] She does so first by making those documents physically present on stage, as newspaper articles, leaflets and photos are displayed on a big screen behind the performers, while old records are played on an antique phonograph. Rather than only seeking to recreate an ambience, this set-up aims at making the 'trace' of the past tangible on stage. Second, all the historical documents highlight the 1917–19 period from the perspective of its underprivileged actors: newspaper articles giving statistics about peasants sent to war; slogans shouted by demonstrators, the so-called 'rabble' who were smashing shop windows while screaming 'long live calm and silence' (*yahya al-hudu' wal sakina*); minutes documenting the courageous complaints by peasant women against the British soldiers who raped them.[14] The performance hence gives flesh to the voices of collective groups usually dismissed in the dominant narrative: peasants, both men and women, and the urban underprivileged.

Presented as sites of erasure and distortion *par excellence*, old songs constitute an essential part of this counter-archive and play a central role in the performance's organisation. The play's 'inner musical structure' (Mudford 2000: 170) is constructed around eight songs, which all give an insight into the narrative of ordinary people about the revolution and the years preceding it. Some are unknown titles like 'Pardon ya Wingate' ('Pardon, Wingate'), a song written on a leaflet found in the British Foreign Office Archive, whilst others are not so well-known, such as 'al-Kuthra' ('Numbers'), and yet others famous, like 'Salma ya Salama' ('Safe and Sound'), 'Ya 'Aziz 'Ayni' ('Apple of my Eye') or 'Zuruni Kull Sana Marra' ('Visit Me Once Each Year').[15] These three last songs play an important role in the structure of the performance. Both their choice and mise-en-scène are meant to emotionally involve the audience in the remembering process the play attempts to trigger.

'Salma Ya Salama', a song probably composed by Sayyid Darwish in 1918, and adapted by the Alexandria-born Italian singer Dalida in 1977, is arguably the most central.[16] Written by Badi' Khayri, its lyrics convey the mixed feelings of peasants conscripted during the First World War as they are finally back home. While it expresses patriotic love, it also deals with memories of war: 'Never mind America, or Europe either/Nothing compares with this country/The ship bringing us home/Is so much sweeter than the one which took us/away'; 'We've seen the guns and we've seen the wars/And we've seen the dynamite'.[17] The adaptation sung by Dalida keeps only two verses 'Safe and Sound/We went and made it back'. The mise-en-scène of the song aptly imbeds it in the structure of the performance. As I mentioned earlier, in the opening scene, the song underlines the omnipresence of the past in the present and the difficulty to grasp it, as the old phonograph systematically crackles. It reappears towards the middle of the play, its melody zooming in the background as Nanda remembers Syria, sadly stating that she is 'not going back'. Then, the performer sings the two first couplets *a capella*, in an expressive mise-en-scène in which she appropriates the peasants' melancholy and relates it to her status as a Syrian living in Cairo. As she acknowledges the relevance of the song to her own feelings, she prompts the audience to connect with its haunting sadness. When Zeinab Magdy remembers that her mother sung it 'without the war bit', her comment invites the audience to also recover the context and the meaning of the song. Drawing our attention to the obliteration of the subaltern's voice in the contemporary version of the song, the director attempts to give life to layers of emotion erased by the dominant narrative.

Figure 7.1 Zeinab Magdy in Hawa al-Huriyya © Ruud Gielens.

Hence the performance is an invitation to reconnect with the past, both intellectually and emotionally. The casting contributes to this process, as both performers enact their own characters, Zeinab as an Egyptian academic, and Nanda as a Syrian singer[18] and actress living in Cairo. The constant back and forth movement between the questions and feelings of the performers and those of the past contributes to drawing parallels between the fear, anxiety and anger of both revolutions, thus bringing the past closer to the present. On stage, Zeinab Magdy explicitly links the revolutionary moment of the past with that of the present, stating that she cannot 'reach into the depths of the triumph of romance of one revolution, because of the disillusion of another', and that, 'at a moment as devoid of romance as this, reading the 1919 revolution is miserable and upsetting'. Through the constant comparison between 1919 and 2011, *Hawa al-Horiyya* builds bridges with the past, thus appropriating its concerns. By excavating the past to understand the present, the play draws intimate bonds with that past, thus integrating the 'historical other'[19] into its reflections upon the 2011 revolution.

While this is done in a fragmentary mode, as I mentioned earlier, the play 'does not project a lack of logic or affect. On the contrary it assumes anomic fragmentation as a condition not only to represent but to work through, and proposes new orders of affective association' (Foster 2006: 145). Through these associations, Soliman in a way gives life to Benjamin's 'flashes of memory'. Rather than remaining in the realm of the intellectual, the past becomes part of an intimate questioning of the present. In that sense, the link Soliman establishes between past, present and future gives her articulation of 1919 a committed dimension. Indeed, as she actively retrieves lost voices from the past, she at once engages in an empowering process of learning from the past, while encouraging her audience to remain vigilant in order not to let the present be lost for the future. That dimension is summarised on stage by Zeinab Magdy, as she asks: 'Where will we find the patience and courage for a revolution if we don't remember that those who came before us were scared and anxious too?'

New Middle-Class Icons

Unlike *Hawa al-Hurriyya*, Ahmad Mourad's *1919* lacks, I contend, that committed dimension. Born in 1978, Mourad roughly belongs to the same generation as Soliman, but unlike her, he is a bestselling author[20] whose trajectory embodies the

> commodification of cultural products, and the rise or come-back of 'middle' cultural forms ... that blur the frontier between a 'high culture' and a 'popular culture' that the literary and artistic Egyptian elites consistently established since the beginning of the Nahda. (Jacquemond 2016a: 64)

Despite his commercial success, and although his third novel, *al-Fil al-Azraq* (*The Blue Elephant*, 2012) was shortlisted for the International Prize for Arabic Fiction in 2013, Mourad remains largely ignored, or even despised, by the 'legitimate' critique.[21] When he was awarded the *tafawwuq* prize, a state prize valued at 100,000 EG (c. £4,735) in June 2018, the news was received by a concert of astonished and scandalised remarks.[22] However, he enjoys a privileged bond with a wide audience of young middle-class readers, as his interactions with large crowds of young people during book signings attest.[23] It is that bond, I argue, that enabled him to articulate a narrative about 1919 that is at once a mirror and a vector of the cultural changes the 2011 revolution triggered.

Mourad began writing *1919* in December 2012, and it took him a year to complete.[24] Unlike his previous novels, which can be classified as political or psychological thrillers, *1919* is a historical novel,[25] whose characters include Saad Zaghlul, Safiyya Zaghlul, King Fuad, Queen Nazli and Wafd secretary general 'Abd al-Rahman Fahmi, as well as lesser-known figures from *al-Yad al-Sawda'* (the Black Hand), an underground organisation which targeted and killed British officers and their Egyptian collaborators. These include Ahmad Kira,[26] the organisation's brain, 'Abd al-Qadir Shihata, the son of a *fitiwwa* who joins after his father is killed by a British officer and Dawlat Fahmi, a teacher originally from an Upper Egypt village. The only entirely fictive character is Ward, a young Armenian who turns to prostitution after her parents die from the Spanish flu at the beginning of the novel.

Mourad publicly asserted that *1919* was explicitly written in an attempt to draw parallels with 2011. His metatextual discourse about his novel further invites readers to view it as an attempt at demystifying the icons of nationalist history. He repeatedly stated that his intention was to re-open the 1919 files in a fashion different from what he describes as the 'propaganda' his generation had been 'taught at school'. It was important, he said, to 'look at those people [the actors of the 1919 revolution] as flesh and blood, not as statues or divine creatures'.[27] But while embarking on this enterprise he was 'afraid' of the reaction of his audience: 'our generation' he said, is 'afraid of history'.[28] His anxiety proved unfounded. *1919* was met with immediate success; the book went out of print within days of its release and has been reprinted several times since.[29] Strikingly, the novel triggered a renewed interest in the historical characters Mourad brought to life. Upon checking Wikipedia entries about Ahmad Kira and Dawlat Fahmi, I found out these had been created *after* the novel's release.[30] A history programme on 'Mekameleen TV' in June 2016 was devoted to 'Abd al-Qadir Shihata.[31] Numerous posts on Facebook paid tribute to Dawlat Fahmi.[32]

This back-and-forth movement between the text and its readers provides a concrete illustration of the argument at the core of this book, namely that literature and film have been central to shaping representations of the 1919 revolution. I argue that Mourad's attempt at rewriting the history of 1919 was met with such popular success not only because its winning formula consisted of sensational scenes and a plot with unexpected developments. Rather, the novel satisfied the broad fascination with the past which had been unleashed in the aftermath of the 2011 revolution. Facebook pages titled 'Egypt Zaman', 'Misr Zaman' ('Egypt in the Past') or 'Magharit al-Dhikrayat' ('The Cavern of Memories') gathered tens of thousands of 'likes'. The enthusiasm went beyond the nostalgia for pre-Nasser Egypt and the fascination for everything black and white, with a genuine interest for stories about ordinary people outside the dominant narratives, as attested by 'Turath Misri' ('Egyptian Heritage'), a page that has gathered more than 250,000 likes.

Mourad's privileged bond with his young readers enabled him to revisit the past in a mode in tune with their expectations. In terms of content, the novel expresses the insistence of a generation to appropriate the realm of history, by establishing its own temporal and spatial frame for the events, choosing its own gallery of heroes and revisiting its own selection of historical documents. In terms of form, the genre of the thriller, as well as Mourad's sensationalist tone, guarantee the page turning effect his readers expect. More fundamentally, the genre ideally allows for a focus on the action of a reduced gallery of middle-class heroes, thereby mirroring prevalent articulations of 2011 as a revolution of middle-class youth.

1919 escapes the temporal and geographical reductions at work in 'dominant narrative configurations' (Ross 2002: 8) as embodied in al-Hakim's *'Awdat al-Ruh* or Mahfouz's *Bayn al-Qasrayn*, which reduce the revolution's time and space frame to the spring of 1919 in Cairo (see Chapter 3). The novel opens with a preface exposing the deep reasons for the revolution's explosion, beyond the event most often underlined as its direct cause, namely Saad Zaghlul's exile. It provides information on elements such as the British occupation of Egypt in 1882, the exile of Ahmad 'Urabi and his companions, and the peasants' ordeal as the 'young men among them were taken into forced labour to serve the occupier's soldiers' (Mourad 2014: 8) during the First World War. The chronology of the novel spans from February 1919 until 1924, thus including all the turmoil years. Moreover, in a clear effort to escape the geographical reduction of the events to the capital, the narrative evokes resistance scenes in Dawlat's village, Ibshaq al-Ghazal. In addition, the novel diversifies its sub-spaces beyond the well-known streets of Cairo that welcomed most of the demonstrations: many scenes take place in the basement under Café Rich and the petrified forest south of Cairo, where Ahmad Kira trains 'Abd al-Qadir Shihata to throw a bomb. The prison is also a space in which the revolutionaries are resisting the investigators and weaving solidarity bonds.

The opening scene of the novel directly introduces the reader to the unusual focalisation used by Mourad. The narrative opens with the epidemic that claims the lives of Ward's parents in February 1919. The dramatic scene evokes al-Hakim's *'Awdat al-Ruh*, which similarly opens with the Spanish flu epidemic. But while *'Awdat al-Ruh*'s sick characters are members of the upper middle class (except Mabruk) who together allegorically refer to the Egyptian Nation, *1919*'s victims of the epidemic belong to the margins of the national community. From the very start, Mourad's intertextual reference thus announces that the novel is adopting a fresh perspective and an unusual reading of the 1919 revolution. Instead of an exclusive male effendi focalisation, he uses a multi-focalised perspective, as each chapter is narrated from the point of view of a different character: two men and two women.

Moreover, unlike *Bayn al-Qasrayn*, and, to a lesser extent, *'Awdat al-Ruh*,

Mourad's novel does not frame the revolution as a series of peaceful demonstrations, but mainly as underground activities such as printing leaflets and preparing political assassinations, which entail the use of violence by the characters. Violence is no longer the exclusive prerogative of the colonial troops as in *Bayn al-Qasrayn* (see Chapter 3), nor of the so-called 'rabble' as in *al-Dahik al-Baki* (see Chapter 2). Rather, similarly to the narratives I analysed in Chapters 5 and 6, violence is narrated on a laudatory mode, framed as the choice of the brave. The novel rehabilitates organised violence as a tool the Wafd used by financing the Black Hand organisation, with Saad Zaghlul's approval.[33] The central element of the plot is the assassination attempt against the minister Muhammad Shafiq Pasha on 22 February 1920, carried out by 'Abd al-Qadir Shihata.

By the characterisation of his male revolutionary heroes, Mourad also takes issue with earlier representations of the revolution's actors, specifically in *Bayn al-Qasrayn*. None of them correspond in any way to the figure of the model child and 'politically correct' student activist imagined by Mahfouz. Rather, the actors of the revolution are devoted members of an underground 'terrorist' organisation, who all have a complicated and dark side to their personal life. There is not much Ahmad Kira shares with *Bayn al-Qasrayn*'s Fahmi, except his social status as a student. Not only does Kira firmly believe in violence as a revolutionary tool; he himself is a cold-blooded murderer who plans the assassinations and secures financing through regular meetings with 'Abd al-Rahman Fahmi. Moreover, while Fahmi is quite predictably in love with the daughter of the neighbours, Kira's romantic life defies tradition as he has two unusual affairs, one with Nazli, the daughter of a pasha who then marries King Fuad, and the other with Ward, although he knows she has worked as a prostitute. As for 'Abd al-Qadir Shihata, he functions as the perfect anti-Fahmi: before joining the nationalist struggle, he was a morally corrupt individual at all levels: in addition to being a cocaine addict and a regular brothel visitor, his first appearance in the text shows him furnishing a British camp with cigarettes, alcohol and cocaine (24–5).

Moreover, unlike the canonical novels *Bayn al-Qasrayn* and *'Awdat al-Ruh* (see Chapter 3), or even less canonical texts like *Qantara* and *al-Faylaq* (see Chapter 6), *1919* grants a prominent role to the female characters in the revolutionary struggle. Loosely inspired by a historical figure,[34] the character of Dawlat[35] attests to the active involvement of women from underprivileged and middle-class backgrounds in the organisation of the anti-colonial struggle. Although she is brought up in a poor peasant family, Dawlat has overcome all barriers burdening women of her class: she works and lives on her own in Cairo and is active in an organisation where she has to spend hours in a cave with men. Like Mariam in *al-Dahik al-Baki* (see Chapter 2) and her homonym in al-Imam's adaptation of *Bayn al-Qasrayn* (see Chapter 4), Dawlat is a courageous woman who saves the man she loves from the gallows. She hides 'Abd al-Qadir when he is on the run after having thrown a bomb at the minister's car, and falsely claims during his trial that he was her lover and that he spent the night with her the day before the attack, so as to provide him with an alibi (344 and 347).

The other central female character in the novel, Ward, an Armenian who successively works as a prostitute, then as a dancer at Badi'a Masabni's theatre[36] before turning into a nun, allows Mourad to question both the trope of national unity and the equation between morality and revolutionary activism. Although the novel refers to the unity between Muslims and Copts in the anti-colonial struggle, mainly through the character of 'Am Ishaq, an old Copt member of the Black Hand, the text does not shy away from mentioning confessional and ethnic strifes that arose during the revolution. Moreover, as it focalises attacks against Armenians through the perspective of one of their potential victims, the novel explodes the binary between 'good revolutionaries' and 'bad British occupiers' that lies at the core of the Mahfouzian narrative and its filmic adaptation.[37] As Ward is attempting to flee the brothel, 'Abd al-Qadir Shihata warns her that people in the streets are attacking Armenians after an Armenian man shot at demonstrators from a window (158). When she is finally able to escape, Ward finds herself in a street where 'a group of revolting people were writing insults and invectives on a closed jewellery shop with an Armenian name after they smashed the window'; she feels 'terrorised' as 'one of them stares at her Armenian features with a mixture of seduction and suspicion' (162). Most importantly, like the other Armenians who publicly voiced their support for the nationalist struggle,[38] Ward objectively supports the revolution. Although her initial reason for doing so is humanitarian rather than political, she hides and nurses a man she finds bleeding in the street, who appears to be a member of the Black Hand organisation – and is in fact none other than Ahmad Kira.

Finally, Mourad's ambition to produce an alternative history about 1919 may be most clearly embodied in the replica of historical documents inserted in the narrative. The content of those documents varies greatly, as it goes from short chronologies of the events to the secret correspondence between Saad Zaghlul and 'Abd al-Rahman Fahmi, including the *qasida* by Hafiz Ibrahim, *Kharaja al-ghawani*. Recognisable by their informative style, they are framed in small grey boxes; the style and lay-out aims at differentiating these documents from the fictional narrative and underlining their historical, *non-fictional* nature. However, though inspired by historical ones, these documents are in fact a pastiche. Dates and content of the letters between Zaghlul and Fahmi have been changed in order to fit the plot. Most of them highlight the theme of organised violence: a concise telegram by 'Abd al-Rahman Fahmi addressed to Saad Zaghlul requests authorisation to 'finance limited operations that leave traces on our friends' (124); reports by General Allenby to Earl Curzon, the British Secretary of State for Foreign Affairs, count the number of British officers killed (258–9), give information about arrested activists and their confessions (262); a short epigraph preceding one of the chapters contains information according to which 'demonstrators attacked the prison in Minya al-Qamh and freed the prisoners and then attacked the railways. Thirty People were killed' (119).

Unlike Soliman's, Mourad's use of archival documents cannot be read as a gesture towards building a 'counter-archive' to that of the state. Rather, the archival documents are submitted to the logic of the literary narrative, to its capacity to entertain and maintain the suspense. Mourad narrates history in the genre he is most familiar with, the thriller. His previous novels, *Vertigo* (2007) and *Turab al-Mas* (*Diamond Dust*, 2010) are political thrillers, and *al-Fil al-Azraq* (*The Blue Elephant*, 2012) is a psychological thriller. The thriller is 'a tense, exciting, tautly plotted and sometimes sensational type of novel . . . in which action is swift and suspense continual. Sex and violence may often play a considerable part in such a narrative, and they have tended to do so (often gratuitously) since the 1960s' (Cuddon 1999: 914–15). All the ingredients of the thriller are present in *1919*. The plot is built in order to maintain the suspense; violence and sex scenes are graphic, often unexpected or indeed gratuitous and depicted in exaggerated sensationalist terms. In the final ambush scene, replete with details worthy of an action movie, Ahmad Kira and 'Abd al-Qadir Shihata manage quite easily to kill five British officers and their Egyptian informer (434–6).

Hence, the sensational prevails over the historical, and it becomes tempting to read Mourad's novel as one that operates a '"spectacularisation" of the past', 'indicative of the commodification of history as a prevalent trend in contemporary culture' (Rousselot 2016: 8). But given the context in which Mourad writes, in addition to his privileged relationship with his readership, I argue for a more complex reading of *1919*. The end of the novel, while it warns against what Mourad calls a simplistic 'black and white reading' of history, mirrors the disillusionment of his readership with the 2011 revolution. First of all, it highlights the bitterness of the nationalist militants as they witness how the existing social structure remains unchanged, through the theme of the persisting gap between a privileged Wafdist leadership and hundreds of disenfranchised members. In a key scene following their release from prison in 1924, 'Abd al-Qadir Shihata and his former cellmate Naguib al-Ahwani are welcomed by Mustafa al-Nahhas, a historical figure well known as an important member of the Wafd's leadership. Al-Nahhas provides them with an envelope containing money 'to face immediate needs' and announces that they will be offered a job. Having served a nine-year sentence for an attempted assassination of Sultan Hussein in 1915, al-Ahwani is furious when he hears that he will be working as a low-ranking employee at the Bank of Egypt for a salary of 8 EG a month: 'Eight pounds! Me! I sacrificed my life in 1915 *ya basha*' (404).

Most importantly, the ending of the novel highlights the limits of gender emancipation and the deadly conflicts taking place at the heart of the nationalist struggle, as two of the revolutionary characters are killed by traitors to the nation. Dawlat has her throat slit by her brother, an illiterate peasant who shot his fellow villagers under the orders of British soldiers.[39] Ahmed Kira is killed in an ambush in Istanbul set by British intelligence officers with the help of a former comrade who betrays him for 10,000 EG – no other than Naguib al-Ahwani.[40] This last unexpected and sensationalist twist of the plot is presented by the author as directly reflecting the political developments of the moment at which the novel is published. According to Mourad, al-Ahwani's hand with its missing thumb is meant to metaphorically refer to the Rabʿa sit-in sign.[41] In his discourse about his own work, Mourad thus implicitly condemns the Muslim Brotherhood as former comrades who stabbed the movement in the back. The author in this manner both articulates the past in the political terms of the present and uses it to comment on the disillusion of the present.

This porosity between past and present, which I discussed at the beginning of this chapter, materialised in very different ways in Mourad and Soliman's work. Although both challenge the dominant trope of national unity, and attempt to trigger alternative remembering processes, their articulations of the 1919 revolution remain very dissimilar. Mourad created for his audience icons in which they could recognise themselves: middle class young men and women who, although defeated, had struggled and resisted against all odds. Although the streets of downtown Cairo are still named after the pashas of the Wafd, Mourad's enterprise of demystifying the revolution's icons by updating them, has at least succeeded in providing his audience with Wikipedia entries about young effendis active in 1919. Soliman's *Hawa al-Hurriyya* on the other hand provides her audience with a 'counter-archive' to that of the states. The archive she proposes is one that seeks to counter the erasure of revolutionary memory and one which is committed to rehabilitating the voice of the underprivileged: a voice systematically erased from the dominant narrative about 1919.

Notes

1. *Hawa al-Hurriyya* is available at <https://vimeo.com/138705682> (last accessed 21 June 2018). The text of the performance has not been published. Unfortunately, I was unable to access any video recordings of another play about the 1919 revolution performed in the aftermath of 2011, *Hikayat al-Nas fi-Thawrat 1919 (The Stories of the People in the 1919 Revolution)*. Directed by Ahmad Ismaʿil, it was performed on the stage of the National Theatre in 2014.
2. For working class strikes during the revolution see Anne Alexander and Mostafa Bassiouny (2014), *Bread, Freedom, Social Justice Workers and the Egyptian Revolution*, Zed Books; Nicholas S. Hopkins (ed.) (2015), *The Political Economy of the New Egyptian Republic*; Contributors Deena Abdelmonem, Yasmine Ahmed, Ellis Goldberg, Dina Makram-Ebeid, Zeinab Abul-Magd, Sandrine

Gamblin, Clement M. Henry, Hans Christian Korsholm Nielsen, David Sims. Cairo: The American University in Cairo Press.

3. More broadly, it is visible in ongoing changes that are the result of decades of 'ordinary citizens' mobilisations, through what Asef Bayat calls nonmovements, or 'the collective endeavours of millions of non-collective actors, carried out in the main squares, backstreets, court houses, and communities.' (Bayat 2013: x). These 'ordinary practices of everyday life' (Bayat 2013: 20–1) are visible among the urban youth in Egypt through initiatives enabling new forms of sociability despite the closure of the public space after 2013.

4. From *Usturat Ard al-Zalam* (*The Legend of the Land of Darkness*), published in the collection *Ma Wara' al-Tabi'a* (Supernatural) of *al-Mu'assasa al-'Arabiyya al-Haditha*, the book becomes *Fi Mamarr al-Fi'ran* (*In the Rats Corridor*), released by a general publisher. Chiti notes, that, in the latter, 'the reference to darkness is coupled with the one to the narrowness and insalubrity of the place, immediately recalling prison imagery, and the term "legend" disappears' (Chiti 2016: 279–80).

5. Graffiti of the revolution has received extensive critical attention in English. See for instance Mona Abaza (2013), 'Walls, Segregating Downtown Cairo and the Mohammed Mahmud Street Graffiti', *Theory, Culture and Society* 30, no. 1; John Lennon (2014), 'Assembling a Revolution Graffiti, Cairo and the Arab Spring', *Cultural Studies Review*, 20, no. 1, pp. 237–75; Enrique Klaus (2014), 'Graffiti and Urban Revolt in Cairo', *Built Environment* 40, March. For books displaying photographs of street art, see Heba Hilmi (2013), *Guwwaya Shahid*, Cairo: Dar al-'Ayn, and Sherif Borie (2012), ed. *Wall Talk: Graffiti of the Egyptian Revolution*.

6. See Mosireen's site (http://mosireen.org/?page_id=). For video material about the revolution, see <https://858.ma/> (last accessed 20 January 2020).

7. For independent theatre, see Nehad Selaiha (2003), *Egyptian Theatre, New Directions*, Cairo: Matabi' al-Hay'a al-'Amma lil-Kitab.

8. See Pauline Donizeau (2011), 'Théâtre de la révolution, théâtre révolutionnaire, révolution du théâtre en Égypte? *No Time for Art* de Laila Soliman', *Acta Litt&Arts* [Online], Les conditions du théâtre: la théâtralisation, Théâtre (du) politique, last updated: 08/10/2017.

9. The performance is produced by a private institution, Shish (Brussels/Cairo), founded by Ruud Gielens and Laila Soliman, and co-produced by Gorki Theater (Berlin), Kaaitheater (Brussels) and the Lift festival (London).

10. From her talk at the Centre for Translation Studies at the American University

in Cairo. Titled 'Bilingualism on Stage: The Case of *Hawa al-Hurriyya* (*Whims of Freedom*)', the lecture was held in Fall 2014 and is available at <https://www.youtube.com/watch?v=S9FgrywR7JM> (last accessed 21 June 2018).
11. Soliman's feminist statement pays tribute both to the individual contribution of 'two female artists and entrepreneurs' to the field of musical theatre – Munira al-Mahdiyya and Na'ima al-Masriyya (see Introduction) and to the collective resistance led by women in the countryside, as they braved local customs by publicly stating that they had been raped. Moreover, she had a nearly all-women staff – the director, historical researcher, performers, dramaturge, costume designer as well as one of the translators, are women.
12. More about Sayyid Darwish and his legacy can be found in Chapters 1 and 4.
13. For performances by women in post-revolutionary Tunisia 'that can function as defiant counter-archives to those of state institutions', see Nevine El Nossery, 'The '*mal d'archives*' and Tunisian Women Revolutionary Art', lecture delivered at the American University in Cairo, Centre for Translation Studies, 24 May 2018.
14. This is the object of another play by Laila Soliman, *Zig Zig*. For this play, see Dina Heshmat (2016), 'Un pan oublié de la révolution égyptienne de 1919', *Orient XXI*, 6 May. Available at <https://orientxxi.info/lu-vu-entendu/un-pan-oublie-de-la-revolution-egyptienne-de-1919,1320,1320> (last accessed 15 June 2018); Daniela Potenza. 'A History Lesson from the Present. Documenting Female Accounts in Laila Soliman's *Zig Zig*'. Proceedings of the 13th Euramal Conference, Naples 28 May-1 June 2018, (forthcoming).
15. Title translations by Kate Halls.
16. The song has been remixed in 2016 by Hamza Namira (1980), a popular singer known for his songs titled 'al-Midan' ('The Square'), 'Baladi ya Baladi' ('Oh My Country') and 'Insan' ('Human Being').
17. The information on, and translation of, this song comes from *Hawa al-Hurriyya*'s poster. Musical research Mustafa Sa'id, translation Kate Halls.
18. By casting a singer as one of the performers, Soliman also reconnects with the musical theatre of the beginning of the twentieth century.
19. Both the expressions 'excavating the past' and 'the historical other' are used by Elodie Rousselot in her study of the neo-Victorian novel.
20. As of 10 November 2019, Ahmed Mourad had a total of 16,6237 ratings on Goodreads, available at <https://www.goodreads.com/author/show/1633682._?from_search=true> (last accessed 10 November 2019). Mourad left his work as a photographer at the presidency (under Hosni Mubarak) to devote himself

entirely to his career as a novelist, after his first novel, *Vertigo* (2007) met with some success. Many of his works were turned into cinematic narratives; *Vertigo* into a television series; both *al-Fil al-Azraq*, (*The Blue Elephant*, 2012) and *Turab al-Mas* (*Diamond Dust*, 2010) were adapted for the screen by Marwan Hamid, respectively in 2014 and 2018.

21. See for instance Galal Amin's article, which describes the novel as 'successful, but 'very perplexing'. Amin acknowledges that Mourad is a writer 'who knows how to narrate an entertaining story' but he then asks himself whether it is only 'entertainement that is requested?' Galal Amin (2014), "An Riwayat 1919 li-Ahmad Mourad. Riwaya Najiha wa lakinnaha Muhayyira Jiddan', *Al-Ahram*, 20 May, available at <http://www.ahram.org.eg/NewsQ/290734.aspx> (last accessed 24 June 2019). See also Sharif 'Azir (2014), 'Ahmad Murad wa madrasat al-istihbal al-adabi', *Mada Masr*, 2 July, available at <http://tiny.cc/9wd5bz> (last accessed 28 August 2019) and Nidal Mamduh (2018), 'Jawa'iz al-Dawla al-Misriyya: Kathir min al-Hajb wal Tarwij lil-Thaqafa al-Istihlakiyya', *al-Hayat*, 14 June, available at <https://bit.ly/2ksu63x> (last accessed 3 September 2019).

22. An article in *al-yaum al-sabi'* refers to the polemic unleashed after Mourad was awarded the prize. The article mentions that the prize is normally awarded to writers having over fifteen years' experience in the field. Available at <youm7.com/story/2018/6/15/3834178-هل-فاز-أحمد-مراد-بجائزة-التفوق-بالمخالفة-للقانون-والأعلى-للثقافة> (last accessed 24 June 2018).

23. See for instance a lecture followed by a book signing at Cairo Opera House in April 2014, available at <https://www.youtube.com/watch?v=byMF_E0aGOo> (last accessed 13 June 2018), and a book signing at Diwan bookshop in Zamalek, available at <https://www.youtube.com/watch?v=5FfcKba74vo> (last accessed 13 June 2018).

24. See interview available at <https://www.youtube.com/watch?v=byMF_E0aGOo> (last accessed 24 June 2018).

25. Mourad takes some liberty with a few historical details. For instance, he replaces Nazli's lover, originally Saad Zaghlul's nephew Sa'id (as narrated by Mustafa Amin in *Min Wahid li-'Ashara*) with one of the main figures of the Black Hand organisation, Ahmad Kira. In another example, Zaghlul addresses the officers who come to arrest him on 8 March in 'perfect English', while Zaghlul spoke French, but not English, as attested in his own diaries in which he relates communication problems with the jailors during his exile due to language.

26. For Ahmed Kira, see Yahya Haqqi (1984), *Nas fil Zill wa Shakhsiyyat Ukhra*.

Cairo: al-Hay'a al-Misriyya al-'Amma lil-Kitab, pp. 188–96. Haqqi relates that he met Ahmad Kira during a trip in Istanbul.

27. See 'Hafl Tawqi' Kitab 1919 lil Katib Ahmad Murad bi Diwan al-Zamalek', available at <https://www.youtube.com/watch?v=5FfcKba74vo> (last accessed 2 September 2019).
28. Ibid.
29. See 'Riwayat Ahmad Mourad Tatasaddar al-Kutub al-Akthar Mabi'an', *al-Bawwaba*. 10 April 2014, available at <https://www.albawaba.com/ar//أدب-وثقافة/أحمد-مراد-1919-الكتب-الاكثر-مبيعا-567795> (last accessed 13 June 2018). No exact numbers are available. A pocket edition of the novel published in June 2018 states on the cover sheet that this is the tenth edition and that editions two through six were published in 2014 (the same year as the first), the seventh in 2016, the eighth and the ninth in 2017. On *Goodreads*, the novel had gathered, as of 10 November 2019, 19,576 ratings and 2,573 reviews, available at <https://www.goodreads.com/book/show/21456940-1919> (last accessed 10 November 2019).
30. The entry 'Ahmad 'Abd al-Hayy Kira', available at <https://ar.wikipedia.org/wiki/أحمد_عبد_الحي_كيرة> (last accessed 15 May 2018) was created in April 2014, and the entry 'Dawlat Fahmi', available at <https://ar.wikipedia.org/wiki/دولت_فهمي> (last accessed 15 May 2018) was created in June 2014. A short documentary about Dawlat was published in June 2014 on YouTube, available at <https://www.youtube.com/watch?v=ptjsdBhY8EQ> (last accessed 12 June 2018).
31. Available at <https://www.youtube.com/watch?v=I1dWRpwosJA> (last accessed 15 May 2018).
32. See for instance <https://ar-ar.facebook.com/king.farouk.faroukmisr/posts/537235929711046> and <https://www.facebook.com/turath.masry/posts/948468745240628:0> (last accessed 15 May 2018).
33. For violence and its use by the Wafd's underground organisation apparatus, see Chapter 5.
34. According to Ahmad Mourad, the existence of Dawlat Fahmi as a historical character has yet to be proven. The only available information about her is in *Asrar Thawrat 1919* by Mustafa Amin and a TV episode about her made in 1987 (also based on a script by Mustafa Amin, no longer available). In those documents, Dawlat (or Hikmat) Fahmi is from a wealthy family in Minya (or Asyut). A member of the Wafd's secret organisation, she falsely declared at 'Abd al-Qadir Shihata's tribunal that he spent the night before the assassination attempt with her (Personal communication with the author, 14 May 2018).

35. Her name suggests an allegorical reading of her character. Dawlat comes from *dawla* (the state). By choosing a name uncommon in the countryside –Dawlat is a name with Turkish consonance more common in upper middle class families – Mourad draws the reader's attention to the allegory.
36. An actress, singer and dancer born in Damascus, Badiʻa al-Masabni (1892–1974) settled in Cairo in the 1910s and was a member of Naguib al-Rihani's theatre troupe. After her divorce from al-Rihani she established her own theatre.
37. See Armbrust 1995: 92 and Chapter 4, note 16.
38. See Introduction, note 36.
39. In accordance with his statement that it was important to look at actors of the 1919 revolution not as statues, but as people of flesh and blood, the narrator hereby states that the Egyptian peasant should not be read as a flawless romantic figure.
40. According to Yahya Haqqi, Ahmad Kira was indeed killed by British Intelligence in Istanbul, but ten years later, in 1934.
41. Personal communication with the author, 14 May 2018. Some of Mourad's readers seem to share this interpretation. During a book-signing at the Diwan Library in Zamalek, a woman in the audience interrupted Mourad while he was talking about the fact that the comparison between 1919 and 2011 imposed itself during the writing proccess. She told him that she personally felt it was the present he was talking about in his novel. She asserted, to the laughing approval of the audience: 'you are talking about particular persons, and I can tell who they are'. See 'Hafl Tawqiʻ Kitab 1919 lil Katib Ahmad Murad bi Diwan al-Zamalek', available at <https://www.youtube.com/watch?v=5FfcKba74vo> (last accessed 2 September 2019).

Conclusion

I started this book with a scene of youth frantically cleaning slogans off fences on Tahrir Square in the immediate aftermath of President Husni Mubarak's resignation; I argued that, as it encapsulated the politics of erasure at work in the memory of the 2011 revolution, the scene could help us imagine how the traces of another revolution were lost and erased, decade after decade. It remained present in my mind while I was reading and watching the literary and cinematic narratives dealing with the 1919 anti-colonial revolution in Egypt that constitute the corpus of this book. I systematically tried to locate *what* exactly had been silenced, and *why*.

The answer to these two questions, however, is not straightforward. There are as many ways of narrating 1919 as there are authors, obviously, but also as there are changing political, economic and cultural contexts. One of the main postulates of this book is that 'every present invents its own past' (Spiropoulou 2015: 119). 1919 was articulated differently in 1924, 1964, and 2014; yet, a dominant imaginary about this revolutionary moment emerges beyond this diversity, shaped through processes of remembering and forgetting coined by successive political and cultural elites.

Canonical novels and films played a central role in this process, presenting 1919 as a key moment for the creation of a modern Egyptian nation and describing the male middle class as leading the revolution, thus marginalising the role of women and underprivileged actors from both urban and rural backgrounds.

This male middle class storyline, however, which has remained dominant until today,[1] is challenged in a wide range of literary narratives about the 1919 revolution. Those novels, plays and short-stories, examined in this book, each question the dominant narrative configurations in which 1919 is enshrined by enlarging the restricted space and time frame beyond Cairo in Spring 1919 and challenging the characterisation of the effendi as the main actor of the revolution, either by turning him into an impotent figure, or by replacing him with underprivileged actors from rural or urban backgrounds. The tone used to celebrate the 1919 demonstrations demanding Saad Zaghlul's liberation is either railed at or used to describe the social dynamics of the revolution. Women from diverse class backgrounds are given a more strategic role than the one they are relegated to in the iconic photographs of the revolution.

By putting these alternative narratives in conversation with the prevailing image of 1919, this book both documents the revolution and contributes to a critical re-evaluation of how it has been narrated, questioning the dominant image of idealised national unity in which 1919 is reified. It shows, through literature and film, that the revolution entailed significantly more class tensions and radical politics than what is generally admitted and allows the reader to imagine the breadth of hope it triggered. It was not only the resistance to colonial occupation that was at stake during the years 1918–23; rather, it was also the struggle against a complex network of gender and class oppressions. These years must be understood as an extraordinary moment during which people envisioned and experienced much more than the well-known iconic demonstrations under the slogan of the united cross and crescent.

As this work comes to a close, I want to evoke a number of initiatives that seem radically opposed to the politics of erasure with which I have been concerned in this book. In 2019, while I was in the process of finishing this work, numerous initiatives commemorating the centennial of the 1919 revolution emerged.[2] Cairo University held a celebration on 13 March, in addition to a number of other universities.[3] The Department of Arab and Islamic Studies of the American University in Cairo held its Annual History Seminar around the theme of the 1919 revolution.[4] The University held a daylong celebration, concluded by a concert, including Sayyid Darwish songs by the group Eskenderella. The Supreme Council of Culture organised a three-day conference titled 'Thawrat 1919 ba'd Mi'at 'Am' (The 1919 Revolution After a Hundred Years).[5]

Similarly, a large number of publications celebrated the centennial. The publisher Dar al-Shuruq devoted an entire collection to re-publishing documents about the revolution. A special issue of the magazine *al-Mussawwar* was published. The issue of the magazine *Kitab Maraya* titled *Al-Thawra wal Tarikh: 1919 ba'd Mi'at 'Am* (*The Revolution and History: 1919 after 100 Years*) gathered together no less than twenty-five contributions.[6] The special edition of the magazine *Dhakirat Misr* devoted to the revolution contained, in addition to a large number of interesting analytical articles and testimonies,[7] a large number of hitherto unseen photographs.[8] Mustafa Musharrafa's novel *Qantara al-Ladhi Kafara* was reedited.[9] A similar frenzy was noted on the screen. In addition to a number of documentaries – including a propagandist one by the Wafd,[10] a contract to turn Ahmed Mourad's novel *1919* into a film was signed; the film will be a big budget affair, directed by Marwan Hamid, featuring the stars Ahmad 'Izz and Karim 'Abd al-'Aziz.[11]

Beyond the commercial trend and the fashion for the centennial, this '1919 mania' reveals a deeper development at work in the Egyptian intellectual and cultural fields. There is a revival of the interest in the past, which participates in a broader worldwide phenomenon (Rousso 2007: 3).[12] This 'memorial reactivation of the past' (Hamel 2006), however, materialises in very different ways. The remembering of 1919 that is taking place is a plural one; rather than one commemoration of 1919, there is a plurality of commemorations taking place. Many of them seek to perpetuate the dominant history of 1919 described in the introduction to this book, or to legitimise the current regime. On the other hand, there is an alternative remembering, seeking to uncover the silences of the dominant narrative. As is happening elsewhere in the world, there is 'the formation of a new public space ... characterised by an increased expression of groups proposing historical narrations tending to reject not only national history but also an important part of scholarly history' (Rousso 2007: 5).

This trend materialises in the work of researchers and artists from the younger generation who are concerned with the gaps in the Egyptian archive, and drawing attention to the silences of the dominant history.[13] Their work seeks to confront what I called in my introduction, following Paul Ricoeur, a 'manipulated' and 'ideologised' memory of 1919, embodied most powerfully in the Nasserist framing of 1919, as exemplified in the history textbook I mentioned in the introduction. A leitmotif in the interventions of younger writers and artists is the urge to go beyond the narrative taught at school. As I have already noted in Chapter 7, both the playwright Laila Soliman and the novelist Ahmed Mourad mentioned the need to question and rewrite dominant narratives about 1919, and about history more generally.

This 'process of recalling' remains

> influenced by collective dynamics that constantly readjust a number of images, impressions and narratives more or less sharp, but always fragmented and partial, in order to form a representation of the past presented as accurate in term of historical veracity and exemplary in term of values. (Hamel 2006)

This seems to suggest that, despite all efforts, the current process of recollection will produce nothing but a new, recontextualised narrative about 1919, as selective as its predecessors. However, Soliman and Mourad's statements, coming from artists belonging to two different areas of the Egyptian literary field, reveal a broad awareness of the politics of erasure referred to earlier. It seems safe to say that the centennial of 2019 marks the end of one period and the beginning of another for the memory of 1919. Whilst the absolute truth about what happened during the years 1918–23 remains methodologically unattainable, the current collective efforts will hopefully open the door for a more pluralistic process of remembering a revolution that has for a century been reduced to a few iconic, reductive images and slogans.

Notes

1. See Hakim Abdelnaeem (2019), 'What's the First Image that Comes to mind When You Think of the 1919 Revolution?' Mada Masr, 26 April, available at <https://madamasr.com/en/2019/04/26/feature/culture/whats-the-first-image-that-comes-to-mind-when-you-think-of-the-1919-revolution/> (last accessed 4 September 2019). In addition, the film by Hassan al-Iman is used to introduce a short documentary made by students of the American University in Cairo about the 1919 revolution.
2. Although I focus on initiatives taken in the Egyptian intellectual and cultural field, a similar phenomenon can be observed outside Egypt. In Paris, the Arab World Institute hosted a seminar around democratic moments in the Arab World, introduced by a panel about the 1919 revolution. In London, the British Egyptian Society, the London Middle East Institute, the School of Oriental and African Studies of the University of London and the Council for British Research in the Levant organised a conference titled 'The Egyptian Revolution

of 1919: The Birth of the Modern Nation'. The annual meeting of the Middle East Studies Association (MESA) held in November 2019 in New Orleans featured three panels under the label 'Rethinking 1919".

3. See for instance Hasan Salih (2019), 'Adab Banha: Thawrat 1919 Jama'at Atyaf al-Sha'b Kullahu', al-Watan, 12/12', available at <https://www.elwatannews.com/news/details/4058552> (last accessed 22 August 2019).
4. See <http://schools.aucegypt.edu/huss/aric/Pages/PROGRAM%202019.aspx> (last accessed 26 August 2019).
5. See <https://bit.ly/2L2aRby> (last accessed 26 August 2019).
6. *Al-Thawra wal Tarikh: 1919 ba'd Mi'at 'Am (The Revolution and History: 1919 after 100 years) Kitab Maraya*, (2019), Cairo: Maraya.
7. See the interesting testimony of Yusuf Darwish, a lawyer and Marxist activist well-known for his support to working class struggles who was a little boy during the revolution: Yusuf Darwish (2019), 'Mudhakkirat Shahid 'Iyan 'Ala Thawrat 1919', *Dhakirat Misr 36*, January.
8. *Mi'awiyyat Thawrat 1919 1919/2019, Dhakirat Misr 36*, January 2019.
9. Musharrafa, Mustafa [1966] (2019), *Qantara al-Ladhi Kafara,* Cairo: Dar Battana, Yusuf Sha'ban (ed.).
10. See 'Film Watha'iqi li-Tarikh al-Wafd fi Mi'awiyyat Thawrat 1919' (2019), al-Masry al-Youm, 9/03, available at <https://www.almasryalyoum.com/news/details/1376612> (last accessed 22 August 2019).
11. See 'Ahmad 'Izz Yuzih al-Sitar 'an Afish 1919 ma' Karim 'Abd al-'Aziz', available at <https://bit.ly/2kUZesH> (last accessed 23 August 2019).
12. This is reflected, among other things, in the resurgence of the historical novel. The past decades have witnessed the publication of historical fiction dealing with all periods of Egyptian history from pharaonic to early colonial, including the mamluk era. See for instance: Ahmed Mourad (2016), *Ard al-Illah*, Cairo: Dar al-Shuruq; Ibrahim Farghali (2011), *Mughamara fi Madinat al-Mawta,* Dubai: Dar Hakaya; Nasser 'Iraq (2015), *al-Azbakiyya,* Cairo: Dar al-Misriyya al-Libnaniyya; Muhammad al-Mansi Qindil (2015), *Katiba Sawda',* Cairo: Dar al-Shuruq; Hajjaj Uddul (2011), *Thalath Burtuqalat Mamlukiyya*, Cairo: Dar al-'Ayn; Ashraf 'Ashmawi (2016), *Kilab al-Ra'i,* Cairo: al-Dar al-Misriyya al-Libnaniyya; Rim Basyuni (2018), *Awlad al-Nas, Thulathiyyat al-Mamalik*, Cairo: Dar al-Nahda lil-Nashr. For the genre of the historical novel in Arabic fiction, see Roger Allen, 'The Arabic Novel and History' in Waïl S.Hassan, ed.(2017) *The Oxford Handbook of Arab Novelistic Traditions*, New York: Oxford University Press.

13. See, for instance: Kareem Megahed (2019), 'Idolized Narratives of 1919: Are They Too Good to Be True?', contribution to the Annual History Seminar held by the Department of Arab and Islamic Civilizations, AUC, 5 April; Ahmad Diya' Dardir (2019), '1919 Fajwat al-Arshif al-Muntija', Cairo: *Kitab Maraya*.

Bibliography

Primary Sources

Abaza, Fikri (1933), *Al-Dahik al-Baki*, Cairo: al-Hilal.
Amin, Mustafa (1977), *Min Wahid li-'Ashara*, Cairo: al-Maktab al-'Arabi al-Hadith.
Al-Badawi, Mahmud (1965), 'Dhata Layla', in Mahmud al-Badawi, *Hadatha Dhata Layla*, Cairo: al-Dar al-Qawmiyya lil-Tiba'a wal-Nashr.
Al-Hakim, Tawfiq [1933] (1998), *'Awdat al-Ruh*, Cairo: al-Hay'a al-'Amma al-Misriyya lil-Kitab. English translation by William M. Hutchins (2012), *Return of the Spirit*, Cairo: The American University in Cairo Press.
'Izz al-Din, Amin (1999), *Al-Faylaq*, Cairo: Markaz al-Fustat lil-Dirasat.
Mahfouz, Naguib [1956] (2014), *Bayn al-Qasrayn*, Cairo: Dar al-Shuruq. English translation by William M. Hutchins and Olive E. Kenny (2001), *Palace Walk*, Cairo: The American University in Cairo Press.
Murad, Ahmad (2014), *1919*, Cairo: Dar al-Shuruq.
Musharrafa, Mustafa [1966] (1991), *Qantara al-Ladhi Kafara*, Cairo: Majallat Adab wa-Naqd. (reedited 2019, Cairo: Dar Battana, Yusuf Sha'ban (ed.).
Sidqi, Amin [1923] (1989), *al-Intikhabat* in Nagwa 'Anus (ed.), *Masrahiyyat Amin Sidqi*. Cairo: Matabi' al-Hay'a al-Misriyya al-'Amma lil-Kitab.
Sidqi, Amin (1924), *Al-Imbratur*, unpublished manuscript.
Tsirkas, Stratis (1994), *Nur al-Din Bumba*, translated by Yani Milakhrinudi, Cairo: Matba'at Atlas.
'Ubayd, 'Isa, 'Mudhakkirat Hikmat Hanim', Cairo: Matba'at Ra'amsis bil-Faggala (publication date not available).
Al-Yusuf, Fatma (2010), *Dhikrayat*, Cairo: Mu'assassat Ruz al-Yusuf.
Wahba, Sa'd al-Din (1967), *al-Masamir*, Cairo: Dar al-Katib al-'Arabi.

Films and Plays

'Awdat al-Ruh, series (1977), directed by Husayn Kamal.
'Awdat Sa'd Zaghlul min al-Manfa (1923), directed by Muhammad Bayyumi.
Bayn al-Qasrayn (1964), directed by Hasan al-Imam, Egypt: Aflam Jabra'il Talhami.
Bayn al-Qasrayn, series (1987), directed by Yusuf Marzuq, Dubai: Mu'assassat al-Khalij lil-A'mal al-Fanniyya.
Gumhuriyyat Zifta, directed by Muhammad Farid, al-Jazeera al-Watha'iqiyya, available at <https://www.youtube.com/watch?v=WTx17i5aa1Y> (last accessed 12 June 2019).
Gumhuriyyat Zifta, series (1999), directed by Isma'il 'Abd al-Hafiz, Egypt: Sawt al-Qahira lil Sawtiyyat wal Mar'iyyat.
Hawa al-Hurriyya (2014), directed by Laila Soliman.
Mustafa Kamil (1951), directed by Ahmad Badrakhan, Egypt: Aflam Ahmad Badrakhan.
Sa'd Zaghlul (2009), directed by Tamir Muhsin, al-Jazeera al-Watha'iqiyya, <https://www.youtube.com/watch?v=IbGbiEcBwMM> (last accessed 21 January 2019).
Sayyid Darwish (1966), directed by Ahmad Badrakhan, Egypt: al-Sharika al-'Amma lil-Intaj al-Sinima'i al-'Arabi.

Periodicals and Others

Al-Tarikh (2019), in *al-Imtihan*, Cairo: al-Dawliyya lil-Tab' wal Nashr wal Tawzi'.

Secondary Sources: Books, Articles and Newspaper Articles in Arabic

Abaza, Fikri (1925), *Majmu'at Maqalat Fikri Abaza al-Muhami: Nushirat bil-Jara'id al-Yawmiyya wal-Usbu'iyya li-Munasabat Siyasiyya Wa-Ijtima'iyya*, Cairo: al-Matba'a al-Tijariyya al-Kubra.
——— (1969), *Hawadit*, Cairo: Dar al-Sha'b.
——— (1969), 'Dhikrayat Nisf Qarn aw Khamsin 'Aman', *Al-Musawwar*, 7 March.
——— (2000), *Al-Dahik al-Baki al-Marhalatan al-Ula wal Thaniya*, Cairo: Dar al-Hilal.
'Abd al-Nasser, Gamal [1954] (1996), *Falsafat al-Thawra*, Cairo: Bayt al-'Arab lil-Tawthiq al-'Asri.
'Abd al-Nur, Fakhri (1992), *Mudhakkirat Fakhri 'Abd al-Nur, Thawrat 1919 wa Dawr Sa'd Zaghlul wal Wafd fil Haraka al-Wataniyya*, Cairo: Dar al-Shuruq.
'Abd al-Rahman, Fahmi (1988), *Mudhakkirat 'Abd al-Rahman Fahmi, Yaumiyyat Misr al-Siyasiyya*, (ed. Yunan Labib Rizq), Cairo: al-Hay'a al-Misriyya al-'Amma lil-Kitab.

Aboul-Hussein, Hiam (1968), *Les Mille et une Nuits dans le théâtre égyptien, inspiration arabe et influence française*, thèse de doctorat de 3ème cycle, unpublished, Paris.

'Aqqad, 'Abbas Mahmud [1952] (1988), *Saad Zaghlul: Za'im Al-Thawra*, Cairo: Dar al-Hilal.

—––– [1936] (2017), *Saad Zaghlul: Sira wa-Tahiyya*, Cairo: al-Hay'a al-Misriyya al-'Amma lil-Kitab.

Abu Bakr, Midhat (1998), 'Gumhuriyyat Zifta Tuwajih al-Nizam al-'Alami al-Jadid', Cairo: *al-Usbu'*, 19 January.

Abu Ghazi, 'Imad (2019), 'Saad wal-Thawra', Cairo, *Majallat Diwan*, 6 January.

Abu l-Magd, Sabri (1987), *Fikri Abaza*, Cairo: Markaz al-Dirasat al-Suhufiyya wal-Tarikhiyya bi-Mu'assasat Dar al-Ta'awun.

Al-'Alim, Mahmud Amin (1967), 'Muqaddima' in Sa'd al-Din Wahba, *al-Masamir*, Cairo: Dar al-Katib al-'Arabi.

—––– (1970), *Ta'mmulat fi 'Alam Naguib Mahfouz*, Cairo: al-Hay'a al-Misriyya al-'Amma lil-Ta'lif wal-Nashr.

Amin, Mustafa [1974] (1975), *Sana Ula Sijn*, Cairo: Mu'assassat Akhbar al-Yaum.

—––– [1974] (1991), *Asrar Thawrat 1919*, Cairo: Mu'assassat Akhbar al-Yaum.

Anis, Muhammad [1963] (2019), *Dirasat fi Watha'iq Thawrat 1919, al-Murasalat al-Sirriyya bayn Saad Zaghlul wa 'Abd al-Rahman Fahmi*, Cairo: Dar al-Shuruq.

'Anus, Najwa Ibrahim (1989), *Al-Masrah al-Dahik: Masrah Amin Sidqi*, Cairo: Dar al-Hilal.

'Ashri, Fathi (1973), *Daqqat al-Masrah*, Cairo: al-Hay'a al-'Amma al-Misriyya lil-Kitab.

Al-'Antabli, Fawzi (1958), 'al-Mujtama' al-Misri, Kama Tusawwiruhu Riwayat Bayn al-Qasrayn', Cairo: *al-Majalla*, March.

'Awad, Luwis (1989), *Awraq al-'Umr: Sanawat al-Takwin*, Cairo: Maktabat Madbuli.

'Ayyad, Shukri (1991), 'Dars al-Ustadh', in Mustafa Musharrafa, *Qantara al-Ladhi Kafara*, Cairo: Kitab Adab wa Naqd, pp. 7–11.

Badr, 'Abd al-Muhsin Taha [1963] (1977), *Tatawwur al-Riwaya al-'Arabiyya al-Haditha fi Misr, 1870–1938*, Cairo: Dar al-Ma'arif.

Barakat, 'Ali (1977), *Tatawwur al-Milkiyya al-Zira'iyya fi Misr wa Atharuha 'ala al-Haraka al-Siyasiyya*, Cairo: Dar al-Thaqafa al-Jadida.

—––– (2009), 'Al-Rif al-Misri fi Thawrat 1919', in Ahmad Zakariyya al-Shiliq (ed.) *Tis'un 'Aman 'ala Thawrat 1919*, Cairo: Dar al-Kutub wal Watha'iq al-Qawmiyya.

Baha' al-Din, Ahmad (1990), 'Imbraturiyyat Zifta' in *Ayyam laha Tarikh*, Cairo: al-Hilal.

Al-Barghouti, Tamim (2007), *al-Wataniyya al-Alifa, al-Wafd wa Bina' al-Dawla al-Wataniyya fi-Zill al-Isti'mar*, Cairo: Dar al-Kutub wal Watha'iq al-Qawmiyya.

Darwish, Yusuf (2019), 'Mudhakkirat Shahid 'Iyan 'ala Thawrat 1919', *Dhakirat Misr* 36, January.

Al-Dusuqi, 'Asim (1981), *Thawrat 1919 fil Aqalim, Min al-Watha'iq al-Britaniyya*, Cairo: Dar al-Kitab al-Jami'i.

Fadl, Bilal (1998), 'Gumhuriyyat Zifta Taksab wa Yusri al-Gindi Yukaffir 'an Sayyi'at "al-Taw'am" wa fi "Zizinya" al-Malik Malik', Cairo: *al-Dustur*, 21 January.

Fawzi, Husayn (1968), *Sindbad fi Rihlat al-Hayat*, Cairo: Dar al-Ma'arif.

Filastin, Wadi' (2009), 'Fikri Abaza', in Hamdi al-Sakkut (ed.), *Qamus al-Adab al-'Arabi al-Hadith*, Cairo: Dar al-Shuruq.

Al-Fishawi, 'Abd al-Fattah (1964), 'Bayn al-Qasrayn.. wal-Mukhrij al-Ladhi I'taqala Nafsahu', *al-Jumhuriyya*, 5 March.

Gabir, Nasir (1998), 'Gumhuriyyat Zifta: Limadha Tawaqqafat Faj'a… bil Sakta al-Tilifizyuniyya?', Cairo: *al-Kawakib*, 27 January.

al-Gawadi, Muhammad (2009), *al-'Amal al-Sirri fi Thawrat 1919, Mudhakkirat al-Shubban al-Wafdiyyin, Ibrahim 'Abd al-Hadi, Sayyid Basha, 'Iryan Yusuf Sa'd, Muhammad Mazhar Sa'id*, Cairo: al-Shuruq al-Dawliyya.

Gayyid, Ramzi Mikha'il (1980), *al-Wihda al-Wataniyya fi Thawrat 1919*, Cairo: al-Hay'a al-Misriyya al-'Amma lil-Kitab.

Al-Gindi, Muhammad Yusuf (1998), 'al-Batal al-Haqiqi li-Thawrat Zifta', Cairo: *Ruz al-Yusuf*, 16 February, pp. 70–1.

Ghurab, Yusuf Amin (1957), 'Bayn al-Qasrayn' *Akhir Sa'a*, Cairo, 23 January, p. 25.

Hafiz, Sabri (2001), 'Awdat al-Ruh wa Ta'sis al-Mutakhayyal al-Qawmi, in *Tawfiq al-Hakim: Hudur Mutajaddid*, Cairo: al-Majlis al-A'la lil-Thaqafa.

Hammad, Muhammad Ali (1933), 'Awdat al-Ruh bayna al-'Amiyya wal 'Arabiyya', *Al-Risala*, Cairo, 15 September, pp. 40–2.

Haqqi, Yahya (1984), ''Abd al-Hayy Kira' in *Nas fil Zill wa Shakhsiyyat Ukhra*, Cairo: al-Hay'a al-Misriyya al-'Amma lil-Kitab.

Ibrahim, Hafiz [1927] (1937), *Diwan Hafiz Ibrahim, Dabatahu wa-Sahhahahu wa-Sharahahu Ahmad Amin wa Ahmad al-Zayn wa Ibrahim al-Ibyari vol.2*, Cairo: Wizarat al-Ma'arif al-'Umumiyya, pp. 218–19.

Idris, Yusuf (1991), 'Qantara al-Ladhi Kafara: 'Alam Khass Mashur', in Mustafa Musharrafa, *Qantara al-Ladhi Kafara*, Cairo: Kitab Adab wa Naqd, pp. 7–11.

Isma'il, Sayyid 'Ali (2006), *Masrah 'Ali al-Kassar*, 2 vols., Cairo: al-Markaz al-Qawmi lil-Masrah wal-Musiqa wal-Funun al-Sha'biyya.

'Izz al-Din, Amin (1969), 'al-Shughl fil Sulta, Qissat Faylaq al-'Amal al-Misri wa Faylaq al-Jimal', *al-Musawwar* 7 March.

J. S. (1964), 'Shay' Ismuhu: Siyadat al-Rajul', *Akhir Sa'a*, no. 1529, 12 February, p. 20.

Kamil, Sa'd (1963a), 'Al-Mukhrij Tawfiq Salih wal Khilaf Hawl Film "Bayn al-Qasrayn', *Akhir Sa'a*, no. 1492, 29 May, p. 34.

—— (1963b), 'Ra'y Naguib Mahfouz fil Khilaf Hawl Film Bayn al-Qasrayn', *Akhir Sa'a* no. 1495, 19 June, no page number available.

—— (1964a), 'Min al-"'Atifa al-Mushina" ila Film "Bayn al-Qasrayn"', *Akhir Sa'a*, no. 1534 18 March, p. 38.

—— (1964b), 'Ma Huwa Dawr al-Qita' al-'Amm fil Sinima?', *Akhir Sa'a*, no. 1537, 8 April, p. 40.

Kassar, Magid (1991), *'Ali al-Kassar: Barbari Misr al-Wahid*, Cairo: Dar Akhbar al-Yawm.

—— (1993), *'Ali al-Kassar wa-Thawrat al-Kumidiya*, Cairo: Dar al-Ma'arif.

—— (2006), *'Ali al-Kassar fi Zaman 'Imad Al-Din*, Cairo: al-Hay'a al-Misriyya al-'Amma lil-Kitab.

Sami Khashaba (1989), 'Fahmi 'Abd al-Gawwad', in Ghali Shukri (ed.) *Naguib Mahfouz: Ibda' Nisf Qarn*, Beirut–Cairo: al-Shuruq.

Lashin, 'Abd al-Khaliq (1975), *Sa'd Zaghlul wa-Dawruhu fil-Siyasa al-Misriyya*, Beirut–Cairo: Dar al-'Awda.

Mahfouz, Naguib (1964), 'Ra'y Naguib Mahfouz fi Hasan al-Imam', *Ruz al-Yusuf*, no. 1867, 23 March, p. 45.

Al-Mazini, Ibrahim 'Abd al-Qadir (1933), "'Awdat al-Ruh' *Al-Balagh*. Cairo. 25 June.

Al-Nahhas, Hashim, (1997), *Naguib Mahfouz fil-Sinima al-Misriyya: ma Qabla Nubil wa-Ba'daha*, Cairo: al-Majlis al-A'la lil-Thaqafa.

Al-Naggar, 'Abd al-Wahab (2010), *Mudhakkirat*, Cairo: Dar al-Kutub wal-Watha'iq al-Qawmiyya.

Al-Naqqash, Raga' (2011), *Safahat min Mudhakkirat Naguib Mahfouz*, Cairo: Dar al-Shuruq.

Al-Ra'i, 'Ali (2003), *Masrah al-Sha'b*, Cairo: al-Hay'a al-'Amma li-Qusur al-Thaqafa.

Al-Rafi'i, 'Abd al-Rahman (1946), *Thawrat 1919, Tarikh Misr al-Qawmi min 1914 ila 1921*, Cairo: al-Nahda al-Misriyya [vol. 2 1999 Cairo: al-Hay'a al-Misriyya al-'Amma lil-Kitab].

Al-Rihani, Naguib (n.d.), *Mudhakkirat Naguib al-Rihani*, Cairo: Hindawi.

Sa'd, 'Iryan Yusuf (2007), *Mudhakkirat 'Iryan Yusuf Sa'd*, Cairo: al-Shuruq.

Al-Saʿid, Rifʿat (1976), *Saʿd Zaghlul Bayna al-Yamin wal Yasar*, Beirut: Dar al-Qadaya.

Al-Sakkut, Hamdi (2000), *al-Riwaya al-ʿArabiyya, Bibliyughrafiya wa-Madkhal Naqdi*, (1865–1995), Cairo: The American University in Cairo Press.

——— (2007), *Naguib Mahfouz: Bibliyughrafiya Tajribiyya wa-Sirat Haya wa-Madkhal Naqdi*. Cairo: al-Hayʾa al-Misriyya al-ʿAmma lil-Kitab

Salim, Latifa Muhammad [1984] (2009), *Misr fil-Harb al-ʾAlamiyya al-Ula*, Cairo: al-Shuruq.

Shaʿrawi, Huda (2013), *Mudhakkirat*, Cairo: Dar al-Tanwir.

Al-Sharuni, Yusuf (1957), 'Bayn al-Qasrayn li-Naguib Mahfuz: Qissat al-Tamarrud wal Thawra ʿala al-Istibdad, Cairo: *al-Adab*, June.

Shuʿayr, Muhammad (2009), "ʿAbd al-Rahman al-Abnudi: fil Shiʿr… Laysa Nadiman ʿala Shay', *Jaridat al-Akhbar al-Libnaniyya*, Beirut, 23 March.

Shukri, Ghali (1982), *Al-Muntami: Dirasa fi Adab Naguib Mahfouz*, Cairo: Maktabat al-Zunnari.

——— (1993), *Tawfiq Al-Hakim: Al-Jil wal-Tabaqa wal-Ruʾya*, Beirut: Dar al-Farabi.

Al-Surbuni, Muhammad Sabri [1919–21] (2017), *al-Thawra al-Misriyya min Khilal Wathaʾiq Haqiqiyya wa Suwar Iltaqatat athnaʾ al-Thawra*, vol. 2, translated by Magdy ʿAbd al-Hafiz and ʿAli Kurkhan, Cairo: al-Markaz al-Qawmi lil-Tarjama.

Shawqi, Ahmad [1927] (1950), *al-Shawqiyyat, vol.3,* Cairo: Matbaʿat al-Istiqama.

ʿUda, Muhammad (1991), 'Qantara wal Ayyam al-Khawali', in Mustafa Musharrafa, *Qantara al-Ladhi Kafara*, Cairo: Kitab Adab wa Naqd, pp. 21–9.

ʿUkasha, Tharwat (2004), *Mudhakkirati fil Siyasa wal Thaqafa*, vol.2, Cairo: Dar al-Shuruq/Maktabat al-Usra.

Wahba, Saʿd al-Din (1997), *al-Aʿmal al-Kamila li-Saʿd al-Din Wahba*, vol 4. Cairo: al-Fajr lil-Intaj al-Fanni wal Thaqafi.

Yusuf, Shaʿban (2017), *al-Mansiyyun Yanhadun*, Cairo: Battana.

Secondary Sources: Books and Articles in English and French

Abaza, [Muhammad] Fikri (1897 – 14 February 1979). (2004), in A. Goldschmidt, *Biographical Dictionary of Modern Egypt*. Boulder, CO: Lynne Rienner Publishers.

Abdalla, Ahmed (2008), *The Student Movement and National Politics in Egypt, 1923–1973*, Cairo: The American University in Cairo Press.

Aboul-Ela, Hosam (2004), 'The Writer Becomes Text: Naguib Mahfouz and State Nationalism in Egypt', *Biography* 27, no. 2, pp. 339–56.

Abul-Magd, Zeinab (2013), *Imagined Empires: A History of Revolt in Egypt*, Berkeley, CA: University of California Press.

Abu-Lughod, Lila (2005), *Dramas of Nationhood: The Politics of Television in Egypt*, Chicago, IL: The University of Chicago Press.

Allen, Roger (1984), 'Arabic Drama in Theory & Practice: The Writings of Sa'dallah Wannus', *Journal of Arabic Literature* 15, pp. 94–113.

—— (2017), 'The Arabic Novel and History', in Wail S. Hassan (ed.) *The Oxford Handbook of Arab Novelistic Traditions*, New York: Oxford University Press.

Anderson, Benedict R. (2006), *Imagined Communities: Reflections on the Origin and Spread of Nationalism*, New York; London: Verso.

Anderson, Kyle J. (2017), 'The Egyptian Labor Corps: Workers, Peasants, and the State in World War I', *International Journal of Middle East Studies* 49, pp. 5–24.

Anishchenkova, Valerie (2014), *Autobiographical Identities in Contemporary Arab Culture*, Edinburgh: Edinburgh University Press.

Armbrust, Walter (1995), 'New Cinema, Commercial Cinema, and the Modernist Tradition in Egypt', *Alif: Journal of Comparative Poetics 15*, pp. 81–129.

Ashour, Radwa, Ferial J. Ghazoul and Hasna Reda-Mekdashi (2008), *Arab Women Writers: A Critical Reference Guide, 1873–1999*, translated by Mandy McClure, Cairo: The American University in Cairo Press.

Badawi, Mohammed M. (1992), 'Modern Arabic Literature', *The Cambridge History of Arabic Literature*, vol. 4, Cambridge: Cambridge University Press.

Badawi, al-Sa'id and Martin Hinds (1986), *A Dictionary of Egyptian Arabic*, Beirut: Librairie du Liban.

Badran, Margot (1995), *Feminists, Islam, and Nation: Gender and the Making of Modern Egypt*, Princeton: Princeton University Press.

Badrawi, Malak (2000), *Political Violence in Egypt, 1910–1924: Secret Societies, Plots and Assassinations*. Richmond: Curzon.

Bal, Mieke (2007), *Introduction to the Theory of Narrative*, Toronto: University of Toronto Press.

Baron, Beth (2005), *Egypt as a Woman: Nationalism, Gender, and Politics*, Berkeley, CA: University of California Press.

Bayat, Asef (2013), *Life as Politics: How Ordinary People Change the Middle East*, Stanford, CA: Stanford University Press.

Beattie, Kirk J. (1994), *Egypt During the Nasser Years: Ideology, Politics and Civil Society*, Oxford: Westview.

Beinin, Joel and Zachary Lockman (1998a), *Workers on the Nile, Nationalism,*

Communism, Islam, and the Egyptian Working Class, 1882–1954, Cairo: The American University in Cairo Press.

——— (1998b), 'Egypt: Society and Economy, 1923–1952', in M. W. Daly (ed.), *The Cambridge History of Egypt. Modern Egypt, from 1517 to the End of the Twentieth Century*, Cambridge: Cambridge University Press.

Benjamin, Walter (1969), 'Theses on the Philosophy of History', in Hannah Arendt (ed.), *Illuminations*, translated by Harry Zohn, New York: Schocken.

Berque, Jacques (1972), *Egypt, Imperialism and Revolution*, translated by Jean Stewart, London: Faber and Faber.

Berridge, W. J. (2011), 'Object Lessons in Violence: The Rationalities and Irrationalities of Urban Struggle during the Egyptian Revolution of 1919', *Journal of Colonialism and Colonial History* 12, no. 3, DOI: 10.1353/cch.2011.0025.

Besa, Josep (1997) 'Title, Text, Meaning', *Textual Practice* 11, no. 2, pp. 323–30.

Bier, Laura (2011), *Revolutionary Womanhood. Feminisms, Modernity, and the State in Nasser's Egypt*, Cairo: The American University in Cairo Press.

Blanchet, Robert, and Margrethe Bruun Vaage (2012), 'Don, Peggy, and Other Fictional Friends? Engaging with Characters in Television Series' *Projections: The Journal for Movies and Mind* 6, no. 2, pp. 18–41.

Boehmer, Elleke (2005), *Empire, the National and the Post-colonial 1980–1920: Resistance in Interaction*, Oxford: Oxford University Press.

Booth, Marilyn (2001), *May Her Likes Be Multiplied: Biography and Gender Politics in Egypt*, Berkeley, CA: University of California Press.

——— (2016), 'Review of Ryzova, Lucie. The Age of the Efendiyya: Passages to Modernity in National-Colonial Egypt. Oxford Historical Monographs. Oxford: Oxford University Press, 2014', *Journal of Arabic Literature*, vol.47, no. 3, pp. 342–8.

Botman, Selma (1998), 'The Liberal Age, 1923–1952'; in M.W. Daly (ed.) *The Cambridge History of Egypt. Modern Egypt, from 1517 to the End of the Twentieth Century*, Cambridge: Cambridge University Press.

Bourdieu, Pierre (1998), *Les règles de l'art. Genèse et structure du champ littéraire*, Paris: Seuil.

Brown, Nathan J. (1990), *Peasant Politics in Modern Egypt: The Struggle Against the State*, New Haven: Yale University Press.

Cardwell, Sarah (2012), 'Literature on the Small Screen: Television Adaptations' in Timothy Corrigan (ed.) *Film and Literature: An Introduction and Reader*, London and New York: Routledge, pp. 74–88.

Casullo, Nicolás (2009), 'Memory and revolution', *Journal of Latin American Cultural Studies* 18, no. 2–3, pp. 107–24.

Chatterjee, Partha (1991), 'Whose Imagined Community?', *Millennium: Journal of International Studies* 20, no. 3, pp. 521–5.

Chiti, Elena (2016) '"A Dark Comedy": Perceptions of the Egyptian Present Between Reality and Fiction', in Stefan Guth and Elena Chiti (eds.), 'Living 2016. Cultural Codes and Arrays in Arab Everyday Worlds Five Years After the "Arab Spring"', *Journal of Arabic and Islamic Studies* 16, pp. 273–89.

Clément, Anne (2005), *Sa'd Zaghlul 'Lieu de mémoire' du nationalisme égyptien*, Cairo: Cédej.

Cole, Juan Ricardo (1981), 'Feminism, Class, and Islam in Turn-of-the Century Egypt'. *International Journal of Middle East Studies* 13, pp. 387–407.

Colla, Elliot (2011), 'The Poetry of Revolt', Jadaliyya, 31 January, available at <http://www.jadaliyya.com/Details/23638/The-Poetry-of-Revolt> (last accessed 14 April 2019).

Corse, Sarah M. (1995), 'Nations and Novels: Cultural Politics and Literary use' *Social Forces* 73, no. 4, pp. 1279–308.

Couser, Thomas G. (2012), *Memoir: An Introduction*, Oxford: Oxford University Press.

Cuddon, J. A. (2013), *A Dictionary of Literary Terms and Literary Theory*, Oxford: Wiley-Blackwell.

Deeb, Marius (1979), *Party Politics in Egypt: the Wafd & its Rivals, 1919–1939*, London: Ithaca Press for the Middle East Centre, St Antony's College, Oxford.

De Moor, Ed (1998), 'Autobiography, Theory and Practice: The Case of *al-Ayyam*', in Robin Ostle, Ed de Moor and Stefan Wild (eds.) *Writing the Self: Autobiographical Writing in Modern Arabic Literature*, London: Saqi Books.

Dever, Susan (2003), *Celluloid Nationalism and Other Melodramas: From Post-Revolutionary Mexico to Fin de Siglo Mexamerica*, Albany, NY: State University of New York Press.

Di-Capua, Yoav (2001), 'Embodiment of the Revolutionary Spirit: The Mustafa Kamil Mausoleum in Cairo', *History and Memory* 13, no. 1, pp. 85–113.

——— (2009), *Gatekeepers of the Arab Past: Historians and History Writing in Twentieth Century Egypt*. Berkeley, CA: University of California Press.

Donizeau, Pauline (2011), 'Théâtre de la révolution, théâtre révolutionnaire, révolution du théâtre en Égypte? *No Time for Art* de Laila Soliman', *Acta Litt&Arts* [Online], Les conditions du théâtre: la théâtralisation, Théâtre (du) politique, last updated: 08/10/2017.

El-Ariss, Tarek (2013), *Trials of Arab Modernity*, New York: Fordham University Press.

El-Enany, Rasheed (1993), *Naguib Mahfouz: The Pursuit of Meaning*, New York; London: Routledge.

—— (2007), *Naguib Mahfouz: His Life and Times*. Cairo: The American University in Cairo Press.

El-Lozy Mahmoud (1990), 'Brecht and the Egyptian Political Theatre', *Alif, Journal of Comparative Poetics* 10, pp. 56–72.

Elsadda, Hoda (2012), *Gender, Nation and the Arabic Novel, Egypt, 1892–2008*. New York: Syracuse University Press and Edinburgh: Edinburgh University Press.

Elsaesser, Thomas (2012), 'Tales of Sound and Fury: Observations on the Family Melodrama', in Barry Keith Grant (ed.) *Film Genre Reader IV*, Austin, TX: University of Texas Press, pp. 433–62.

Fahmy, Ziad (2011), *Ordinary Egyptians: Creating the Modern Nation through Popular Culture*, Cairo: The American University in Cairo Press.

Foster, Hal (2006), 'An Archival Impulse', in Charles Merewether (ed.) *The Archive*. London: Whitechapel; Cambridge, Mass.: MIT Press, pp. 143–8.

Gaffney, Jane (1987), 'The Egyptian Cinema: Industry and Art in a Changing Society', *Arab Studies Quarterly* 9, no. 1, pp. 53–75.

Garcia, Alberto N. (2016), *Emotions in Contemporary TV Series*, Basingstoke: Palgrave Macmillan.

Gershoni, Israel (1995), 'An Intellectual Source for the Revolution: Tawfik al Hakim's Influence on Nasser and His Generation', in Shimon Shamir (ed.), *Egypt from Monarchy to Republic: A Reassessment of Revolution and Change*, Boulder, CO: Westview Press, p. 230.

—— (1983), 'Between Ottomanism and Nationalism: The Evolution of "National Sentiment" in the Caireen Middle Class as Reflected in Naguib Mahfouz *Bayn al-Qasrayn*', *Asian and African Studies* 17, no. 3, pp. 227–63.

——, and James P. Jankowski (2004), *Commemorating the Nation: Collective Memory, Public Commemoration, and National Identity in Twentieth-Century Egypt*, Chicago: Middle East Documentation Center.

Al-Ghitani, Gamal (2007), *The Mahfouz Dialogs*, translated by Humphrey Davies, Cairo: The American University in Cairo Press.

Gitre, Carmen (2011), *Performing Modernity, Theatre and Political Culture in Egypt, 1869–1923*, PhD Dissertation, New Brunswick, New Jersey.

Goldberg, Ellis (1992), 'Peasants in Revolt - Egypt 1919', *International Journal of Middle East Studies* 24, no. 2 (May), pp. 261–80.

Goldschmidt, Arthur (1968), 'The Egyptian Nationalist Party, 1892–1919', in P. M. Holt (ed.) *Political and Social Change in Modern Egypt: Historical Studies from the Ottoman Conquest to the United Arab Republic*, London: Oxford University Press.

Gordon, Joel (2002), *Revolutionary Melodrama: Popular Film and Civic Identity in Nasser's Egypt*, Chicago, IL: Middle East Documentation Center.

―――― (2018), 'Viewing Backwards: Egyptian Historical Television Dramas in the 1990s', *Review of Middle East Studies* 52, no. 1, pp. 74–92.

Gran, Peter (1978), 'Modern Trends in Egyptian Historiography: A Review Article', *International Journal of Middle East Studies* 9, no. 3, pp. 367–71.

―――― (2004), 'Upper Egypt in Modern History: a "Southern Question"?', in Nicholas S. Hopkins and Reem Saad (eds.), *Upper Egypt, Identity and Change*, Cairo: The American University in Cairo Press.

Gued Vidal, Fina (n.d.), *Safia Zaghlul*, Cairo: R. Schindler.

Hafez, Şabry (1993), *The Genesis of Arabic Narrative Discourse: A Study in the Sociology of Modern Arabic Literature*, London: Saqi Books.

Hamel, Yan (2006), *La bataille des mémoires*, Montréal: Presses de l'Université de Montréal.

Heshmat, Dina (2012), 'Tahrir, L'obsession du balai', in Wassyla Tamzali (ed.) *Histoires minuscules des révolutions arabes*, Montpellier: Chèvre-feuille étoilée, pp. 99–102.

―――― (2015), 'Egyptian Narratives of the 2011 Revolution: Diaries as a Medium of Reconciliation with the Political', in Friederike Pannewick and Georges Khalil (eds.), *Commitment and Beyond: Reflections on the Political in Arabic Literature since the 1940s*, Wiesbaden: Reichert, pp. 63–75.

Hopkins, Nicholas S. (2009), ed. *Political and Social Protest in Egypt*, Cairo Papers 29, nos. 2/3: Cairo: The American University in Cairo Press.

Hutcheon, Linda (2012), 'How? (Audiences)', in Timothy Corrigan (ed.) *Film and Literature: An Introduction and Reader*, London and New York: Routledge, pp. 385–402.

Jacob, Wilson Chacko (2010), *Working Out Egypt: Effendi Masculinity and Subject Formation in Colonial Modernity, 1870–1940*, Durham, NC: Duke University Press.

Jacquemond, Richard (2008), *Conscience of the Nation: Writers, State, and Society in Modern Egypt*, translated by David Tresilian, Cairo: The American University in Cairo Press.

―――― (2016a), 'Une révolution culturelle ?', *Vacarme* 2016 1, no. 74, pp. 57–65.

―――― (2016b), 'Satiric Literature and Other "Popular" Literary Genres in Egypt Today', in Stefan Guth and Elena Chiti (eds.), 'Living 2016. Cultural Codes and Arrays in Arab Everyday Worlds Five Years After the "Arab Spring"', *Journal of Arabic and Islamic Studies* 16, pp. 349–67.

Junge, Christian (2015), 'On Affect and Emotion as Dissent: The Kifāya Rhetoric in Pre-Revolutionary Egyptian Literature', in Friederike Pannewick and Georges Khalil (eds.), *Commitment and Beyond: Reflections on the Political in Arabic Literature since the 1940s*. Wiesbaden: Reichert, pp. 253–71.

Khalifah, Omar (2016), *Nasser in the Egyptian Imaginary*, Edinburgh: Edinburgh University Press.

Kholoussy, Hanan (2010), *For Better, for Worse: The Marriage Crisis That Made Modern Egypt*, Stanford, CA: Stanford University Press.

Kuhn Annette and Guy Westwell (2012), *Dictionary of Film Studies*, Oxford: Oxford University Press.

Lanfranchi, Sania Shaarawi (2012), *Casting off the Veil: The Life of Huda Sha'rawi, Egypt's First Feminist*, London: I. B. Tauris.

Lejeune, Philippe (1989), *On Autobiography*, translated by Katherine M. Leary, Minneapolis: University of Minnesota Press.

Lockman, Zachary (1994), 'Imagining the Working Class: Culture, Nationalism, and Class Formation in Egypt, 1899–1914', *Poetics Today* 15, no. 2, pp. 157–90.

Löwy, Michaël (2005), *Fire Alarm: Reading Walter Benjamin's 'On the Concept of History'*, translated by Chris Turner, London and New York: Verso.

Mark, Joshua J. (2016), 'Osiris', in *Ancient History Encyclopedia*, Available at <https://www.ancient.eu/osiris/> (last accessed 16 June 2019).

Martinelli, Alberto (1968), 'In Defense of the Dialectic: Antonio Gramsci's Theory of Revolution', *Berkeley Journal of Sociology* 13, pp. 1–27.

Mehrez, Samia (1993), 'Respected Sir', in Michael Beard and Adnan Haydar (eds.) *Naguib Mahfouz, From Regional Fame to Global Recognition*, New York: Syracuse University Press.

―――― (1994), *Egyptian Writers between History and Fiction*, Cairo: The American University in Cairo Press.

―――― (2012), *Translating Egypt's Revolution: The Language of Tahrir*, Cairo: The American University in Cairo Press.

Mitchell, Timothy (1988), *Colonizing Egypt*, Berkeley, CA: University of California Press.

Mossallam, Alia, 'Strikes, Riots and Laughter: A Close Reading of al-Himamiyya Village's Experience of Egypt's 1918 Peasant Insurrection', *Social Movements and Popular Mobilisation in the Middle East and North Africa Series*, London: London School of Economics and Popular Sciences (Forthcoming).

Mudford, Peter (2000), *Making Theatre: From Text to Performance*, London; New Brunswick, NJ: Athlone Press.

Al-Nahhas, Hashim (1991), 'The Role of Naguib Mahfouz in the Egyptian Cinema', in Trevor Le Gassick (ed.), *Critical Perspectives on Naguib Mahfouz*, Washington: Three Continents Press.

Nessim, Tewfiq (1951), *Fikri Abaza Pasha as a Stylist*, unpublished BA Thesis, The American University in Cairo.

Nussbaum, Martha (2001), *Upheavals of Thought: The Intelligence of Emotions*, Cambridge, New York: Cambridge University Press.

Omar, Hussein (2014), '"And I Saw No Reason to Chronicle My Life": Tensions of Nationalist Modernity in the Memoirs of Fathallah Pasha Barakat' in Marilyn Booth and Anthony Gorman (eds.), *The Long 1890's in Egypt, Colonial Quiescence, Subterranean Resistance*, Edinburgh: Edinburgh University Press, pp. 287–314.

——— (2019), 'The Arab Spring of 1919', *LRB Blog*, available at <https://www.lrb.co.uk/blog/2019/april/the-arab-spring-of-1919> (last accessed 3 December 2019).

Powell, Eve M. Troutt (2001), 'Burnt-Cork Nationalism: Race and Identity in the Theater of 'AH al-Kassar', in Cherifa Zuhur, *Colors of Enchantment: Theatre, Dance, Music and the Visual Arts of the Middle East*, Cairo: The American University in Cairo Press.

Radwan, Noha (2008) 'A Place for Fiction in the Historical Archive', *Critique: Critical Middle Eastern Studies* 17, no. 1, pp. 79–95.

Al-Ra'i, 'Ali (1992), 'Arabic Drama Since the Thirties' in Mohammed Mustafa Badawi (ed.) *Modern Arabic Literature*, The Cambridge History of Arabic Literature vol. 4, Cambridge: Cambridge University Press.

Ramdani, Nabila (2013), 'Women in the 1919 Egyptian Revolution: From Feminist Awakening to Nationalist Political Activism.' *Journal of International Women's Studies* 14, no. 2, pp. 39–52.

Reynolds, Dwight F. (2001), *Interpreting the Self: Autobiography in the Arabic Literary Tradition*, Berkeley, CA: University of California Press.

Ricœur, Paul (2000), 'L'écriture de l'histoire et la représentation du passé', *Annales. Histoire, Sciences Sociales* 55e, no. 4, pp. 731–47.

——— (2004), *Memory, History, Forgetting*, Chicago, IL: University of Chicago Press.

Rooke, Tetz (1998), 'The Arabic Autobiography of Childhood' in Robin Ostle, Ed de Moor and Stefan Wild (eds), *Writing the Self Autobiographical Writing in Modern Arabic Literature*, London: Saqi Books, pp. 100–14.

Ross, Kristin (2002), *May '68 and its Afterlives*, Chicago, IL: University of Chicago Press.

——— (2004), 'Rencontre avec Kristin Ross autour de "L'imaginaire de la Commune"' <https://www.youtube.com/watch?v=c-rXTMzAZF4> (last accessed 30 May 2019).

Rousselot, Elodie (2016), *Exoticizing the Past in Contemporary Neo-Historical Fiction*: Basingstoke: Palgrave Macmillan.

Roussillon, Alain (1998), 'Republican Egypt Interpreted: Revolution and Beyond', in M. W. Daly (ed.), *The Cambridge History of Egypt: Modern Egypt, from 1517 to the End of the Twentieth Century*, Cambridge: Cambridge University Press.

Ruiz, Mario M. (2013–14), 'Photography and the Egyptian Labor Corps in Wartime Palestine, 1917–1918' *Jerusalem Quarterly* 56 and 57, pp. 52–66.

Ryzova, Lucie (2007), 'My notepad Is My Friend: Efendis and the Act of Writing in Modern Egypt', *The Maghreb Review* 32, no. 4, pp. 323–48.

——— (2014), *The Age of the Efendiyya. Passages to Modernity in National-Colonial Egypt*, Oxford: Oxford University Press.

Saad, Reem (1999), 'State, Landlord, Parliament and Peasant: The Story of the 1992 Tenancy Law in Egypt', in Alan K. Bowman and Eugene Rogan (eds.) *Agriculture in Egypt from Pharaonic to Modern Times*, Proceedings of the British Academy, Oxford: Oxford University Press for the British Academy.

——— (2016), 'Before the Spring: Shifting Patterns of Protest in Rural Egypt' in Amal Ghazal and Jens Hanssen (eds.), *The Oxford Handbook of Contemporary Middle-Eastern and North African History*.

Sabaseviciute, Giedre (2011), 'Re-creating the Past: The Manipulation of the Notion of Rupture in Egyptian Revolutions', in *La Révolution française* [Online], Rupture(s) in Revolution. Perceving and Managing Ruptures in Revolutionary Times, Online since 17 December 2011.

Said, Edward (1993), *Culture and Imperialism*, London: Vintage.

Sansot, Pierre (1994), *Poétique de la ville*, Paris: Méridiens Klincksieck.

Sartre, Jean-Paul (1988), 'Situation of the Writer in 1947', in *What Is Literature? and Other Essays*, Cambridge, MA: Harvard University Press.

Sayyid-Marsot, Afaf Lutfi (2007), *A History of Egypt: From the Arab Conquest to the Present*, Cambridge: Cambridge University Press.

Schulze. Reinhard C. (1991), 'Colonization and Resistance: The Egyptian Peasant

Rebellion, 1919', in Farhad Kazemi and John Waterbury (eds.), *Peasants and Politics in the Modern Middle East*, Miami, FL: Florida International University Press.

Schulze, Reinhard C. (2012), 'Saʿd b. Ibrāhīm Zaghlūl', in P. Bearman, Th. Bianquis, C .E. Bosworth, E. van Donzel, W. P. Heinrichs (eds.), *Encyclopaedia of Islam*, Second Edition, available at <ttp://dx.doi.org.libproxy.aucegypt.edu:2048/10.1163/1573-3912_islam_SIM_6397> (last accessed 21 June 2019).

Selaiha, Nehad (2003), *Egyptian Theatre, New Directions*, Cairo: Matabiʿ al-Hayʾa al-ʿAmma lil-Kitab.

Selim, Samah (2003), 'The Narrative Craft: Realism and Fiction in the Arabic Canon', *Edebiyat: Journal of Middle Eastern Literatures* 14, nos. 1–2, pp. 109–28.

——— (2004), *The Novel and the Rural Imaginary in Egypt, 1880–1985*, London, New York: Routledge.

——— (2009), 'Languages of Civilization: Nation, Translation and the Politics of Race in Colonial Egypt', *The Translator* 15, no. 1, pp. 139–56.

Shafik, Viola (2001), 'Egyptian Cinema' in Oliver Leaman (ed.), *Companion Encyclopedia of Middle-Eastern and North-African Film*, London, New York: Routledge, pp. 23–129.

——— (2007a), *Popular Egyptian Cinema: Gender, Class, and Nation*. Cairo: The American University in Cairo Press.

——— (2007b), *Arab Cinema History and Cultural Identity*. Cairo: The American University in Cairo Press.

Shalan, Jeff (2002), 'Writing the Nation: The Emergence of Egypt in the Modern Arabic Novel' *Journal of Arabic Literature* 33, no. 3, pp. 211–47.

Sinor, Jennifer (2005), 'Diary' in Victoria Boynton and Jo Malin (eds.) *Encyclopedia of Women's Autobiography*, Westport, CT: Greenwood, pp. 190–2.

Spiropoulou, Angeliki (2015), 'History and Literature: An Interview with Hayden White', *Synthesis* 8, Fall, pp. 118–24.

Spivak, Gayatri C. (1987), 'A Literary Representation of the Subaltern: A Woman's Text from the Third World' in *In Other Worlds: Essays in Cultural Politics*, Methuen: New York and London.

Stam, Robert (2012), 'Beyond Fidelity: The Dialogics of Adaptation' in Timothy Corrigan (ed.) *Film and Literature: An Introduction and Reader*, London and New York: Routledge, pp. 74–88.

Starkey, Paul (1987), *From the Ivory Tower: A Critical Study of Tawfiq al-Hakim*, London: Ithaca Press.

Stuhr-Rommereim, Helen (2011), 'Lessons in Revolting: The Revolution Continues',

Egypt Independent, 21 August, available at <https://ww.egyptindependent.com/lessons-revolting-revolution-continues/> (last accessed 18 June 2019).

Tawwaf, *Egypt, 1919, Being a Narrative of Certain Incidents of the Rising in Upper Egypt*, Private Papers of F. M. Edwards in the Centre for Middle Eastern Studies, Saint Antony, Oxford University.

Thoraval, Yves (1975), *Regards sur le cinéma égyptien*, Beirut: Dar el-Machreq, pp. 107–8.

Venuti, Lawrence (2012), 'Adaptation, Translation, Critique', in Timothy Corrigan (ed.) *Film and Literature: An Introduction and Reader*, London and New York: Routledge, pp. 89–103.

Verstraten, Peter (2011), *Film Narratology*, translated by Stefan van der Lecq, Toronto: University of Toronto Press.

Waites, Kathleen J. (2005), 'Memoir', in Victoria Boynton and Jo Malin, *Encyclopedia of Women's Autobiography*, Westport, CT: Greenwood, pp. 379–81.

White, Hayden (1978), *Tropics of Discourse. Essays in Cultural Criticism*. Baltimore, MD: The John Hopkins University Press.

Yousef, Hoda A. (2016), *Composing Egypt. Reading, Writing, and the Emergence of a Modern Nation, 1870–1930*, Stanford, CA: Stanford University Press.

Other

'Revolution' in The Editors of Encyclopedia Britannica (eds), *Encyclopedia Britannica*, published May 2019, available at <https://www.britannica.com/topic/revolution-politics> (last accessed 21 June 2019).

'Memoir' in The Editors of Encyclopedia Britannica (eds), *Encyclopedia Britannica*, published 29 June 2017, available at <https://www.britannica.com/topic/memoir-historical-genre> (last accessed 21 June 2019).

Index

Note: Names beginning with al- are classified under the second element of the name: Tawfiq al-Hakim under Hakim, Tawfiq al-. References to notes indicate the page on which they occur.

Abaza, Fikri, 61–2, 64
al-Dahik al-Baki, 59–63, 65–74
'Abd al-Hadi, Ibrahim, 129n18
   character in film 112, 114, 115, 123
'Abd al-Nur, Fakhri, 75n5, 142, 153n24
'Abd al-Rahman, Fahmi, 18, 19, 34n25, 141, 149, 151n3
   character in novel, 194, 196
Aboul-Hussein, Hiyam, 51–2, 57n27, n29 and n30
Abu-Ghazi, 'Imad, 7
Abu-Lughod, Lila, 159, 172, 173
'Awad, Luwis, 75n5, 83, 86–7, 103n16
'Alim, Mahmud Amin, al-, 160, 103n17
Amin, Mustafa, 31n3, 34n25, 53n3, 133, 150n1, 201n25, 202n34
   Asrar Thawrat 1919, 135
   Min Wahid li-'Ashara, 136–48
Anderson, Benedict R., 23, 79
Anderson, Kyle J., 13, 34n28, 36n39
Anis, Muhammad, 36n41, 151n3
Anishchenkova, Valerie, 62, 63
'Anus, Nagwa, 49, 53n5
'Aqqad, 'Abbas, 32n9, 85, 120
archival documents in literature
   in *Hawa al-Hurriya* 187–8
   in *1919*, 196
Armbrust, Walter, 106, 108, 110–11, 113, 114, 128n8
Asyut, 14, 35n30, 36n43
   in *al-Dahik al-Baki*, 59–60, 65–73
autobiography, 62–3, 76n9 and n10, 154n28
   autobiographical recollections of the revolution, 148–50, 153n24 and n25
   memoirs 17–18, 136–9, 142

Badawi, Mahmud, al-, 28
   'Dhata Layla', 66, 70
Badr, 'Abd al-Muhsin Taha, 104n29
Barakat, 'Ali, 14, 34n27, 36n43
Barakat, Fathallah, 154n28
Barakat, Hidiya [or Hidaya], 73, 153n25
Barghouti, Tamim, al-, 7, 31n6
Baron, Beth, 10, 104n25
Beinin, Joel, 14–16, 35n32, 39, 52n1
Benjamin, Walter, 21, 182, 190
Berque, Jacques, 20
Berridge, W. J., 77n20
Bey, 8, 39, 41–7, 55n19, 75n8, 162–4
Bier, Laura, 119–20

Boehmer, Elleke, 16, 82
Booth, Marilyn, 67, 76n11
Botman, Selma, 39, 63, 88, 142
Brown, Nathan J., 14, 62, 75n4, 114

canon formation, 83–4
Casullo, Nicolás, 1, 4, 21
Chatterjee, Partha, 23
Chiti, Elena, 184, 199n4
Clément, Anne, 6–7, 8, 9, 136
Cole, Juan Ricardo, 75n7, 78n22, 142
colloquial, 9, 30, 83, 170, 172, 177, 180n25

Dusuqi, 'Asim al-, 35n30, 77n16
Darwish, Sayyid, 8, 29, 36n37, 41, 53n4, 56n20, 124, 187–8, 205
   Sayyid Darwish (film), 128n11, 131n28
Di-Capua, Yoav, 6, 7, 126

effendiyya, 6, 8, 25, 32n8, 39, 41, 60–1, 71–2, 73–4, 75n8, 80
   effendi autobiography, 62–3
   representation in literature, 42, 46, 47, 66–7, 69, 71, 93, 96, 113–14, 146, 162–4, 172–4, 193, 198, 205
El-Enany, Rasheed, 87, 102n13, 103n19, 104n24
Elsadda, Hoda, 61, 107
Elsaesser, Thomas, 122
emotions, 26, 176, 189, 37n48
   compassion 68–70
   fear, 68–70, 94–5, 125, 173, 182, 190
   in films and TV series, 121–2, 125, 172, 176

fallah, in literature, 41, 46–8, 98–9, 136, 141, 143, 147
   see also Revolution of 1919 and peasants
Fahmi, 'Abd al-'Aziz, 91, 147, 173

Fahmi, Dawlat, 202n30 and n34
   in literature 78n28, 191–3, 195, 197, 203n35
Fahmy, Ziad, 17–18, 36n37, 39–41, 73, 115–16, 124, 129n19
Farid, Muhammad, 91, 132n35, 153n22
Fawzi, Hussein, 17–18
focalisation 68, 70, 80, 82, 90–2, 123, 125, 141, 162, 169–70, 172, 175, 193
Foster, Hal 187–8, 190

Ghawgha', 35n36, 59, 66–9, 74n3, 78n23, 94, 188
Gindi, Yusri al-, 155–6, 160, 171, 173
Gindi, Yusuf al-, 35, 50–1, 52, 54, 56n25, 155
   in TV series, 172, 174, 175
Goldschmidt, Arthur, 72
Gordon, Joel, 108, 109, 122, 126, 128n11, 159
Gran, Peter, 12, 60
Gued Vidal, Fina, 152n12

Hafez [or Hafiz], Sabri, 24, 79, 80, 105n31
Hakim, Tawfiq al-, 85, 96, 101n1, 104n28
   'Awdat al-Ruh, 24–5, 28, 79–80, 83, 84, 85, 96–100, 167, 193
   'Awdat al-Ruh (play), 101, 105n35
   'Awdat al-Ruh (series), 101, 131n27
Haqqi, Yahya, 201n26, 203n40
Hutcheon, Linda, 124
Husayn, Taha, 83, 86, 101n5, 138, 180n25

Ibrahim, Hafiz, 9, 11, 95–6, 196
'Izz al-Din, Amin, 168, 180
   al-Faylaq, 168–71
Idris, Yusuf, 88, 121, 130n22, 167, 170

Imam, Hassan, 106–7, 110–12, 113, 127n5
   Bayn al-Qasrayn (film), 28, 106–26, 127n4 and n6, 128n8, n9 and n12, 135
Irish struggle for independence, 16, 81–2

Jacquemond, Richard, 86, 102n8, 108, 135, 157, 159, 184, 186, 191
Jahine, Salah, 120

Kamil, Mustafa, 31n6, 64, 132n35
   in literature 91, 113
   Mustafa Kamil (film), 128n11
Kassar, Ali, al- 39, 41, 53n4 and n6
Kholoussy, Hanan, 61
Kira, Ahmad, 103n20, 201n26, 202n30, 203n40
   literary character 191–3, 195–7, 201n25

Lockman, Zachary, 14–16, 23, 35n32, 61

Mahdiyya, Munira, al-, 8, 200n11
Mahfouz, Naguib, 85–6
   Bayn al-Qasrayn, 25, 28, 83–96, 100, 103n16, 104–5n30, 194
   Bayn al-Qasrayn (play), 101, 105n35
   Bayn al-Qasrayn (series), 101
Mahmud, Muhammad, 67, 71
Masriyya, Na'ima, al-, 8, 32n13, 200n11
Mehrez, Samia, 25, 86, 145, 158, 159
melodrama, 109, 110, 121–5, 172, 176
memoirs *see* autobiography
   prison memoirs, 135–6, 149, 153n27
memory, 3, 4, 9, 11, 21, 64, 74, 80, 104n25, 107, 132n35, 182–3, 184, 187–8, 190, 197, 204, 207
   dominant (official), 4, 22, 25–6, 206
Mossallam, Alia, 12, 13, 34n26, 34n28
Mukhtar, Mahmud, 117, 130n25

Mourad, Ahmad 183, 185, 190–2, 196, 200n20, 201n22, 207, 208n12
   1919, 190–8, 201n21, 202n29
   1919 (film) 206
Musharrafa, Mustafa, 166–7, 180n22
   Qantara al-Ladhi Kafara, 30, 167–8, 179n18, 206
music (in film), 122, 123–4, 131n31
   songs 8–9, 43, 101n2, 121, 124–5, 152n18, 153n21, 177, 188–9

Nabarawi, Ceiza, 154n25
Naggar, 'Abd al-Wahab, 18, 35n36, 149–50
Naqqash, Raga' al-, 89, 102n13 and n14, 103n16, 110
Nasser, 79, 86, 107–8, 114, 119, 121, 126, 133, 135, 159, 160, 179n15
   nasserism (and Nasserist rhetoric, discourse and regime), 115–17, 119, 120, 126, 132n35, 164, 172, 173
   post-Nasser period, 136, 156–9
National Party (NP), 31n6, 64, 71, 72, 74, 76n12 and n13, 91, 132n35
Nussbaum, Martha, 26, 68, 69, 176

Omar, Hussein, 32n8, 153n22, 154n28
One Thousand and One Nights tale, 51, 52, 57n28

pashas, 8, 136, 143
   in literature and TV series, 70–1, 100, 155, 168, 173–4, 180n28, 181n34
pharaonic themes, 79, 85, 99–100, 105n32, 118, 208n12

Radwan, Noha, 25, 159, 163
Ra'i, 'Ali, al- 41, 42, 53n5, 54n12, 55n15, 85
Rafi'i,'Abd al-Rahman, al- 13, 34n24, 59, 74n2, 77n18, 102n12, 119, 132n35, 162

realism, 82, 83–7
Revolution of 1919
and Armenians, 16, 18, 35n36; in literature 191, 195
and Copts, 18, 73, 115, 35n35; in literature and film, 115–16, 142, 195,
and Jews, 16–17, 35n36, 36n37, 93, 129n19, 174; character in TV series, 174, 181n32
and national literature, 24–5
and peasants, 6, 12–14, 34n27 and n28; in literature 71, 81, 88, 94, 98, 146, 156, 160, 162–5, 171–4, 193; see also *Fallah*
and violence, 6, 19, 52–3n2; in literature, 65–6, 68, 98, 114–15, 135, 146–7, 168–9, 194, 196; *see also* Wafd, underground organisation
and women, 11, 17, 18–19, 36n39; in literature, 46–7, 72–4, 81, 93–4, 95–6, 98, 101, 101n2, 116–21, 131n27, 144, 149, 170, 188, 195, 200n11
and working class, 14–16, 61; in literature and film, 114, 168
Revolution of 1919 in fiction
  1919 (novel), 190–8, 201n21, 202n29
  'Awdat al-Ruh (play), 101, 105n35
  'Awdat al-Ruh (novel), 24–5, 28, 79–80, 83, 84, 85, 96–100, 167, 193, 101, 105n35
  'Awdat al-Ruh (series), 101, 131n27
  Bayn al-Qasrayn (film), 28, 106–26, 127n4 and n6, 128n8, n9 and n12, 135
  Bayn al-Qasrayn (novel), 25, 28, 83–96, 100, 103n16, 104–5n30, 194
  Bayn al-Qasrayn (play), 101, 105n35
  Bayn al-Qasrayn (series), 101
  al-Dahik al-Baki (novel), 59–63, 65–74
  'Dhata Layla' (short story), 66, 70

  al-Faylaq (novel), 168–71
  Gumhuriyyat Zifta (series), 155–7, 160, 171–8
  Hawa al-Hurriya (performance), 185–90, 198
  Imbratur Zifta (play), 39, 40, 48–52
  al-Intikhabat (play), 39, 40, 41, 42–8
  al-Masamir (play), 160–6, 171
  'Mudhakkirat Hikmat Hanim' (short story), 80–2, 95, 99, 100
  Mustafa Kamil (film), 128n11
  'Nur al-Din Bumba' (short story), 66, 77n19
  Qantara al-Ladhi Kafara (novel), 30, 167–8, 179n18, 206
  Sayyid Darwish (film), 128n11, 131n28
Revolution of 1919 in memoirs *see* autobiographical recollections of the revolution
Revolution of 2011, 1–4, 59, 182–7, 190–3, 197
Ricœur, Paul, 4, 22, 206
Rihani, Naguib al-, 41, 53n4 and n5, 203n36
Ross, Kristin, 1, 22, 23, 25, 80, 89, 90, 100, 108, 126, 193
Rousselot, Elodie, 30, 197, 201n19
Ryzova, Lucie, 61, 62, 138, 148

Sa'd, 'Iryan Yusuf, 35n35, 103n20, 149
Saad, Reem, 156, 178
Sayyid Darwish (film) *see* Darwish, Sayyid
Schulze, Reinhard C., 8, 13
Selim, Samah, 24, 83–4, 171
Sergius, 18, 116, 130n20
Sha'rawi, 'Ali, 91, 142, 144, 149, 173
Sha'rawi, Huda, 11, 19, 33n20, 34n22, 46, 118–19, 149
Shafik, Viola, 109, 110, 123, 127n5
Shalan, Jeff, 24, 84–5, 97, 98
Shawqi, Ahmad, 9, 16, 35n34

Shukri, Ghali, 102n7
Sidqi, Amin, 39, 41, 52, 53n4 and 5, 57n29
   Imbratur Zifta, 39, 40, 48–52
   al-Intikhabat 39, 40, 41, 42–8
Soliman, Laila, 183, 185–7, 200n11 and n14, 206–7
   Hawa al-Hurriyya (performance), 185–90, 198
songs *see* music
Stam, Robert, 111

Tsirkas, Stratis *Nur al-Din Bumba*, 66, 77n19

'Ubayd, 'Isa, 28, 80, 93
   'Mudhakkirat Hikmat Hanim', 80–2, 95, 99, 100
'Uda, Muhammad, 166, 179n17, 180n22
'Ukasha, Tharwat, 108, 161, 162, 179n13

Venuti, Lawrence, 111–12

Wafd, 5–7, 10, 11, 12, 14, 15, 17, 19, 63–4, 65, 67, 71, 87, 105n33, 137, 141, 142–4, 146, 147, 148, 149, 177, 197, 198, 206
   criticism of, 38, 42, 44, 46, 48, 52n1, 71
   and underground organisation, 19, 34n25, 56n25, 129n18, 135, 136, 141, 166–7, 172, 194, 202n34
Wahba, Sa'd al-Din, 160–1, 163, 179n14
   al-Masamir, 160–6, 171
White, Hayden, 20–2
Wisa, Esther 153n25

Yad al-Sawda', al (Black Hand, organisation), 30, 65, 115, 129n17, 191, 194–6, 201n25
Yusuf, Fatma al- (also Ruz al-Yusuf), 153n25

Zaghlul, Saad, 2, 5, 7–8, 12, 18, 20, 31n6, 32n8, 53n3, 150n2, 152n10
   critics of, 38–9
   in literature, 63–4, 71, 89–94, 99–100, 113, 133–6, 139–43, 149–50, 152n8, 153n24, 167–8, 191, 194, 196, 101n25
   in poetry, 8–9
Zaghlul, Safiyya, 7, 9–11, 19, 33n18 and n19, 38, 52n2, 133–5, 139
   in literature, 140, 142, 143–4, 147, 149, 191
Zifta, 14, 35n31, 49, 50, 54n8, 155, 156
   Gumhuriyyat Zifta (series), 155–7, 160, 171–8

EU representative:
Easy Access System Europe
Mustamäe tee 50, 10621 Tallinn, Estonia
Gpsr.requests@easproject.com

www.ingramcontent.com/pod-product-compliance
Lightning Source LLC
Chambersburg PA
CBHW070345240426
43671CB00013BA/2411